Integrated Digital Marketing in Practice

Integrated Digital Marketing in Practice is a comprehensive guide to the transformative effect of digital technologies on all of the key practices of marketing. Considering a broad range of organization types, sizes and markets, this book provides an all-encompassing view of how digital technologies help marketers understand, anticipate and deliver on customer needs as efficiently and effectively as possible. Students will benefit from the clear structure and rich learning features, including case studies, key concepts in brief, digital and research insight boxes, review questions and skills development boxes. Instructor resources include model answers to practice exam questions, teaching slides, group discussion ideas, and practice activities.

Andrew Corcoran is Associate Professor in Marketing at the Nottingham University Business School, where he leads institutional initiatives to enhance educational practices and the student experience. He has won teaching awards at Aston University, the University of Warwick and the University of Nottingham.

"In this book, Professor Andrew Corcoran deploys all his knowledge and professional expertise in the field to analyse the transformative impact of new digital technologies on Marketing. Digital transformations affect not only business models and common business practices, but also impact the strategy, creativity, innovation processes, customers' behaviour, and the ways customers and firms interact. The book's format allows a vivid description of the panoply of different issues linked to digitalisation and new marketing trends. Especially interesting and instructive is the section "End of chapter case" which applies the findings of each chapter to real situations. *Integrated Digital Marketing in Practice* is an invaluable guide to understanding all the challenges and opportunities opened by the profound transformations of the digital age. Indeed, an obligatory reference book."
Dr. Félix-Fernando Muñoz, *Universidad Autónoma de Madrid (Spain)*

Integrated Digital Marketing in Practice

Andrew Corcoran Nottingham University Business School

CAMBRIDGE
UNIVERSITY PRESS

CAMBRIDGE
UNIVERSITY PRESS

Shaftesbury Road, Cambridge CB2 8EA, United Kingdom

One Liberty Plaza, 20th Floor, New York, NY 10006, USA

477 Williamstown Road, Port Melbourne, VIC 3207, Australia

314–321, 3rd Floor, Plot 3, Splendor Forum, Jasola District Centre,
New Delhi – 110025, India

103 Penang Road, #05-06/07, Visioncrest Commercial, Singapore 238467

Cambridge University Press is part of Cambridge University Press & Assessment, a department
of the University of Cambridge.

We share the University's mission to contribute to society through the pursuit of education,
learning and research at the highest international levels of excellence.

www.cambridge.org
Information on this title: www.cambridge.org/9781009204361

DOI: 10.1017/9781009204323

First published 2023

Printed in Great Britain by Ashford Colour Press Ltd.

A catalogue record for this publication is available from the British Library.

Library of Congress Cataloging-in-Publication Data
Names: Corcoran, Andrew, 1970– author.
Title: Integrated digital marketing in practice / Andrew Corcoran.
Description: 1 Edition. | New York, NY : Cambridge University Press, [2023] |
    Includes bibliographical references.
Identifiers: LCCN 2022056945 (print) | LCCN 2022056946 (ebook) | ISBN 9781009204361
    (hardback) | ISBN 9781009204378 (paperback) | ISBN 9781009204323 (ebook)
Subjects: LCSH: Internet marketing. | Marketing–Management.
Classification: LCC HF5415.1265 C677 2023 (print) | LCC HF5415.1265 (ebook) |
    DDC 658.8/72–dc23/eng/20221128
LC record available at https://lccn.loc.gov/2022056945
LC ebook record available at https://lccn.loc.gov/2022056946

ISBN 978-1-009-20436-1 Hardback
ISBN 978-1-009-20437-8 Paperback

Additional resources for this publication at https://www.cambridge.org/corcoran

For Jo, Poppy, Tallulah, Finley, and Callum.
My best people.

Brief Contents

Contents

Preface

Context

The digital revolution has brought about a significant shift in how customers connect with suppliers and with each other; in turn, this has led to a paradigm shift in how professionals engage with marketing as a business discipline. This book equips students of business/management and marketing with the latest digital techniques for understanding and delivering customer needs in a wide range of organisations. It signposts readers to emerging trends and demonstrates how they can embrace change and be ready for future challenges.

The primary distinguishing feature of this text is its consideration of digital technologies with respect to every component of the marketing mix. Traditional texts tend to be one of the following: (1) those focused on e-commerce, essentially about web design; (2) higher-level strategic texts; and (3) books about social media. This book provides an integrated approach to how digital technologies have impacted upon **all** aspects of marketing – for example, to include product co-creation, integrated delivery channels, and negotiated and dynamic pricing. This book is distinct from other texts in helping students to develop key skills that are essential to embracing change in a fast-moving field.

Students using this book will be expected to have an undergraduate grounding in business/management with a component module in the principles of marketing or marketing management.

Features and Benefits

This book addresses the three most significant course challenges when teaching digital marketing.

Challenge 1: Breadth of Coverage

Digital marketing has become synonymous with the mastery of websites and social media – that is, the 'promotion' component of the marketing mix: this has become the dominant focus of the prevailing academic textbooks on the subject.

However, the impact of the Internet and digital technologies has had a transformative effect upon all aspects of the marketing mix: products are becoming anticipative and more tailored; pricing is dynamic to take account of supply/demand/competitive conditions; placement is becoming more integrated as the lines between online and offline purchases blur and the time a consumer expects to wait from purchase to gratification continues to shorten. This all has a significant effect upon how we understand, anticipate, and deliver our customers' needs in as efficient a manner as possible. It is a challenge for lecturers to encourage their students to consider the broad spectrum of marketing tools provided by current and emerging digital technologies.

Challenge 2: Case Studies and Examples (Linking Theory to Practice)

Lecturers are faced with the challenge of finding good examples to illustrate the theory from a range of different organisations to provide comparative examples, and to better reflect the range of organisations that their students will ultimately go on to work for. This book considers a broad range of organisation sizes, types, and markets. Providing this rounded view will save lecturers' time in finding relevant examples for lectures and seminars, as well as enabling students to understand how digital technologies are used in a wide range of contexts, better preparing them for their future careers.

Challenge 3: Student Competencies

It is impossible to predict with any degree of certainty the direction of change in the digital age. A challenge for students is to develop a strong set of competencies and positive attitudes to change that will leave them well equipped to embrace and capitalise upon uncertainty. The book supports students to be adaptable, pragmatic, and open to new ideas – skills which are essential in reacting to change, and which their future employers will be looking for. This approach helps the text to remain useful and relevant to students beyond the classroom: it will be of practical use to them in a professional capacity. By encouraging students to develop professional and personal competencies as they progress through the book, it also serves the dual purpose of consistently reinforcing the practical value and relevance of the module to their future careers.

Organisation

Chapter 1 provides helpful background regarding the origins, drivers, and impacts of the Internet and the worldwide web. Chapter 2 discusses how this infrastructure provides a rich and varied flow of data to support marketers' efforts to gain ever more detailed customer insight. Chapter 3 sets this capability in the context of the organisation, with an explanation of how digital technologies play a significant part in providing strategic options to deliver value to the organisation's target customers. Chapter 4 looks at how the behaviour of consumers has changed due to the varied adoption of digital technologies, with Chapter 5 examining the new basis for marketing relationships between consumers and organisations and the increased importance of the customer experience. Chapter 6 looks at how value is delivered to consumers using increasingly sophisticated digitally enabled networks of partnerships. Chapter 7 gives an overview of the complex field of digital promotion (including social media). Chapter 8 considers the creative uses of digital technologies and their role in innovation. Chapter 9 sets the scene for future development by signposting emerging challenges and opportunities. Lastly, Chapter 10 helps students to understand the practical issues of working in digital marketing, and how they might best prepare themselves.

Pedagogy

Each chapter begins with an Introduction which sets the context and provides clear learning objectives. A Case Insight section provides a detailed example to give the reader a practical viewpoint of the issues addressed in the chapter. As the text develops and explains the key concepts, these are further illustrated by shorter sections which offer Digital Insights into practice, and Research Insights which introduce the reader to seminal papers in area. At the end of the main text there is a longer End-of-Chapter Case with discussion questions. Finally, the Develop Your Skills section discusses a relevant practical skill and explains why it is important to the digital marketer, along with advice on how to develop and practise that skill.

1 Origins

Definition, Drivers, and Impact

Introduction

This chapter establishes the key digital technologies that have emerged within and across the structure of the Internet and the World Wide Web. We also discuss how these technologies have caused disruption to established markets but also have created new opportunities for growth. The technologies have also changed the ways that organisations relate to their customers and vice versa, a relationship which is overseen by the marketing function of an organisation. The fundamental changes in consumers, markets, and organisations that have resulted from the emergence of digital technologies call for a radical rethink of the diverse and detailed knowledge, behaviours, and skills we need to succeed as marketers in this new environment.

Learning Objectives

- Define digital marketing.
- Identify key events in the development of the infrastructure of digital technologies.
- Categorise key themes in the evolution of the digital ecosystem.
- Consider the disruptive and convergence effects of digital technologies.
- Evaluate the challenges and opportunities for the practice of marketing.

CASE INSIGHT: AMAZON – THE EVERYTHING FROM A-TO-Z STORE

Amazon.com, Inc., launched by the former New York hedge fund manager Jeff Bezos in 1994, has radically changed the way that we shop. Previously, if we wanted to buy a product we went to a store, selected the product, took it to the checkout for payment then dutifully packed it away with our other purchases to take home. We may have indulged in the occasional impulse purchase that would have been stimulated by point-of-sale displays or by the persuasive skills of the sales assistant. A detailed understanding of our needs and the frequency and scale of our purchases only became clear if we built individual connections with store personnel over years of custom.

Bezos initially sought to use the Internet to offer greater choice to book buyers, whose options were limited to the titles that stores carried on their shelves. These often niche small businesses had to choose between carrying a small number of popular titles in large volumes, denying the customer choice, or many titles in small volumes, leaving the sellers poorly equipped to cope with demand should sales suddenly spike due to a favourable review. By using the Internet to provide a single, massive, always-open virtual store with seemingly unlimited stocks, Amazon positioned itself as a mass intermediary in the book market. From this reconfiguration of the publishing retail chain, choice and convenience grew, and costs fell – a challenge previously impossible in the incumbent 'bricks and mortar' model. This model not only exploited operational efficiencies, but also the knowledge gained from massive amounts of detailed sales data. The greater the understanding that Amazon gained about your reading habits, the better it became at recommending other books, effectively combining the point-of-sale displays and knowledgeable sales assistant into one dynamic role, instantly and on a global scale.

The idea that Amazon once existed as an online global bookstore today seems to us an example of small thinking which is lacking in vision and ambition. Since those early days, Amazon has gone on to disrupt a wide range of retail chains. But, as in the early days when bookshop sales assistants would welcome customers who would browse the book selection then search their smartphones for better offers and purchase online, retailers quickly realised that it was not a straight battle between online and offline – they had to coexist to some degree.

The resources and knowledge that Amazon has developed has led to broader and deeper disruptions beyond retail activities. Its cloud computing service, AWS, has changed the way we use software and store our data. Its streaming services have further disrupted the publishing industry (to include film, television, books, and audio). Its Kindle and Alexa devices have changed how we interact with the Internet. Its studios are creating original content to feed into its entertainment networks. Amazon is indisputably a dominating force in the online retail space, but has also shown its intention to reinvent the physical retail experience too. In an experimental shop in

Seattle, customers can choose items and pay automatically, without stopping at the checkout, thanks to sensors and machine learning. Is Amazon truly Earth's most customer-centric company?

Questions

- Discuss whether Amazon has been visionary in its approach, or unfocused.
- To what degree does Amazon achieve advantage through its philosophy or its technology?
- What have been the positive and negative social impacts of our changing buying habits?

1.1   What Is Digital Marketing?

Digital marketing first appeared as a term in the 1990s, when Web 1.0 comprised static screen-based content with extraordinarily little interaction and no real communities. With the arrival of banner advertising in 1993 and the first web crawler in 1994, search engine optimisation (SEO) as we know it today was born. At this point users had a largely passive engagement with material that was reproduced from physical channels. As a result, this new technology was mainly seen by marketers as another form of broadcast media that was similar in nature to newspapers, posters, radio, and television, and as such digital marketing was considered to be a sales and advertising vehicle.

It was not until the emergence of Web 2.0 around the turn of the century that a truly interactive Internet emerged, allowing the Web to be a more social place and an enabler for online communities. The main types of services that developed as part of Web 2.0, which still underpin social media interaction, are free to use, advertisement-supported, web-hosted services or interactive applications for different media formats: Instagram for images; YouTube and TikTok for video; Bing for maps; blogging services such as Wordpress.com; and rating of travel destinations and services through TripAdvisor. This significant change in functionality and utility led to a redefining of the term in the practitioner literature as 'the process of using digital technologies to acquire customers and build customer preferences, promote brands, retain customers and increase sales' (*Financial Times*, 2018) or 'activities, institutions, and processes facilitated by digital technologies for creating, communicating and delivering value for customers and other stakeholders' (American Marketing Association, 2013). Both definitions highlight the importance of creating a symbiotic 'digital relationship' with customers. Within the academic literature, Kannan and Li (2017) recognised this shift in the supplier–customer relationship to be more interactive and refined the definition of digital marketing as 'an adaptive, technology-enabled process by which firms collaborate with customers and partners to jointly create, communicate, deliver, and sustain value for all stakeholders', capturing the dynamic and co-operative nature of digital marketing.

1.2   Origins of the Internet

Understanding the origins of the Internet helps us as marketers to appreciate its nature, behaviours, risks, and opportunities. Inspired by, and expanding upon, the work of Gribbin (2011), Ryan and Jones (2013), and Arthur (2017) we explore the evolutionary cycles that have been driven by the emergence of new families of technologies, fundamentally altering the paradigm of the digital economy.

- **Conglomeration:** The 1950s and 1960s saw the establishment of the principles of scientific collaboration and communication using digital means, led by the US Department of Defense in response to the strategic threat posed by the launch of the Sputnik satellite by the USSR in 1957. The need to share information quickly and securely within the military-scientific community led to the development of a 'packet' protocol in 1965 that enabled two computers to communicate with each other over a network of academic and industrial organisations.
- **Collection:** The 1970s and 1980s saw the arrival of integrated circuits – tiny processors and memory storage on microchips that miniaturised and greatly speeded calculation. This fundamentally changed how we stored, retrieved, transferred, and analysed data. Modern and fast personal computation had arrived. By 1971 email had arrived as users began to send messages between machines (rather than to different mailboxes on the same machine) across a network. From 1974, with a growing array of networks the need to standardise the way different host computers communicated led to the evolution of the Transmission Control Protocol /Internet Protocol (TCP/IP) suite that is still used to pass packets of information across the Internet to this day. In 1989, Tim Berners-Lee, a British developer working at CERN, proposed a system of information cross-referencing, access, and retrieval. This system, 'The World', was the first internet service provider that was also open to the public.

- **Connection:** The 1990s and 2000s saw institutional, corporate, and personal computers linked together into local and global networks and a new 'virtual' marketplace was born. Up until the mid-1990s the Internet had been the realm of technologists and scientists at research institutions. But the advent of the web changed the landscape, making information accessible more quickly to a much broader audience. With more websites and more people going online every day, it was only a matter of time before marketers started to notice the web's potential as an avenue for the marketing message. It is here that the importance of geographical locality fades. With market communication becoming global and instantaneous, offshoring took off and production concentrated where it was cheapest – fundamentally changing the balance of national economies. Modern globalisation had arrived. Existing products and services became digitised (e.g., films, music, auctions, banking) and new services emerged (e.g., search engines, social media, cloud computing).
- **Capability and capacity:** The 2010s have been characterised by the ubiquity of sensors (e.g., gyroscopic sensors, magnetic sensors, blood-chemistry sensors) and the machine learning processes that are required to make sense of the oceans of data that they produce. The full capability of sensors can only be realised if this data is transferred rapidly and accurately to form a coherent response – this is where wireless networks come in. Intelligent algorithms are used for recognising things and doing something with the result. If we could collect images of humans, we could use these to recognise their faces. If we could 'see' objects such as roads and pedestrians, we could use this to automatically drive cars. This also gave us the ability, through natural language processing, to talk to a computer as we would to another human being. We now have digital language translation, face recognition, voice recognition, inductive inference, and digital assistants. Machine learning has arrived.

1.3 Principal Architecture

The essential infrastructure for digital marketing has been enabled by the Internet, which consists of a network of servers and the communication links between them that are used to hold and transport vast amounts of information. The growth in the use of the Internet occurred because of the development of the World Wide Web, a medium for publishing information and providing services that is accessed through web browsers, which display site content on different web pages. The content making up websites is stored on web servers and is accessed through web browser software such as Google

Chrome, Microsoft Edge, Apple Safari, or Mozilla Firefox, which display the information and allow users to interact with and select links to access websites. This 'computer-mediated environment' (CME) is characterised by Hoffman and Novak (1996) as a 'dynamic distributed network, potentially global in scope, together with associated hardware and software' that enables consumers and firms to communicate and access digital content.

1.4   Contemporary Development Themes

While precise predictions are difficult to make with a high degree of certainty, the work of Spivack (2007) (Figure 1.1) makes some attempt to track trends and developments towards an Internet which integrates a wide range of connected technologies (i.e., sensors, networks, and processing power) and highly embedded into our lives (i.e., automation, apps, and artificial intelligence (AI)). While we are perhaps some way away from the 'singularity' predicted by Kurzweil (2006), there are nevertheless clear themes that have a significant impact upon the current and future practice of marketing.

- **Cloud/software as a service** will grow with the continuing migration towards the use of web-based applications and services, moving away from local software applications based on individual desktops and closed networks, with all the attendant risks of outdating and cost of updates

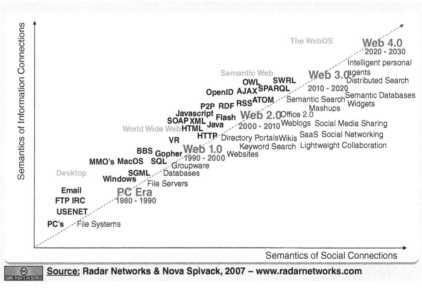

Figure 1.1 Evolution of web technologies (Spivack, 2007). Reprinted with permission of Nova Spivack.

and processing power. Workers will operate globally, and the importance of their physical location will be redundant since all they will need to work is access to a computer with a web browser. For marketing this means a truly global workforce of ideas and talents that will refine existing marketing mixes and develop new ones in a highly dynamic and decentralised fashion. There may be threats to hierarchical organisation, but the firms that thrive will be those that grant freedom and latitude to their workforce to work within comparatively loose organisational frameworks.

- **Social media sharing** will mature through the increased incorporation of syndicated content and services from other sites, or a network into a site, the increased use of streamed video and user-generated content, and increased use of immersive virtual environments such as Second Life. Users will continue the trend of being less passive consumers of content and more active in their engagement with experiences. This largely unmediated interaction between large and diverse communities will gain the attention of legislators as inevitably some users will abuse the global reach and anonymity that the Internet gives them. The responsibility to deal with 'bad actors' will be as big a matter for debate in online communities as it has been in offline communities for centuries. There will be no quick or easy solution that keeps all parties happy. Trust will be key for marketers who seek to engage directly with end users, maintain strong and consistent brand messages that are not distorted by malicious third parties (e.g., aggressive competition or criminal interests) or vexatious customer or shareholder activists.

- **The semantic Web** will continue to integrate datastreams which are aimed at anticipating and precipitating the needs of consumers. This is driven by the increased exchange of data between social networks and the increased use of semantic mark-up, which is an essential prerequisite for the development of AI applications that recommend content and services to web users. For marketers this offers significant quantitative insight into the behaviours of customers, enabling tracking and attribution across multiple online promotional channels, campaigns, and tactics. Engagement and conversion will be tracked to assess effectiveness and value for money. Analysis of this data in real time allows for further timely and relevant purchasing recommendations to be made. However, these processes will have their limitations since whatever has happened in the past may only be an indication of what may happen in the future. Creativity, an innate human trait (especially of marketers), will be required to refresh and renew this process.

- **Intelligent personal agents**, through their use of AI, will be our principal method of interacting with the Internet in the age of Web 4.0. Distributed intelligence will tailor experiences to our needs and preferences. For example, automated shopping comparison services will make decisions on the behalf of users, without them actively having to seek out choices and apply their own judgement as to the best products and brands.

1.5 The Effect of the Changing Digital Ecosystem upon the Organisation

So far in this chapter we have set the scene by identifying the evolution of digital technologies, but now need to explore their impact upon organisations and their relationships with customers. It is important to realise that not all changes are immediately identifiable as positive ones; digital globalisation has come under criticism from many sides as being responsible for industry decline, job losses, wealth destruction, and social inequality. To understand these effects, and corresponding benefits and opportunities that arise when industries transform, it is time to delve into economic and innovation literature. This section will describe the disruptive effects of individual innovations, how innovations often come in groups to create even greater levels of change, and where innovations can occur together not only to replace established practices but also to create completely new industries, opportunities, jobs, and wealth.

1.5.1 The Disruptive Effects of Digital Technologies

Christensen (1997) describes how a disruptive innovation is an advance that creates new market value, potentially disrupting or replacing an existing market in the process. Traditionally these disruptions start on a small scale as incremental changes that, over time, gain market momentum and a secure establishment of new practices and attitudes within the value chain. This acceptance and establishment of the innovation then leads to quicker and more radical innovations that will eventually destroy previously stable industries. In the non-digital world, the main barrier to more rapid and radical adoption of innovations (leading ultimately to disruption) was the time required to acquire, deploy, and fine-tune the factors of production at scale to achieve a sustainable position. Factors of production include working capital, employees, manufacturing equipment, storage, and transportation, which on a global scale represent a significant investment risk. However, the force of digital disruption does not just reduce these barriers, it obliterates them (McQuivey, 2013). Such technologies allow the disruptor to take new ideas of any size and potential impact and rapidly pursue target customers at almost no marginal average cost and in the space of a few days, rather than years. Where digital disruption differs in comparison to its non-digital predecessor is the reach of its influence. Imagine using sensor and data techniques across the value chain. Your inventory of raw materials could be optimised, freeing up space and money that could be put to other good uses; product quality could be more closely monitored within the manufacturing process so as to quickly locate and solve problems before completion; logistics could be optimised to reduce wasted products and wasted journeys; real-time sales data could be used to inform manufacturing priorities by predicting demand; customer behavioural data could feed into product development and promotional campaigns (both online and offline), significantly increasing both the effectiveness and the efficiency of the organisation. These effects no longer act upon isolated aspects of the organisation but throughout, multiplying their impact and disruptive power, not only to competitors but to the organisation itself.

DIGITAL INSIGHT 1.1 Higher Education in High Definition

In *The Digital Economy – Rethinking Promise and Peril in the Age of Networked Intelligence*, Tapscott (2015) provides an assessment of the scale and scope of digital adoption in Higher Education:

> Ironically, no institutions have been more resistant to change than universities. They have used technology primarily to improve administration rather than changing the model of pedagogy. In higher education this is all changing rapidly today, not because faculty and administrators have awoken to the new opportunities, but because the entire model of higher education is being challenged by the emergence of Massive Open Online Courses (MOOCs). Major universities are putting recorded lectures and course content online for free. Some analysts say that half of the universities in the United States will be gone within a couple of decades. Some universities want to develop a way to give students credit for MOOCs they complete. In a similar vein, a new kind of training programme, designed by businesses, will prepare thousands of workers and job seekers for high-demand jobs in the tech industry. AT&T and Udacity have launched the first 'nanodegree' programme using the MOOC format. The first courses focus on entry-level software skills. Udacity manage the programme with

DIGITAL INSIGHT 1.1 (cont.)

personalized coaching and career services, and AT&T provide direction on course content and offer paid internships for nanodegree graduates. Students are certified for the skills they learn, and the nanodegree is fully recognised for entry-level software jobs at AT&T. With technology, it is possible to offload rote learning to multimedia computers or tablets that are used outside class time. The computer customises the material to each student's pace and abilities. Rather than devoting class time to a lecture, it can be used to discuss material that the students have learned. So, it is now possible to embrace new collaboration models that emulate the nature of the small seminar and capture its benefits. The technology gives educators opportunities to develop a deeper and richer relationship with their students.

1.5.2 Waves of Innovation

According to Schumpeter (1961), a normal, healthy economy was not one in equilibrium, but one that was constantly being 'disrupted' by technological innovation. It is an accepted fact in nature that a disrupted ecosystem, through painful change, leads to a stronger and more enduring environment for actors to coexist. However, stable ecosystems with no external challenge lead to calcification, decline, and death. Schumpeter's work built upon that of Kondratieff (1925), who first drew attention to identifiable waves of change that emerge from analysis of data on prices, wages, and interest rates, as well as industrial production and consumption. In Schumpeter's view, however, each of these business cycles was unique in that they were driven by entirely different technological breakthroughs that impacted upon specific clusters of industries. According to Mathews (2013), a long upswing in a cycle started when a new set of innovations came into general use – as happened with waterpower, textiles, and iron in the late eighteenth century; steam, rail, and steel in the mid-nineteenth century; and electricity, chemicals, and the internal combustion engine at the turn of the twentieth century. Each upswing drew a corresponding growth in investment and an expansion of the economy. These booms eventually petered out as the technologies matured and returns to investors declined, only to be followed by a wave of fresh innovations that destroyed the old way of doing things and created the conditions for a new upswing. Using this methodology, it has become evident that the durations of these economic waves are shortening, from 50–60 years to around 30–40, indicating a hastening in the rate of change, possibly due in some part to the instant and ubiquitous access to information enabled by the Internet and the World Wide Web.

1.5.3 Technological Convergence

Technology convergence occurs when different forms of technologies co-habit in a single device, sharing resources and interacting (Roland, 2017). This occurs when any type of terminal can access any type of data, which in turn is able to be transmitted through any kind of 'pipe'. The Internet has been the catalyst of this process through the Internet Protocol (IP), which allows the routing and transmitting of data such as text, image, and voice (Borés et al., 2003). The European Commission (1997), in its Green Paper on Technological Convergence, illustrates this idea and defines technological convergence as 'The ability of different network platforms to carry essentially similar kinds of services, or the coming together of consumer devices such as the telephone, television, and personal computer.' Kurzweil (2006) explains that technology is accelerating at an exponential pace because of the intersection of different disciplines. Everyone seems to approve when innovation makes our lives easier and saves lives, and when new technology allows us to do more with less. Roland (2017) identifies the key benefits of technology convergence as follows:

- time- and cost-saving devices;
- improving human performance;
- allows and encourages new ways to communicate;
- more active, less passive audiences;
- a single piece of technology simply does more;
- one set of infrastructures is cheaper to operate; and
- access via a wide range of devices.

Borés et al. (2003) observed the information and communication technologies (ICT) sectors as they converged towards a unified market. Determinant factors in this process were the liberalisation of the telecommunications markets and the acceleration of technological change. Technological convergence was made possible because of a confluence of technological and economic factors. On the technological side, the key factor is the evolution of communications and information technologies. On the economics side, the most important factor is the global liberalisation of the telecommunications markets. In addition to these macro-level factors there were also significant driving forces within the industry. The possibility of digitising all types of signals gave rise to technological convergence across networks and platforms, which had implications both for the supply (merging of different sectors that were previously separated) and the demand (the sheer ubiquity along with cheap and easy access to information and connectivity greatly heightening the rate at which they were used by organisations and individuals alike). Also, the costs of voice and data transmission had experienced a remarkable decrease, made possible thanks to an improvement in compression techniques and the reduction in the costs of infrastructures.

DIGITAL INSIGHT 1.2 Divergent Audiences through Convergent Technologies

Media convergence is the joining together of different mass communication formats and the Internet. This is especially apparent in the creative media sector – think photography (Google Images, iStock, Instagram), films (YouTube, Netflix, Amazon Prime), games (App Store), television (BBC iPlayer), and music (Spotify, iTunes). For example, think about *Harry Potter and the Philosopher's Stone* in printed book form. Media convergence has put the book put onto your Kindle to read, made it available to download as an audio book from Audible to listen to when travelling, made it into a movie that can be downloaded or streamed to your tablet or PC, and even made it into an interactive video game for people to play on their games console. This phenomenon is not merely an adaptation from one form of media to another, such as toys being produced from films, but a deepening of your original content to make it more complex and accessible. Display advertisers also provide website links, either in the form of uniform resource locator (URL) addresses or quick recognition (QR) codes that can be scanned by the camera in your smartphone to access richer content, creating a deeper sensory relationship with more informed customers who are now hopefully loyal as they may be accessing this content through the company's proprietary app, which by definition excludes the prospect of competition that a simple search using a web browser would reveal.

Source: Roland (2017)

The most well-known and understandable type of convergence is the smartphone itself, where ICT, computer networks, and media came together into one platform (Roland, 2017). Many experts contend that the first 'real' smartphone was the original iPhone, which was launched in 2007. As more stable versions of the smartphone were released, other devices such as music players, personal digital assistants (PDAs, incorporating diary, address book, and note-taking functionality), web access (to include browsing and email), cameras, reading materials, and maps were redundant since their singular functions were now aggregated into one convenient device.

Although the smartphone is a strong example of how technological convergence consolidates traditional industries (Grover and Vaswani, 2000; Roland, 2017), it also shows how it creates the effect of blurring the lines between industries, often causing unprecedented crossovers (e.g., Microsoft's Xbox would have once been part of the information technology industry, but is now part of the entertainment industry) and entirely new industries. Just think how digital convergence has changed the way we consume the traditional television product (i.e., delivery of television over the Internet vs as a traditional broadcast, recording/downloading, catch-up/on-demand/streaming, interactions such as voting).

However, disruption and convergence need not spell the end of an organisation. The ability to identify threats/opportunities, plan the necessary change responses, and respond at a time when the organisations have sufficient funds to reinvest (i.e., before their entire business model is at the mercy of declining demand and cut-price competitors) can be a core competence of an organisation. International Business Machines (IBM), one of the largest information technology companies in the world, offers hardware, software, and services principally to corporate clients and is an example of network convergence, combining voice, video networks, and data networks. Its latest development, termed 'cognitive computing' by the organisation, represents a significant investment in its AI capabilities. Through a series of algorithms and application programming interfaces (APIs), the IBM Watson™ Conversation service combines machine learning, natural language understanding, and integrated dialogue tools to create conversation flows between an organisation's apps and its users. The technology uses different language analysis algorithms to find answers to questions. Once the system has some potential answers, it checks them against a database for the most likely correct solution to a question.

1.5.4 The Near Future of Disruption and Convergence

Many believe that the full potential of the Internet and the World Wide Web has yet to be realised. With a borderless network of users, a common language in its universally accepted communication protocols, and a vast audience eager to engage and consume content across multiple channels and devices, what does the future hold? Roland (2017) identified three big technologies that now underlie the next big crop of convergent breakthroughs:

- **Artificial intelligence (AI)**, also known as machine learning (ML), is when machines can perceive and interpret the environment, recommending actions you should take to achieve your goals within it. This involves a deep analysis of your response behaviours in relation to specific environmental stimuli, and also the encoding of your knowledge, reasoning, problem-solving skills, planning, learning, and ability to manipulate other people and objects. Deep learning is when these artificial neural networks enable machines to learn on their own, adapt, and get better. Coupled with robotics, AI/ML not only has the capability to think (i.e., to collect data, analyse it, and recommend a plan of action), but also to actively pursue these goals through positive action without the need for human intervention.

- **Blockchain** is a distributed database that grows as 'blocks' (i.e., sets of recorded transactions) are added to it. These recordings cannot be changed or deleted, and may be publicly viewed or seen by anyone with access to the network. It is claimed to be an incorruptible, unhackable, global spreadsheet that has the potential to revolutionise how transactions on the Internet are made and secured. It also presents significant transaction cost and time savings as the authorisation and recording of transactions is automated (i.e., no need for retail banks or state treasuries) and is charged at an extremely low cost to the 'miners' who facilitate the transaction. Its principal use today has been in the development of cryptocurrencies (e.g., Bitcoin), which is actively disrupting the banking system overseen by state treasuries, but it is also moving into 'smart contracts', which will disrupt the legal profession overseen by state judiciaries.

- **The Internet of Things (IoT)** is when physical devices contain sensors that connect to the Internet, usually via Wi-Fi, collect data, exchange data, make decisions, and remotely control the device, all without direct human interference or oversight. At a basic level this might involve your choice in groceries that will also give you the best deal on accompanying products, or even provide recipe suggestions. At a more complex level your Tesla car will analyse the condition of the key components of your car in real time, offering proactive notifications of potential problems. New data can also be uploaded to the vehicle's operating system to alter its performance – for example, by boosting power. Besides anticipating and precipitating consumer choices, IoT throws up other potential convergent possibilities. For example, the diverse fields of nanotechnology, biotechnology, information technology, and cognitive science are converging, to improve social productivity, emergency response, communication and performance, age-related deterioration, and evolutionary advancements (Roco and Bainbridge, 2003).

1.6   Challenges and Opportunities for the Practice of Marketing

Now it is time to focus directly upon the specific digital drivers that impact upon the practice of marketing, both now and in the future. Tapscott (2015) highlights issues that have a direct impact upon the marketing relationship, which are distilled as follows:

- Knowledge is more easily captured, catalogued, and accessed in digital form. Data can be analysed and decisions made within ever-shorter stimulus–response timescales. This change in the format and use of knowledge has created choice for the consumer and significantly changed the role of the market intermediary (i.e., the agent that brokers transactions between the producer and the consumer). In the early years of the World Wide Web it was thought that the role of the intermediary was redundant since the two main parties could now communicate directly. An example of this might be an insurance sales representative. While it was possible for consumers to deal directly with insurers, the sheer number of options led to poor choices; the intermediary reappeared in virtual form as price comparison websites. While data increases the feeling of choice and empowerment, it still needs to be made meaningful by a skilled interpreter, be they human or machine. Such a reimagining of the role of knowledge, especially with the evolution of Web 2.0, which enabled a truly interactive web, has led to the emergence of 'prosumers', which in the new age of networked intelligence brings forward the possibility of mass customisation. Thus, the distinctions between producers and customers begin to overlap and every consumer on the information highway is now also a producer, creating and sending a message to order or specify their opinions, additions, adjustments, and specifications about the product or service they are purchasing.
- Globalisation has accelerated to unprecedented levels due to the wide and rapid adoption of compatible internet hardware and World Wide Web software standards. This 'always on' matrix-style network of individual users has enabled largely free, easy, and fast connections across national, linguistic, economic, and social boundaries. The effect has been to truly open a world market largely free from artificial barriers that prevent people and companies from working together. There have been significant costs (i.e., national protected industries that struggled against better or cheaper external competition), but also significant benefits (e.g., access to new medicines, foods, cultures, and friendships). This paradigm shift in the locus of power in trading relationships (from governments

and companies to customers and consumers) has led to discordance at economic, social, and technological levels between the 'haves' and the 'have-nots' which is growing and may cause significant societal stresses in the future.

- Innovation thrives when human imagination and creativity are the main sources of value. Any platform for the sharing and collaboration of ideas (such as the World Wide Web) will lead to the development of new products and services. The digital economy has created opportunities for technological convergence, particularly in the areas of computing, communications, and content. These together create the interactive multimedia that is one of the platforms on which the new age is dependent. New convergence opportunities have also been created in finance (e.g., online banking, cryptocurrencies, cashless transactions), transport (e.g., ridesharing), and disposal (e.g., eBay, Amazon) markets.

DIGITAL INSIGHT 1.3 Your Virtual Doctor Will See You Now

Digital technologies have few more opportunities to positively impact individual human wellbeing than in the healthcare sector. From global drug companies, through national public and private healthcare systems, to local welfare and rehabilitation groups, the ready access to reliable information can make a life-or-death difference through the accurate diagnoses of illnesses (or their prevention) and timely treatment interventions. In the United States 80 per cent of internet users look for health and medical information online and 98 per cent of physicians are online and 'spend at least 50 minutes per night online researching disease information, drug information, and to a lesser degree, Continuing Medical Education (CME) information' (Schiavo, 2008). Similarly, searching for medical or health-related information is 'the third most popular use after e-mail and general browsing' among internet users in Canadian households. The appetite among healthcare professionals, patients, and carers for healthcare information is served by sophisticated and visually appealing websites, podcasts, webinars, chat forums, audio and video files, animations, virtual support groups, audience feedback mechanisms, and disease simulators, which have become widespread among different kinds of health organisations. Interactive health communications is a well-established area of health communication and has been defined as the 'interaction of an individual – consumer, patient, caregiver or professional – with or through an electronic device or communication technology to access or transmit health information or to receive guidance and support on a health-related issue'. Healthcare, however, is a challenge where access to resources and treatments is often unequal and illnesses frequently present differently, with many central and peripheral complicating factors. As such the credentials and experience (both personal and as part of a wider network of practitioners) of the medic is not something that can be easily coded to give the right response every time. As for other kinds of mass media channels, the Internet is not intended to replace the human touch of interpersonal communications, but for some of its applications (e.g., virtual support groups, professional and consumer blogs) it is well positioned to build and maintain communities and groups.

1.7   Digital Technology Has Driven Changes in the Marketing Relationship

Yadav and Pavlou (2014) offer a framework that examines consumer and firm activities in CMEs, depicting a set of behavioural interactions. Their work offers an important overview of how the digital ecosystem impacts upon the conduct of market relationships (Table 1.1) and how these are likely to change with the emergence and adoption of new technologies. Since marketing acts as the nexus between the firm and its customers, their analysis establishes an understanding of the process dynamics required of the marketing function.

RESEARCH INSIGHT 1.1 Dynamic Digital Marketing Relationships

Yadav, M., and Pavlou, P. (2014). Marketing in computer-mediated environments: research synthesis and new directions. *Journal of Marketing*, 78(1): 20–40.

This paper provides structure and guidance to the rapidly increasing digital marketing research stream which has previously been fragmented and lacking in overall direction. The authors organise and synthesise findings from the literature using a framework structured around four key interactions in CMEs: consumer–firm interactions, firm–consumer interactions, consumer–consumer interactions, and firm–firm interactions.

> **RESEARCH INSIGHT 1.2 The Shifting Foundations of Digital Marketing**
>
> Lamberton, C., and Stephen, A. (2016). A thematic exploration of digital, social media, and mobile marketing: research evolution from 2000 to 2015 and an agenda for future inquiry. *Journal of Marketing*, 80(6): 146–172.
>
> This paper examines how over the period 2000–2015, digital media platforms have revolutionised marketing, offering new ways to reach, inform, engage, sell to, learn about, and provide service to customers. This article tracks the changes in academic research perspectives across the three key themes of digital, social media, and mobile marketing.

Table 1.1 The impact of CMEs upon the interactions between and across firms and consumers (adapted from Yadav and Pavlou, 2014).

	From: Consumer	From: Firm
To: Consumer	*Established behaviours* • Online community participation enhances loyalty and influences new product adoption • Communication originating in online communities has more pronounced long-term effects than firm-initiated communication • Negative word-of-mouth behaviours are motivated primarily by a desire to address a perceived injustice. Their unfavourable impact on stock prices, volatility, and cash flows can be substantial and long term	*Established behaviours* • Recommendation systems must incorporate consumers' stated and unstated preferences • Presenting real-time, personalised products based on online browsing patterns increases purchases • Website investments to increase interactivity increase trust in the firm • Customer-initiated communication is significantly more effective than firm-initiated communication • Price customisation increases profitability, but it can also create evaluation difficulties for customers and trigger perceptions of unfairness • Buyers at online stores are less price-sensitive than those at offline stores
	Emerging behaviours • Leveraging and monetising social media assets through 'social commerce' • Generation and management of curated multimedia collections that are more complex than textual content	*Emerging behaviours* • Digital augmentation of products creates a new class of personalisation (e.g., apparel recommendations, 3D printing of products) • Customised pricing offers create a significantly more engaged and empowered customer base • Same-day fulfilment infrastructure and strategies

Table 1.1 (cont.)		
	From: Consumer	**From: Firm**
To: Firm	*Established behaviours* • Drivers of online trust vary significantly across websites • Excessive search may lead to poor choices • Decision tools improve consumers' decision quality and reduce effort • In online auctions, bidders' experience level, past outcomes, future expectations, product descriptions, reference prices, and bidding format affect bidding behaviour	*Established behaviours* • A shift is occurring from hierarchical to networked organisational structures • Despite declining search costs, price competition may not increase as much as expected • Finer segmentation, product design changes, and behaviour-based discrimination potentially increase firms' power and mitigate competition. • Open-bid reverse auction formats can be detrimental to long-term relationships
	Emerging behaviours • A desktop-centric perspective dominates, but consumers now rely on a significantly expanded set of devices (e.g., interaction with gestures, augmented-reality glasses) • Search criteria and outcomes are no longer limited to textual content (e.g., voice-based search, location-based mobile search) • Consumers are increasingly making decisions by integrating information across multiple devices	*Emerging behaviours* • A new generation of B2B intermediaries, with an emphasis on new functionalities and efficiencies, remains unexplored • Implications of platform-based competition between firms (e.g., third-party marketplaces, platforms for payments, platforms for apps and content) • Application of online reverse auctions to non-procurement contexts such as sustainability and environmental protection

1.8   A New Practice of Marketing

Digital technologies have fundamentally changed the way in which organisations and customers interact with one another. Since marketing is a management discipline tasked with brokering this relationship, a fundamental rethink is required to understand in detail how marketing practice is changing. The work of Kannan and Li (2017) provides a holistic framework that takes a systematic approach to the work of the marketer. Their framework first considers the environment, which is driven by consumer interactions via digital platforms. Assuming an existing relationship with these customers, the model then translates customers' needs through the prism of the marketing mix, which helps the firm assess to what degree the relationship meets the ongoing needs of the organisation. Should the organisation seek to maximise these outcomes – and most do – it will then need to engage in a market research process to understand how best to achieve these goals. This overall relationship is governed by the marketing strategy of the organisation.

RESEARCH INSIGHT 1.3 New Directions for Marketing in the Digital Ecosystem

Kannan, P., and Li, H. (2017). Digital marketing: a framework, review and research agenda. *International Journal of Research in Marketing*, 34(1): 22–45.

This paper establishes a framework for research in digital marketing that focuses upon the key tactical and strategic aspects of the firm's marketing processes, where digital technologies have made the biggest impact. They go on to identify future research in digital marketing.

From chatbots to wearables, and from mobile customer relationship management to hands-free payment apps, rapid technological advances are changing the way marketers connect with audiences (Benady, 2016). But the value that these transformative technologies create is enabled only if marketers constantly update their skills, stay on top of how these new techniques can be applied to their challenges, and learn how to implement them effectively and efficiently. It is the mission of this book to acknowledge and keep pace with advancements in marketing practice, particularly regarding the enabling power of technology in marketing.

1.9   The Eight Drivers of Digital Marketing

Marketers will need to fully understand both the technical and strategic implications of a wide range of existing and emerging digital marketing practices. The effect upon physical marketing activities is illustrated by the eight drivers of digital marketing:

- **Product:** Product lifecycles will shorten, and the number of variants expected within and across product families will rise significantly. There will be an expectation for products/services to be both 'connected' and 'smart' because of technology convergence. Customisation at scale will become the norm. New products will succeed or fail quickly.

- **Price:** Pricing will become dynamic, with cost, inventory, and sales data coalescing in real time. This will mobilise larger numbers of buyers, allowing the economically and socially disadvantaged to access products previously unaffordable in the days of fixed or segmented prices. 'Pay what you think it is worth' programmes will become more widespread.
- **Place:** The switch from retail 'collection' to online 'delivery' models will increase environmental damage through vehicle pollution and packaging waste. Analytics, enhanced apps, local delivery hubs, and aerial drones will be the key to efficient distribution.
- **Promotion:** Message, creative content, and channel effectiveness will largely remain a mystery to advertisers and influencers. The big challenge here is that of consumers' attitudes to their personal privacy. Sophisticated biometric tracking and behavioural data collection, interpretation, and actioning techniques exist, but so do the ethical frameworks and consumer suspicion of financial/political exploitation. Regulation of the worst excesses of personal data exploitation will arrive. On the whole, consumers and states will loosen their resistance so that their needs can be met more effectively and more efficiently through technology. Cybercrime will be a major industry.
- **People:** The 'always on' nature of the Internet, which allows massive amounts of data to be accessed through multiple channels, will change how we interact with work, leisure, and each other. The mental health implications of the Internet, and the behaviours it empowers, will drive regulation. Employment rights and taxation regulations will need to adapt to how people work in the growing 'gig' economy. Work pressures and opportunities will rise. It is the ability of workers to identify and adapt that will ensure survival and success. Traditional curricula in compulsory and post-compulsory education will no longer be fit for purpose as educational institutions build more dynamic lifelong learning models to equip a rapidly changing global workforce.
- **Processes:** The need for sustainable production, consumption, and re-use will push organisations to become 'resource intelligent' – using sensors, networks, and data to eliminate waste from the extended value chain (i.e., from product design to its post-consumption redundancy). Customer relationship management will develop more sophisticated approaches that will build more post-purchase value for customers (particularly through communities and experiences) while being less intrusive to the customer. This follows the realisation that traditional loyalty schemes and feedback programmes are no longer fit for purpose.

- **Physical evidence:** As an aspect of the marketing mix this element will be largely subsumed into product, price, place, and process. What will emerge is a greater emphasis upon the physical experience, which will focus upon entertainment, engagement, and emotion.
- **Partnerships:** As markets change so will the nature of the organisations that form them. Traditional analysis and deployment activities need fewer people, and more operational tasks become automated. Rapid and radical change will lead to flexible organisations and adaptable workers. The required rate of innovation will be too fast and too radical for traditional hierarchies to keep up. With the global scope of both online and offline marketplaces it will be more cost-effective to collaborate, for whatever duration, than to build and own a full value chain.

CHAPTER SUMMARY

This chapter sets the scene for the discussion and detailed development of the practice of marketing within a digital ecosystem. The key infrastructure of the World Wide Web and the Internet is discussed, along with their origins. The mass adoption of this new capability has changed the way that firms and consumers interact with one another and has fundamentally redefined many established industries, rendering some obsolete and giving rise to many new ones. The changing nature of the marketing relationship within this new paradigm requires new disciplines and practices that will be explored further within this book.

Review Questions

- What technological, economic, and social factors helped the Internet and World Wide Web to move from a specialist niche collaboration tool to a global network of interconnected technologies with mass appeal?
- How has the customer–organisation relationship changed in the last few years and what changes do you envisage in the near future?
- What are the main drivers for the new practice of digital marketing and what is their relative importance to each other?
- What opportunities and threats exist due to the disruptive and convergence effects of digital technologies?
- How will the practice of marketing need to change to be relevant in the evolving digital ecosystem?

END-OF-CHAPTER CASE: BLOCKBUSTER AND NETFLIX

Dominance of Blockbuster

In 1985, in the midst of a sharp downturn in the oil and gas industry – to which he sold software – David Cook opened the first Blockbuster store in Dallas, Texas. In a period of limited television channels, movie rental had given consumers unheard-of choice of viewing. Within two years Blockbuster was sold for $18.5 million and by 1992 it was the undisputed video rental leader, with over 2,800 stores worldwide. The company's growth was driven by acquisitions of other retailers such as Britain's Ritz and US chains Major Video and Erol's Video. Media conglomerate Viacom bought Blockbuster for $8.4 billion in 1994. In 2004 Blockbuster was at the peak of its powers, with 25,500 employees at 8,000 stores dispensing movie rentals and a parallel distribution system of 6,000 DVD public vending machines (Halal, 2011).

Emergence of Netflix

Software engineers Reed Hastings and Marc Rudolph founded Netflix in 1997 to use the Internet to rent movies (they had no physical store locations) only in the new DVD format, even though the VHS cassette was prevalent at that time. Users could search through the collection and select the desired title. The DVD was mailed to the customer using the United States Parcel Service. The mail-rental model offered customers a far greater choice against the few hundred available in a typical Blockbuster store and needed only a few centralised distribution centres, as against a labour-intensive network of retail stores. However, Netflix soon realised that this business model was inefficient as it was spending $100–200 for a customer to make one $4 rental. As a solution, in 1999 Netflix moved to the prepaid subscription-based model, which had the triple effect of building customer loyalty through frequency of use, turning the long delivery time to an advantage since choices were likely to be predictable based on tastes and not impulse purchases, and allowing Netflix to offer 'unlimited' DVDs per month, taking away patchy transaction costs, per-day rental, and late return fees. The next hurdle Netflix faced was how to deal with high demand for hit and new movies, and the user frustration when the chosen movie was unavailable. They achieved this through a recommendation system that made suggestions of movies that were available and might be of interest based on preferences and history. The success of the recommendation system decreased the demand for newer releases to 20 per cent of the total demand, compared to the 70 per cent for traditional video rentals (Deshpande, 2010).

Competing Business Models

Although Blockbuster and Netflix competed in the same video rental market, they really did different jobs for consumers. Blockbuster had made its core business the idea of a 'movie night', which assumed that most movie rentals were impulse decisions for people who wanted to watch a movie straight away. These films were typically new releases and thus were the majority of films that Blockbuster stocked in their nationwide retail network. Netflix, on the other hand, had evolved to view movie watching as a regular part of daily entertainment and instead appealed to the customers who did not see 'movie night' as an infrequent event, but instead as an ordinary form of regular entertainment like watching television. Monthly fees instead of rentals, mail delivery instead of pickup, and a wide choice of movies instead of just new releases were all a part of the Netflix operations strategy. While Netflix's model clearly had some compelling aspects, it also had some obvious disadvantages. Without retail locations it was hard for people to find it. With its mail order distribution strategy, service was somewhat slow and renters could not just pick up a movie for the night on impulse on their way home. This forced a change in consumer behaviour: limited choices with instant availability but potentially high fees (the Blockbuster model) versus a wide range of choices that required patience and planning but was rewarded with lower fees (the Netflix model).

Netflix saw the opportunity to take their business model entirely online, dealing with the costly and expensive process of storing and processing thousands of titles and the operational and financial limitations to growth implicit in the cassette/disc rental model. Even when few Americans had broadband in 2000, they knew that renting video cassettes would soon yield to streaming movies over the Internet. Thus, Netflix set to work on a TV box that would stream movies, but due to bandwidth, processor, and storage limitations it required 16 hours of download time per movie. Blockbuster also knew that this disruptive technology shift was coming, but it had its own financial and governance problems and would not take the plunge. Instead, they tried to beef up sales by diversifying their stores into outlets for books, toys, drinks, snacks, and other merchandise.

Confluence

In 2000, Reed Hastings flew to Dallas to propose a partnership to Blockbuster CEO John Antioco and his team. The idea was that Netflix would run Blockbuster's brand online and Blockbuster would promote Netflix in its stores. Hastings was laughed out of the room (Satell, 2014). When Hastings proposed his deal Blockbuster sat atop the video rental industry. With thousands of retail locations, millions of customers, massive marketing budgets, and efficient operations, it dominated the competition. This dominance may have led to complacency and overconfidence in the brand they had worked hard to build. Yet Blockbuster's model had a weakness that was not clear until a competing model highlighted this to consumers, giving them an alternative. Blockbuster earned an enormous amount of money by charging its customers late fees (which in 2000 amounted to almost $800 million – roughly 16 per cent of its revenue), which made penalising its patrons essential to the viability of the business. Netflix had the antidote to this unhappy relationship. By eschewing retail locations, it lowered costs and could afford to offer its customers far greater variety. Instead of charging to rent videos, it offered subscriptions, which made annoying late fees unnecessary. Customers could watch a video for as long as they wanted or return it and get a new one.

Demise of Blockbuster

Netflix proved to be a very disruptive innovation because Blockbuster would have to alter its business model – and damage its profitability – to compete with the start-up. Despite being a small, niche service at the time, Netflix had the potential to upend Blockbuster's well-oiled machine. Blockbuster responded by launching its own online rental service in 2004, with customers able to return their DVDs simply through a local store. Although Blockbuster began a rentals-by-mail and streaming service belatedly to fight competitors like Netflix, they didn't come on strong enough or soon enough. It was a battle between old technology and new technology, and new technology won out in the end (Satell, 2014).

Once John Antioco became convinced that Netflix was a threat, he used his authority as CEO – as well as the credibility he had earned by nearly doubling Blockbuster's revenues during his tenure – to discontinue the late fees that annoyed customers and invest heavily in a digital platform to ensure the brand's future. While he convinced the board to back his plan, Carl Icahn (a major investor) pointed out that the costs of Antioco's changes – about $200 million to drop late fees and another $200 million to launch Blockbuster Online – were damaging profitability. Antioco lost the board's confidence and stepped down in 2007. A new CEO immediately reversed Antioco's changes to increase profitability. In 2009 Blockbuster closed more than 1,800 stores and withdrew from some national markets altogether. After continued heavy losses Blockbuster filed for bankruptcy a year later, in 2010, when it lost $1.1 billion. The company at the time was valued at around $24 million, while Netflix's worth had risen to around $13 billion.

Subsequent Development of Netflix

When faster broadband and better video compression allowed YouTube and other Web 2.0 sites to erupt on the scene around 2005, Hastings realised that the time had come to cannibalise his DVD rental business in favour of streaming video. He also knew that developing a 'box' was too limiting, and that an open-source approach would allow Netflix to distribute movies on TVs, DVD players, desktop computers, mobile phones, or almost any device. As internet capacity had improved, in 2007 Netflix began to stream movies straight to customers' computers. With the rise in availability of broadband Internet and Internet-connectible devices, the video-on-demand (VOD) business model had gained prominence. VOD is a pay-per-view ability to access any multimedia content via an individual web browser or TV set based on user requests (Deshpande, 2010). VOD systems either stream content through a set-top box, a computer, or other device, allowing viewing in real time, or download it to a device such as a computer, digital video recorder, or portable media player for viewing at any time. To help their customers give up DVDs, Netflix did the unthinkable – they gave away streaming movies and made it easy. To split its DVD and streaming businesses, Netflix created Qwikster for DVD distribution in 2011. Within a month consumer protests prompted the company to drop the idea.

By 2013 the company had moved into original programming with *House of Cards*, a series about Washington intrigue produced by David Fincher (Downes and Nunes, 2013). Netflix had invested $100 million for two 13-episode seasons – a huge risk – but the first season earned eight Emmy nominations and greatly increased Netflix's visibility.

What can be learned from this case? Netflix illustrates the central role that emerging technology plays in transforming an industry. Because Hastings is a Stanford computer scientist and a Silicon Valley entrepreneur, he knew it would soon be feasible to stream movies, but he also knew the switch had to be timed quite precisely. Taking such a big risk too early would invite a bleeding-edge failure, while a few years later the field would be left to competitors. He also knew that having employees run shops, charging for rentals, late fees, etc. were outmoded relics of the past, while online service delivered by a virtual organisation offered unbeatable value.

DISCUSSION QUESTIONS

- With reference to the models discussed earlier, what were the key factors in Netflix's success and Blockbuster's failure in their ability to adapt to the evolving digital infrastructure?
- Could Blockbuster have survived? If so, how would you have advised the company and how would you provide a compelling case to deal with their concerns?

Develop Your Skills

· ·

What Is the Skill?

Customer experience (CX) is the product of an interaction between an organisation and a customer over the duration of their relationship. This interaction is made up of three parts: the customer journey, the brand touchpoints the customer interacts with, and the environments the customer experiences (including digital environments) during their experience. A good customer experience means that the individual's experience during all points of contact matches the individual's expectations, which could lead to satisfaction, loyalty, profitability, and competitive advantage.

Why Is It Important?

Digital technologies have revolutionised business. New entrants often emerge rapidly and unexpectedly, aggressively threatening and displacing the leaders. Technologies such as cloud computing, social media, and smart mobility provide challengers with global scale and enterprise-grade infrastructure at little cost. With the resource and cultural limitations of incumbency removed, new companies are left to compete on the quality of their offerings, and, increasingly, the distinguishing feature is the experience customers are offered. Consumers are seeing service levels increase dramatically, and as consumers become more enriched and empowered, their expectations grow accordingly. In Australia alone, poor customer experiences are estimated to cost business a staggering A$122 billion each year. A big part of the problem is that in the rush to digital, many organisations are losing track of the importance of the human element (Association for Data-Driven Marketing & Advertising, 2016). Factor into this that 90 per cent of customers and prospects say it is important for retailers to let them shop for products in a way that is convenient for them no matter what channel they choose. Also, 94 per cent of customers and prospects will end a relationship with a brand because of irrelevant ads or promotions. Customers with the best experiences spend 140 per cent more in the subsequent year compared to those with the poorest experiences.

How to Develop It

Harvard Business Review (2016) offers the following lessons in CX management:

- Think like a customer. What primary and peripheral connections do you have with a similar organisation (or one that is more sophisticated)?

What delights and frustrates you about every interaction? Think aspirationally, developing ideas by starting thoughts with the phrase 'Wouldn't it be great if . . .?'

- Expand the definition of CX success across multiple touchpoints. This will include offline (i.e., in a person-to-person interaction) or online in a more automated environment, not forgetting that the experience should be consistent across multiple devices.
- Understand what drives value, both on a transactional basis (i.e., conversion and up-sell rates) and also the longer-term relationship (i.e., customer lifetime value, indirect traffic, social media sentiment). This insight is easily available through a range of metrics. But before you delve into the huge range of possible measurements, start with a list of what should be measured. This might not be more than 10 things, but should represent the full experience from being drawn to an organisation all the way through to paying for the purchase (and possibly even returning it!).

How to Apply It

Develop a checklist for a service you receive and rate your experience each time. What improvements would you recommend? Which might be the costs and benefits of making such an improvement? Not everything is a great idea and many organisations must choose between competing priorities by making 'opportunity-cost' decisions to benefit the organisation in the longer term.

References

American Marketing Association (2013). About AMA [online]. Available from: www.ama.org/AboutAMA/Pages/Definition-of-Marketing.aspx [Accessed 10 March 2018].

Arthur, W. B. (2017) Where is technology taking the economy? *McKinsey Quarterly.* October.

Association for Data-Driven Marketing & Advertising (2016). Driving stronger returns from customer experience [online]. Available from: www.adma.com.au/system/files/article/ADMA_CX_Whitepaper%202016.pdf [Accessed 9 June 2018].

Benady, D. (2016). The shock of the new. *Exchange Magazine.* Chartered Institute of Marketing.

Borés, C., Saurina, C., and Torres, R. (2003). Technological convergence: a strategic perspective. *Technovation*, 23(1): 1.

Christensen, C. (1997). *The Innovator's Dilemma: When New Technologies Cause Great Firms to Fail.* Boston: Harvard Business School Press.

Deshpande, A. (2010). Netflix vs. Blockbuster [online]. Available from: http://amitadeshpande.blogspot.co.uk/2010/12/Netflix-vs-blockbuster.html [Accessed 5 January 2018].

Downes, L., and Nunes, P. (2013). Blockbuster becomes a casualty of big bang disruption [online]. Available from: https://hbr.org/2013/11/blockbuster-becomes-a-casualty-of-big-bang-disruption [Accessed 5 February 2018].

European Commission (1997). Green paper on the convergence of telecommunications, the media and the information technology [online]. Available from https://ec.europa.eu/digital-single-market/en/news/green-paper-convergence-telecom munications-media-and-information-technology-sectors-and   [Accessed 21 February 2018].

Financial Times (2018). Definition of digital marketing [online]. Available from http://lexicon.ft.com/Term?term=digital-marketing [Accessed 10 March 2018].

Gribbin, A. (2011). A brief history of the internet. *New Statesman*, 140(5066): 30.

Grover, V., and Vaswani, P. (2000). Partnerships in the U.S. telecommunications industry. *Communications of the ACM*, 43(2): 80–89.

Halal, W. E. (2011). How Netflix beat Blockbuster: an exemplar of emerging technologies [online]. Available from: http://billhalal.com/?p=295 [Accessed 5 February 2018].

Harvard Business Review (2016). Lessons from the leading edge of customer experience management [online]. Available from: https://hbr.org/resources/pdfs/tools/SAS_Report_April2014_webview.pdf [Accessed 9 June 2018].

Hoffman, D., and Novak, T. (1996). Marketing in hypermedia computer-mediated environments: conceptual foundations. *Journal of Marketing*, 60(July): 50–68.

Kannan, P., and Li, H. (2017). Digital marketing: a framework, review and research agenda. *International Journal of Research in Marketing*, 34(1): 22–45.

Kondratieff, N. D. (1925). The static and dynamic view of economics. *Quarterly Journal of Economics*, 39(4): 575–583.

Kurzweil, R. (2006). *The Singularity Is Near.* London: Duckworth.

Lamberton, C., and Stephen, A. (2016). A thematic exploration of digital, social media, and mobile marketing: research evolution from 2000 to 2015 and an agenda for future inquiry. *Journal of Marketing*, 80(6): 146–172.

Mathews, J. A. (2013). The renewable energies technology surge: a new techno-economic paradigm in the making? *Futures*, 46(February): 10–22.

McQuivey, J. (2013). *Digital Disruption: Unleashing the Next Wave of Innovation.* Las Vegas: Amazon Publishing.

Roco, M., and Bainbridge, W. (2003). *Converging Technologies for Improving Human Performance.* Dordrecht: Kluwer Academic Publishers.

Roland, C. (2017). The complete and modern guide to technology convergence [online]. Available from: https://shape.att.com/blog/technology-convergence [Accessed 21 February 2018].

Ryan, D., and Jones, C. (2013). *Understanding Digital Marketing: Marketing Strategies for Engaging the Digital Generation.* London: Kogan Page.

Satell, G. (2014). A look back at why Blockbuster really failed and why it didn't have to [online]. Available from: www.forbes.com/sites/gregsatell/2014/09/05/a-look-back-at-why-blockbuster-really-failed-and-why-it-didnt-have-to/#2cad deb11d64 [Accessed 5 January 2018].

Schiavo, R. (2008). Digital marketing: the rise of e-health: current trends and topics on online health communications. *Journal of Medical Marketing*, 8(1): 9–18.

Schumpeter, J. A. (1961). *Capitalism, Socialism and Democracy*, 4th ed. London: Allen and Unwin.

Spivack, N. (2007). How the WebOS evolves? [online]. Available from: http://novaspivack.typepad.com/nova_spivacks_Weblog/2007/02/steps_towards_a .html [Accessed 6 March 2018].

Tapscott, D. (2015). *The Digital Economy: Rethinking Promise and Peril in the Age of Networked Intelligence*. New York: McGraw-Hill.

Yadav, M., and Pavlou, P. (2014). Marketing in computer-mediated environments: research synthesis and new directions. *Journal of Marketing*, 78(1): 20–40.

2 Insights
Big Data and Analytics

Introduction

This chapter looks in detail at the beginning of the digital marketing process and how the key 'fuel' of data is created, collected, analysed, and utilised to support the organisation's goals. These processes require an understanding of how our online behaviours are tracked and the challenges to the organisation making use of this data, sometimes collecting and exploiting personal data to subsequently influence the subject's decisions and actions. Having real-time and historical data that can be interrogated in depth to see key trends informs the strategic approach of the organisation. Additionally, granular detail of the behaviours of customers and consumers helps us to track and predict purchase behaviours to make sure that the right offering is in the right place at the right time, with a purchasing action triggered by the right stimulus. Overall, this ability to amass, interrogate, and interpret data sets over time gives us some idea of future directions of market needs, hopefully ahead of our competitors.

Learning Objectives

- Summarise how digital data is captured, stored, and utilised by organisations.
- Consider the legal and ethical drivers for the correct use of personal data.
- Recommend approaches to market research and testing.
- Appraise trustworthiness in the digital marketplace.

CASE INSIGHT: BIG DATA MEETS BIG BROTHER

Imagine a world where many of your interactions are recorded and scored as either positive or negative to distil them into a single number, creating your Citizen Score. Plus, your rating would be publicly ranked against that of the entire population and used to determine your eligibility for a mortgage or a job, where your children can go to school, or even just your chances of getting a date. Development of this system is underway in China, where the government is developing the Social Credit System to rate the trustworthiness of its citizens.

Individuals are assessed across five factors. These are credit history (whether you pay your electricity or phone bill on time), fulfilment capacity (the ability to meet your contractual obligations), personal characteristics (verifying personal information such as someone's mobile phone number and address), behaviour and preference (indicating a sense of responsibility), and interpersonal relationships (group and individual connections and interactions). Higher scores represent less risk and grant the holder not only access to higher amounts of loan credit and VIP customer experiences, but also access to enhanced government services – for example, the ability to apply for travel without supporting documents such as an employee letter, or getting a fast-tracked application to a coveted pan-European Schengen visa.

Currently the system does not directly penalise people for being 'untrustworthy', but lower scores will mean that untrustworthy people won't be able to rent a car or may have lower or more expensive access to credit (this is not news in the consumer economy). It will, however, reach more deeply into lives by restricting access to restaurants, nightclubs, or golf courses, removing social security benefits, and limiting employment prospects (for example in the civil service, journalism, and legal fields). Students who cheated on national examinations could also be made to pay in the future for their dishonesty.

Adapted from Botsman (2017).

Questions

- Produce arguments for and against the Social Credit System from the viewpoints of citizens, companies, and the government.
- Judge the reliability of the measures and whether they truly reflect an individual's trustworthiness.
- Evaluate the risks of the misinterpretation and misuse of the scoress.

2.1   The Internet of Things

In Chapter 1 we established how digitisation enables us to collect and move data. For this data to translate into useful information that determines subsequent action, it needs to be timely and appropriate to the organisation's or individual's requirements. The development of miniature wireless sensors and the local communications networks that communicate with them has enabled greater numbers of diverse devices to become connected to the common network of the Internet using the common language of the World Wide Web. This widespread and automated collection of data has the profound potential to remove mundane and repetitive tasks from our lives. For example, your weekly online grocery purchases, through sensors in your refrigerator, can be automatically reordered based on frequently used products and brands. Car insurance apps assess your risk and tailor your insurance premium based upon an assessment of how safe a driver you are, and even when and where you drive. Wearable health monitors monitor your vital statistics such as pulse, temperature, blood pressure, and blood glucose level. For the less vulnerable this might serve as a route to weight loss or increased fitness. For the more vulnerable it serves to identify developing chronic health conditions, maybe by alerting your family doctor to call you in for a check-up, or to summon emergency help in the event of an acute event such as a heart attack, stroke, or accident. This transformation of the physical world into an infor-mation system has led to the Internet of Things (IoT). As with any system, the quality of the inputs determines the likely usefulness of the outputs. The work of Chui et al. (2010) differentiates between IoT inputs (i.e., data collected and analysed in the system in order to create useful information) and outputs (i.e., how that information is deployed though commands to act) via the IoT platform (Table 2.1). They build a complex picture of the proactive role of data available to marketers within the organisation.

Table 2.1 Organisational implications for IoT (adapted from Chui et al., 2010).

Inputs: information and analysis	Outputs: automation and control
Tracking behaviour • Products embedded with sensors allow companies to monitor their movements and interaction with other products, leading to tailored product and price packages for the customer • Shops use sensors to obtain customers' profile data to provide targeted recommendations or discounts at the point of sale	**Process optimisation** • Real-time data from sensors means that manufacturers can detect and fix quality problems immediately, without building up defective stock or stopping the process • Processes can also be fine-tuned to achieve major reductions in waste, energy costs, and human intervention
Enhanced situational awareness • Data from sensors in infrastructure (such as roads and buildings) to reports on weather conditions can give logistics, emergency service, and infrastructure planners clear insight into real-time events	**Optimised resource consumption** • Networked sensors and automated feedback mechanisms such as 'smart' meters, by making users aware of the real-time costs of consumption, can change usage patterns for scarce resources, including energy and water

Table 2.1 (*cont.*)	
Inputs: information and analysis	Outputs: automation and control
• Security personnel can use sensor networks that combine video, audio, and vibration detectors to spot unauthorised individuals who enter restricted areas	• Commercial customers can shift energy-intensive activities away from high-priced periods to low-priced off-peak hours
Sensor-driven decision analytics • Longer-range, more complex human planning and decision-making are supported. • In the oil industry valuable deposits can be found using extensive sensor networks placed in the Earth's crust. This leads to lower development costs and improved oil flows • In healthcare, sensors and data links monitor a patient's behaviour and symptoms in real time and at relatively low cost, allowing timely diagnosis and treatment. This leads to reduced lifetime treatment costs, quicker recovery and enhanced quality of life for the patient	**Complex autonomous systems** • Unpredictable conditions can be detected in real time, leading to instantaneous responses from automated systems • The automobile industry invests in systems that can detect imminent collisions and take evasive action. This leads to a potential annual saving of $100 billion in accident costs • Environmental scientists are testing robots that maintain facilities or clean up toxic waste, with potentially major gains in safety, risk, and costs

2.2 Cookies

When you visit a website, your browser sends the domain a hypertext transfer protocol (HTTP) message which requests access and gives a user-name and password if required. The website responds to your browser's request with both the content you asked for and any cookies it would like your browser to save. A cookie is a miniature text file which contains information about your visit to the web page; it is designed to identify you as a unique visitor and to understand your preferences to enable signposting to useful content. When you request another page from the website, your browser sends the cookie back to the server to recognise you. Every future visit that you make to the domain will add further cookies which create a richer picture of your interests, enabling the organisation to create content and offers that are customised for you. For example, online retailers often use cookies to record any personal information that you enter, as well as any items in your shopping cart, so that you do not need to re-enter this infor-mation each time you visit the site. From the organisation's point of view, less popular pages can be identified with a view to retiring them or making them more relevant to visitors. It is possible for websites to measure the volume of visits without the need for cookies. All they need to do is look at the server logs to know how many requests their server received. The problem with this approach is that it does not allow for any understanding of cause and effect (i.e., what marketing actions most likely led to what results within the sales campaign) or, more importantly, it does not allow the organisation to understand how individuals and groups behave. So, cookies make tracking even more powerful and personal, allowing an understanding of how individual users are interacting with their website. This might be to improve their product, serve targeted advertisements, or tailor prices.

Anyone wishing to increase their privacy online starts by installing an adblocker that restricts requests from your browser to domains known to belong to trackers, and further restricts the types of cookies that domains can set. As the functionality of cookies becomes less reliable and easier to defend against, many trackers are moving to new techniques to understand our online behaviour. These methods include exploiting your browser's cache and fingerprinting your device (Heaton, 2017).

DIGITAL INSIGHT 2.1 **Towards a Fully Integrated and Proactive Health System?**

The primary healthcare system has changed markedly since the emergence of the Internet and the World Wide Web. General practitioners (GPs) can quickly access patient histories and clinical data, such as test results from hospitals, enabling more accurate clinical diagnoses. The days of the printed prescription are now limited, with the arrival in the UK of the Electronic Prescription Service which sends electronic prescriptions from GP surgeries to pharmacies. However, consumers have become accustomed to on-demand features and access to information anywhere, at any time, on any device. In addition, they want products tailored to themselves. With an increasing and ageing population, the primary healthcare system seeking to deliver such a service requires the ability to collect the right sources of data, combine them, and analyse them to provide insights and enable improved experiences for patients and physicians. There is nothing more frustrating for a patient, or more wasteful for the healthcare system, than having patients bounced around to different specialists based on archaic paper-based systems which give incomplete diagnoses and rarely integrate.

The IoT offers new approaches to primary healthcare. Streaming applications allow doctors to remotely visit patients, improving efficiency for the practice and reducing stress for the patient and their carers. We have

DIGITAL INSIGHT 2.1 (cont.)

smartwatches that can capture heartrate, disposable patches that transmit streaming ECG, beds that track our quality of sleep, and onesies that can track the activity of new-borns. With nanotechnology and RFID devices that fit in a pill it is possible to transmit your essential body condition and tweak your prescription accordingly. Artificial intelligence (AI) could even change the way that patients and doctors interact: chatbots harnessing natural language processing can assess the patient's condition, making related recommendations or redirecting them to medical professionals (who will have received pre-notification) for more detailed answers. The use of sensors connected to the IoT platform will also allow for a more proactive approach to healthcare. Imagine being able to predict when a patient may need urgent care in real time, by using the results of a blood test, sensors that track the environment that they are living in, and the heartrate application on a smartwatch.

It is important to consider the role of the clinician. As with other automated functions (manufacturing, banking, travel) the role of the expert does not become redundant – it largely moves from a functional role to a design and monitoring role. The growth of AI to support decision-making could lead to better diagnoses and predictions, but while AI has less bias and a better memory, GPs are better at patient relationships.

2.3   Collation of Browser Data through Aggregators

For all these small packets of cookie data to be interpreted into meaningful information we use the services of aggregators to represent the data in a visual form as either statistics or figures. Currently the most popular free analytics tool is Google Analytics, which operates as a single-website tracker that tracks the activity only from the target website, keeping the data of each client website separate from the others. This makes them less powerful but better for consumer privacy, as the tracker is unable to join up a user's activity on different websites. This approach rarely attracts privacy or ethical objections since the analysis is principally focused upon how an audience utilises a website rather than the behaviour of individuals. On the other hand, multi-website trackers, such as AdRoll, track and connect behaviour across multiple, unrelated websites. They are much more powerful due to the integration of data from multiple sources, and can assemble a much more complete picture of a user's online activities. Due to the range of free-to-user data-rich services it provides, Google is one of the main data aggregators. Its browser can track users across most websites (Krishnamurthy and Wills, 2009), storing search histories of text and image visits as it goes. Searches in Google Maps can reveal the user's home address and their favourite places. Google also runs one of the most popular email systems, Gmail, and therefore potentially has access to emails of millions of users. By combining these different types of information coming from different sources, Google can build accurate profiles of their users.

The number of trackers that exist in any website depends upon how many the owner has decided to include. Some websites will have over 60 trackers, belonging to a multitude of companies whose primary goal is to build up a profile of who you are: how old you are, where you live, what you read, and what you are interested in. This information can then be packaged and sold to others: advertisers, other companies, or governments (Tactical Technology Collective, 2017). Others might have only one – perhaps to track visitor numbers, or see where these visitors are coming from, or to enable a certain functionality. Some might have none.

2.4   Digital Footprint

We have already established that whenever you interact on the Internet you leave behind a distinct set of traceable digital activities – whether it is as simple as click-through links or online purchases, all the way through to the unique content you have created and who you have collaborated with. These individual tracers create a 'digital footprint' which allows analysts to understand your past behaviour, not only in terms of browser searches and purchase transactions, but also the activities (online and offline) that may have influenced you every step of the way, creating a rich picture of your online behaviour. We discuss this further in Chapter 5. There are two main classifications for digital footprints:

1. Passive digital footprints are created when data is collected without the owner's knowledge and is sometimes referred to as the 'data exhaust'. Such data may be stored in a database as a 'hit' and would record information such as the IP address, date and time of the transmission, and its origin (which may include country of origin, browser, or referral site). Strictly speaking this data cannot be irrefutably linked to individuals, but reasonable assumptions can be made, given the developing data picture, of who engaged in the activity.
2. Active digital footprints are created when personal data is released deliberately by a user for the purpose of sharing information about

oneself by means of websites or social media. In this way there is a registered name that can be connected to the data. In this situation users have surrendered all expectation of anonymity, which in turn enables analysts to create rich histories of individuals that enable the precise targeting of tailored products or services that are likely to commend a high degree of relevance and acceptability to the recipient.

Your digital footprint helps the organisation to tailor their offering within the eight drivers of digital marketing. Table 2.2 is an example of how browser data could be interrogated to tailor the organisation's offering. This will vary across organisations, campaigns, and products:

Digital footprints have uses outside traditional marketing. They have 'cyber-vetting' uses in the field of recruitment, where interviewers could research applicants based on their online activities, and in law enforcement agencies. The lesson here is that whenever you post anything online it is fair to assume that this data is both permanent and universal. Permanent in the sense that as you get older your views and interests will change. There have been many cases of public careers being delayed, diverted, and even completely derailed due to the personal posting of injudicious opinions in their wild youth. Inevitably, defence of these opinions can make the candidate seem offensive (or not, in the case of more radical populists), but refuting the opinion can be seen as at least lacking in commitment or at worst dishonest.

2.5 Location Tracking

More and more systems and applications record users' locations and movements in public places. For example, RFID cards allow users to open security doors or pay for their transportation tickets, while Global Positioning Systems (GPS) help users to navigate and recommend the closest restaurant or hotel to the destination. While such services are helpful, they pose a considerable threat to location privacy, which is the ability of an individual to move in public space with the expectation that their location will not be systematically and secretly recorded for later use (Blumberg and Eckersley, 2009). This is not a new phenomenon, but technologies such as sensors, wireless networks, cameras, and microphones make it cheaper and easier to create a rich picture of the target's behaviour and their environment. Geolocational data shared on social media could also infer whether an individual is at home. The emergence of 'reality mining' raises even more privacy concerns since it infers human relationships and behaviours from information collected from cell phones, which includes duration and numbers dialled and is used to identify things to do or new people to meet (Greene, 2008).

Table 2.2 Digital footprints and the eight drivers of digital marketing

Digital footprint	\[Driver of digital marketing\] Product	Price	Place	Promotion	People	Processes	Physical experience	Partnerships
How did you find us? Directly from the URL, via a browser search, or from another referring website?			X	X				X
What kind of device are you using? TV, PC, tablet, phone?				X		X	X	
When are you visiting us? Date, day, time?	X	X		X				
Where are you visiting from? Location – fixed or mobile?				X		X	X	X
Which of the different design styles, ad placements, and timings proved most effective in getting you to click through to the website?				X	X		X	
Once on the website, what information did you engage with before making a purchase?	X	X				X	X	
How many times did you revisit the website/product before you made the purchase? On the first visit or did you come back multiple times before making up your mind?		X	X	X		X	X	X
Which other products did you consider? Unrelated, competing, complementary?	X	X			X	X		X
Which pages were of most/least interest to you?	X					X	X	
What was your 'dwell time' on each page?	X				X	X	X	
Did you place your order in a basket before you left the site? (You may have gone away to seek a better a deal, which would indicate price sensitivity.)		X		X				X
Which FAQ searches/themes did you visit?					X	X	X	

2.6   Behavioural Tracking

The concept of behavioural profiling consists of collecting data (recording, storing, and tracking) and searching it for identifying patterns (with the help of data mining algorithms) which are attributable to a single originating entity, to gain information relating to the originating entity. Profiling is not about data but about knowledge (Hildebrandt, 2006). This ability to observe, measure, and test customers at an individual level and in real time through digital means is the holy grail of marketing intelligence. Done in an unobtrusive and accurate manner, online behavioural tracking should provide all the benefits of the consumer–supplier relationship (i.e., signposting to the desired content without having to frequently reidentify yourself, proactively making recommendations for additional or subsequent purchases, or offering special discounts) without any of the downsides (i.e., price gouging, sharing data with unauthorised and unrelated third parties with perhaps more nefarious objectives, infiltration of your reference groups via social media).

The consumer's blissful ignorance of the effects of behavioural tracking is being steadily undermined by significant increases in identity theft, property fraud, and the manipulation of facts. These challenges exist not only in the business-to-consumer space, but also in the manipulation of commodity markets and the democratic process of choosing our political representatives. Let us not delude ourselves. The Internet did not invent lies – it simply provided a global and instant platform for alternative views to be shared (and challenged). We should also remember that marketing is the practice of using influence techniques to get consumers to do things. This may be to lose weight, to treat yourself to that expensive watch, or to persuade you that those you follow no longer serve your best interests, instead making the case for radical alternative candidates as being better placed to create a bold and fresh new vision of the future. Marketing should create and communicate viable options, but it should also support consumers to make good choices. Therein lies the dilemma of online behavioural tracking for marketing purposes. For example, financial comparison websites may encourage you to spend money – by taking that loan or this credit card, thus potentially jeopardising your financial situation – but will do so in as convenient and easy a way as possible, quickly and with lots of alternatives to choose from (many of which will have been pre-vetted against your likely eligibility based on your cookie history). Do you consider this to be intrusive of your privacy or abusive of the trust that you place within the supplier, or is it a useful help in our increasingly busy lives for which we are happy to abdicate personal responsibility or consideration of the darker uses of our personal information, against ourselves or others? After all, there can be no satisfactory, durable relationship between buyer and seller without a sense of trust and confidence on the part of both parties. These issues are being considered by consumer groups, legislators, and businesses, and will be discussed later in this chapter. As argued by Hildebrandt (2006), 'profiling shifts the balance of power between those that can afford profiling (mostly large organisations) and those that are being profiled (mostly individual citizens), because the profilers have a certain type of knowledge to which those profiled have no effective access.' The big question in new markets experiencing significant growth – whether financial, property, or information – is to what degree the consumer–supplier relationship is unfairly balanced in favour of the supplier (potentially through the oligopolistic effects of superior information) and if, to correct that imbalance, oversight, regulation, or possibly stronger intervention is required such as that seen in the telecommunications, energy, and finance industries in the twentieth century.

RESEARCH INSIGHT 2.1 Analytics: Evolution and Revolution

Wedel, M., and Kannan, P. (2016). Marketing analytics for data-rich environments. *Journal of Marketing*, 80(6): 97–121.

This article traces the historical development of marketing analytics practices and considers their application in relation to structured and unstructured data generated both within and outside the organisation. The role of analytics in the process of making marketing decisions is critically evaluated. The authors identify future research opportunities that seek to understand the developing role of analytics to support the practice of optimising marketing-mix spending in a data-rich environment, the personalisation of products and services, and protecting customers' privacy and data security. They examine the impact upon organisations that implement big data analytics. Turning to the future, the article identifies trends that will shape marketing analytics as a discipline as well as marketing analytics education.

2.7 Netnography

Social networks enable individuals to share some of their personal information with a multitude of other entities, such as their friends, companies, or even the public at large. It is possible to make new friends, reconnect with old friends, find work, and receive leisure and travel recommendations. The main purpose of these networks is to make individuals or groups visible; then it is necessary to share personal information to ensure some form of identifiability. This also enables anyone accessing this information to infer further private information, thus causing a privacy breach. While it is possible to make individual profiles inaccessible to other users, the friendship links and group affiliations often remain public.

The application of ethnographic principles to understand discussions within and across internet communities led to the emergence of the practice of netnography, which is an interpretive method devised specifically to investigate the consumer behaviour of cultures and communities in contemporary digital communications contexts to predict trends, which may in turn inform product development and innovation within the organisation. It is a process that observes and interprets digital public conversations (e.g., social media) to study the interactions and experiences manifesting through digital communications (Kozinets, 1998). Rich data samples are collected in the form of internet communications (e.g., text, images, audio, and audio-visual) that are interrogated using content analysis, semiotic visual analysis, social network analysis, and the big data analytic tools and techniques (Kozinets, 2015). These techniques are employed to find the emotional story behind a subject. Netnography has an advantage over ethnography in that it focuses primarily on the context of textual communication and any affiliated multimedia elements, whereas ethnography focuses primarily on physical forms of human communication (e.g., body language) (Bartl et al., 2016). Since netnography uses freely available public data, collected in an unobtrusive manner, it is regarded as more naturalistic than other approaches such as interviews, focus groups, surveys, and experiments.

2.8 Big Data

Digital marketers are fortunate (and some may say also unfortunate) to have endless tools and data at their disposal to enable full transparency. Chen et al. (2012) identify the following five areas as 'big impact' areas of big data research: e-commerce and market intelligence, e-government and politics, science and technology, smart health and wellbeing, and security and public safety.

The definition of what constitutes big data to the organisation depends on whether the data can be ingested, processed, and examined in a timeframe that meets an organisation's requirements. For one company or system, big data may be 50 TB (terabytes); for another it may be 10 PB (petabytes). However, across business sectors there is a considerable gap in the understanding of its challenges and its potential. This has led to confusion and inaction from organisations regarding how to proceed. It does not help that, since the industry is still in the early stages of development, the range of potential solutions is highly fragmented. To understand the challenges and opportunities of big data it is important to explore its component parts of volume, variety, veracity, velocity, and value – known as the five Vs. This combination and integration of multiple valid data sources and types defines the true strength and potential of big data.

- **Volume:** Driven by the increased level to which we digitise information, increased data inputs from the ever-growing IoT, and the proliferation of user-generated content since the emergence of Web 2.0, the total amount of information is growing exponentially every year.
- **Variety:** The increased capabilities of the Internet have enabled the creation and sharing of rich content. This data can be broadly categorised into two types:
  1. Structured data includes items that would fit into a relational database, for example the contents of a bank statement such as transaction type, date, times, amount, and balance.
  2. Unstructured data does not have a set of rules to frame a concept or idea; it defines a class of information, for example social media posts, audio files, images, videos.
- **Veracity:** This refers to the trustworthiness of the data. Can the analyst be sure that the data is complete, accurate, and collected for specific analyses? Every researcher knows that to get a good answer you first need to ask a good question.
- **Velocity:** This is the frequency of incoming data that needs to be processed. In large and busy organisations that provide a wide range of products and services to many customers globally 24/7 (e.g., telecoms, banking, retail, media) this is a key consideration that will determine the techniques for sampling data, analysing its meaning, and responding with timely and determined action.
- **Value:** This helps us to understand the likely impact on the organisation in terms of the potential minimisation of risk and sustained maximisation of reward. For example, will the insights you gather from analysis create a new product line, a cross-sell opportunity, or a cost-cutting measure? Or will your data analysis lead to the discovery of a critical causal effect that results in a cure for a disease?

In marketing decision-making, the understanding of contextual relationships is key. Marketing relies more and more on information technology to model explicit and implicit interactions derived from vast amounts of data. With big data functionality, these interactions are now visible.

2.9 Analytics

The field of web analytics itself lacks definitive standards, and the few standards which do exist are rarely implemented consistently within analytics software. Discrepancies often occur because systems are measuring things differently or have ambiguous terminology, leading to confusing and often contradictory results. To use a quote popularised by the author Mark Twain (1906), 'There are three kinds of lies: lies, damned lies, and statistics.' In this sea of data we can find anything that we wish to find to justify our own subjective viewpoint. To make sense of this data we create a frame of reference to support a meaningful interpretation which helps us to reflect on existing processes with a view to making sure they remain useful and relevant to the developing needs of the organisation. So, let us put some structure into this. Starting from the end (i.e., what the business wants to achieve in terms of sustained and profitable sales, possibly trending into growth) helps us to understand which processes and their associated measures can understand the resources and their relationships that lead to a satisfying outcome. It is helpful to map the customer's relationship with the organisation at various stages of development, known as the *sales funnel*, which works in descending order of a closer marketing relationship from **suspects**, to **prospects**, to **leads**, and ultimately to **customers**.

The **suspect** stage is where your promotional activity reaches out to *engage* audiences (more on how this is done in Chapter 7) who have a *general* interest in your organisation or its products, who will subsequently *visit you*. You should be mindful that not all digital communications will result in a solely digital response, they may even lead to a physical response, for example a store visit. However, to avoid overcomplicating the issue, this section will focus upon wholly digital communications. Those with *no prior knowledge* of the organisation, or indeed even a current and specific need for the product or service that the organisation provides, may be stimulated by social media recommendations or by display advertising triggered by associated browser searches.

- Tracking click-through rates for these messages gives some indication of their creative appeal, but also the effectiveness of the ad platform used, such as affiliate or comparison websites.
- Understanding the browser and device that were used can assess the accessibility of the ad.
- Knowing the geographical origin could help to fine-tune the language and cultural references that could be used in future creative efforts.

- The date, day, and time would indicate browsing patterns, which could then be used to maximise return on investment for pay per click (PPC) campaigns.

The **prospect** stage is where you seek to *build* upon the first tentative engagements to understand the *specific* interest in your organisation or its products, and who will subsequently make an *enquiry*. Users may have registered their details and downloaded your app, perhaps browsing a range of content that relates to the organisation and its products. The customer's objective here might not be for an immediate online purchase, but instead they could be checking out your opening hours, locating the nearest store, comparing products, or just checking for availability/special offers. The interaction may not lead to a financial transaction, but important information is available.

- **Landing and leaving page.** There is a risk of misinterpretation of the visit duration and frequency data. For example, a landing page with consistently short visits might be so because the content is confusing or irrelevant to the keyword search that brought in the visitor. Longer dwell times might not be due to the attractiveness or positive engagement of the page but might be because of poor design as the visitor labours to find what they want. There is a risk in making your domain's home page the landing page (as determined by your search engine optimisation (SEO) approach) or for visitors who will access your site directly via the URL. Consider the contrasting approaches of www.google.com, who simply provide a search bar on the homepage urging visitors to specify what they want to see, versus www.amazon.com, which leaves nothing to chance by providing a search bar, category lists, and recommendations based on the current promotions and your user history. There is also potential confusion with the leaving page. If this is the order confirmation page, then all is well and good since the objective has been achieved. If it is a product or service information page, or even a 'basket' page, does this mean that the customer is dissatisfied, or simply that they are delaying a decision/action?
- **Pages visited and dwell time.** When we know the landing and leaving pages it is helpful to know the interim steps to improve the navigability of the website. Also, how long on a page is long enough? Many authors have tried to establish benchmark figures for the optimum number of pages for the visitor to find what it is they need, or the need of the visitor to spend a maximum amount of time on a website before departure. The truth is that every customer and organisation has different approaches to

information searching and processing. Rigid measures only risk forcing too much content in too little time, effectively overwhelming the visitor, or simply insufficient information which leaves the visitor feeling neglected. Analysts that understand this issue well track the behaviour of categorised visitors that result in the desired outcome. Only then can you truly know the 'right' behaviour for your customer and your organisation.

- **Long-term behaviour.** Is there a pattern to users' searches that might help you identify why they did not go through with the purchase? As you begin to build a picture of the behaviour of registered users you can reach out with personalised emails. For unregistered frequent visitors you could revisit the content and presentation of the most popular (yes, and the least popular) pages to get the desired response.

The **lead** stage is where you *convert* an inquiry into an *offer* that will hopefully be *accepted*.

- Lapsed customers create an opportunity for the organisation to reconnect to understand why it is that they no longer engage. They may simply not need your product any more or have completely disengaged from your brand for whatever reason. Before you go pestering these people to reconnect, remember that while you may have no prospect of rekindling the relationship there is every chance, through nuisance contacts, that you may end up creating a 'brand enemy' who through word-of-mouth processes complains to their contacts about your conduct, potentially eliminating avenues for new business. On a more positive note, the customer may have forgotten to, or simply not been able to get around to, contact your organisation due to the demands of a busy life or changed circumstances. A warm and friendly invitation to reconnect, preferably with an incentive, that enables an updated understanding of their new needs could be well received.
- This is where shopping basket data comes into its own. Movement from a basket item to a purchase is of course the goal. But an understanding of why the customer chose to buy one variant over another, delay purchase, or buy a combination of products offers insight into the motivators and limitations in the customer decision-making process. Organisations respond by sending reminders (hopeful that the transaction was delayed by external factors and that there is an inevitability to the sale), making price offers (item or multi-buy discounts), or stating that there is limited item or time availability on the offer.

The **customer** stage is where you extend the relationship with the buyer from the *first transaction* to develop product or category *loyalty*.

- **Purchase timing.** An understanding of when a customer makes a purchase helps the organisation to back-track to reasonably estimate when that customer might have identified the need to make a purchase and following the process through to deciding to act (more about this in Chapter 5).
    - Seasonal products have different appeals and behaviours for different types of buyers. Take, for example, Halloween on 31 October:
        - frugal buyers will have sought to buy supplies at disposal prices from 1 November the previous year;
        - organised buyers may begin to plan their events a month or two in advance; and
        - panic buyers may leave it until days or hours before the event and make largely impulse purchases.
    - Special-interest purchases largely work to a predictable calendar. Tax consultants may find an increased market for their offerings in the months leading up to the legal deadline for filing personal and company returns. Recruitment companies may see a surge in interest after the festive or summer holiday periods, or even before the start of the new work week. Statutory education providers such as colleges and universities may choose to boost their online campaigns from January in preparation for a September/October annual start date.
- **Purchase volume** considers overall purchase behaviour within a given timeframe and how the initial purchase can be expanded to greater volume, with greater frequency, or with the integration of additional items. Imagine a provider of school supplies. At the start of the academic year the student will buy the school uniform, possibly several copies of different garments to allow for cleaning, damage, and loss throughout the year. This pattern should repeat in subsequent years as the student outgrows their clothes or they are no longer fit for purpose. Besides the standard uniform, perhaps the student can also be persuaded to buy similarly branded sports equipment, shoes, shirts, jumpers, bags, note-books, and stationery. The business can make multi-buy offers and send reminders to registered users, all the time analysing the response to their campaigns, and testing and adapting accordingly. There will also be the opportunity for customers to 'share' their purchases on social media, providing a positive view of your organisation and gaining new prospects/leads from their networks.

RESEARCH INSIGHT 2.2 Analytics at Light Speed

Henke, N., Bughin, J., Chui, M., et al. (2016). The age of analytics: competing in a data driven world. McKinsey Global Institute.

Data and analytics capabilities have made a leap forward in recent years. The volume of available data has grown exponentially, more sophisticated algorithms have been developed, and computational power and storage have steadily improved. The convergence of these trends is fuelling rapid technology advances and business disruptions that are discussed in detail in this paper. The key aspects of the discussion include the value of data, its innovative and competitive potential, and the barriers to successful realisation.

2.10 Attribution Modelling

A tool for understanding the effectiveness of the components of different communication channels and campaigns is *attribution modelling,* which is freely available in most analytics packages. The general approach is to look backwards from the sale, whether to an anonymous user or loyal customer, to determine which communications or channels played a major role in securing the deal. Promoters then use this data to target their spending and effort across a wide range of tools, including tweets, blog posts, and PPC advertisements to get the best possible return. These hard measures in real time enable organisations to test, review, and respond to their audience's reaction to promotional activity. They are based on three broad approaches:

1. The **linear** model seeks to maintain contact with potential customers and keep the company's products fresh in the customer's mind. It is useful in extremely competitive markets where the protection of market share is key to sustained success. It is a steady drip-feed of communication that will credit equally all aspects of the promotional mix. It is possible to differentiate campaigns aimed at different segments or using different channels to allow some comparison. It assumes that all campaign communications make an equal contribution to this goal.

2. The **first/last interaction** model helps to understand which efforts bring new customers into the sales process. However, complications can occur here if an 'interaction' lacks clear definition. For example, are we measuring when the respondent clicks through a PPC advertisement

('suspects' as discussed above), or when they make a specific product enquiry or place an item in the online basket (i.e., 'leads')?

3. The **position-based** model looks at individual aspects of the consumer journey on a step-by-step basis from first contact to completion. Different stages will necessarily have different measures, often based on the percentage conversion to the next stage. It is also possible to use this approach to discern purchase patterns, which, for example, might include frequent buyers who have regular needs that might be predictable, 'binge' buyers who will buy infrequently but in large volumes meaning that choice is important, product-specific buyers who will generally have interests in a small number of categories, and impulse buyers who are open to suggestion and often buy based on recommendations. Attribution based on segmentation allows us to target spending at the stages of the process that are the key decision points for the buyers.

These approaches are quite broad-brush and require an understanding of nuance in customer behaviour. We should also be mindful that the needs of individuals change, as do the dynamics of groups/segments. The effects of competition will impact upon the effectiveness of a campaign. Attribution modelling can only help us to quantify the response. The drivers of that response and the highest-level potential response both require deeper insight into the customer, and constant experimentation.

The key to finding the 'right' one for your organisation is to be clear about the end goal of your campaign and which model will best support you to make decisions that directly impact upon this. This experimentation will require courage to ask the difficult questions, creativity to identify and combine the critical measures, and commitment to stick with a tried-and-tested approach or to reinvigorate your approach. It is important to accept that you will not get the perfect answer, but that doesn't mean you shouldn't aim for the best. In other words, find something that is good enough, then move on to avoid getting stuck in 'analysis paralysis'.

2.11 Testing

The tools that we have to hand take us only so far since they can tell us *what* has happened but not necessarily *why* it happened. That is where the human element comes into play: the ability to analyse the 'what' and infer the 'why'. Their utilisation will help us to understand some of the key numbers in our organisation, which helps us to determine the effort (i.e., time, money, people, creativity) and the effect (i.e., visitors, enquiries, sales volume, sales value, and profit). There is almost always more than one explanation for why your users are behaving in a certain way on your site. However, the Internet has no loyalty to our business model and challengers can emerge and overtake us in double-quick time. We need to keep moving. To do this we need to keep learning. However, learning involves making mistakes and since no one can see reliably into the future to determine how a rapidly changing competitive environment will evolve, we need to be creative, making informed decisions that we can measure through tangible intended (and sometime unintended) results. To do this we need to establish a testing approach that enables us to sense and respond to challenges and opportunities. In the field of digital marketing the two most popular techniques are the following:

- **A/B testing** (also known as split testing), which involves running two versions of a message (i.e., an advertisement, page, email, tweet, post, blog, or keywords campaign) and measuring the results to identify which version produces better results in the desired areas. Due to the small number of variables being tested – 'A' and 'B' versions of a single element at any one time – and requirement for the campaign to run its natural course to collect a sample of data that will allow for meaningful analysis, this can be a relatively time-consuming approach.
- **Multivariate testing** enables marketers to test multiple message components simultaneously in real time to determine which combination of variables produces the best results, allowing for far more complex testing options than simple A/B tests. For example, you may want to compare the effectiveness of alternative messages for a new sales campaign. You could try two different titles, two different images, and two different calls to action. This is a $2 \times 2 \times 2$ variation that gives eight possible combinations to test. With a tool such as the Google Website Optimizer (other commercial multivariate testing tools are available) you set up an experiment that will present variations of your page to your visitors and record the corresponding conversions. The subsequent report will show how each of the different combinations performed, allowing you to take key learnings and adapt your approach.

2.11.1 What Activities Could/Should We Test?

We have already discussed a range of marketing touch points that the organisation has with its market. The specific research methods above, however, help us to fine-tune activities specifically within the promotional mix based on detailed statistical considerations of their relationships to each other, and the likelihood that they will lead to positive progression through the buying cycle. Focusing upon the questions that need to be asked to improve effective communication with customers includes the following elements:

- Media type – comparing the effectiveness of owned (e.g., blog or website), earned (e.g., PR/editorial comment or social media), or paid-for exposure (e.g., sponsorship or advertisements). This will inform a return-on-investment calculation for each campaign.
- Medium – e.g., in social media you could compare the relative effectiveness of Facebook, Twitter, Instagram, and Pinterest – all of which allow for different targeting approaches, allowing the effectiveness of each to be measured.
- Timing – this helps to focus upon when customers might be most receptive to offers, coincide with their anticipated web browsing or social media time, or to fit in with the decision-making stage of their purchasing cycle for a regular or predictable need.
- Frequency – we do not want our customers to think that we rarely contact them because they are unimportant to us. Likewise, we do not want to bombard potential customers with excessive messaging, thereby creating a nuisance and alienating a previously friendly contact.
- Position – this could be within the site itself, which is ideal for direct visitors who will do their own navigation, or more likely the location within a single page or post. The proximity to other key content (i.e., reviews or prices) might impact upon the response.
- Size – we can be too bold or too modest in our artwork design, with the 'right' approach lying somewhere in between.
- Creative treatment – meta-tags, headers, images, colours, typeface; static (such as a single photo) or dynamic (as with a scrolling gallery of photos); podcast/vodcast/video; 'how to' guides.
- Offer – some sales promotions are more effective than others for different audiences. Examples include early release of a new product to preferred customers, single-item discounts, multi-buy discounts, recommendations based on your interests, special features, competitions, 'refer a friend' incentives, and same-day delivery.
- Response methods – sharing with other users, buy now, quick registration for future updates, and chatbots.

2.11.2 Reliability

Testing only becomes 100 per cent reliable when it is possible to attribute a specific response to a specific stimulus, and since marketing activities do not take place in controlled environments with reliable respondents (i.e., humans) we will need to exercise judgement in the interpretation of the data presented to us. The reliability of testing can be improved (but not guaranteed) through measures such as pausing other channel/message activity to avoid multiple unattributable stimuli, creating unique attribution codes for each channel/message, or making a limited-time offer to encourage users to act and not defer a decision.

RESEARCH INSIGHT 2.3 Who Can You Really Trust?

Bart, Y., Shankar, V., Sultan, F., and Urban, G. (2005). Are the drivers and role of online trust the same for all web sites and consumers? A large-scale exploratory empirical study. *Journal of Marketing*, 69(4): 133–152.

   This paper proposes a conceptual model that links website and consumer characteristics, online trust, and behavioural intent. The results show that the factors that influence online trust are different across categories and consumers. Privacy and order fulfilment are the most influential determinants of trust for sites in which both information risk and involvement are high, such as travel sites. Navigation is strongest for information-intensive sites, such as sports, portal, and community sites. Brand strength is critical for high-involvement categories, such as automobile and financial services sites.

2.12 Ethics, Privacy, and the General Data Protection Regulation

With the intimate insights into our personal behaviours and the sensitive nature of the information that we share (e.g., our identities and those of our friends and family; professional information; financial data), we hope that the user of this information will do so with our own wellbeing as a priority. However, logic makes clear that, as in the offline world, there will always be parties who choose to exploit others for personal gain. Concern for user privacy is rising. A report by J. D. Power (Pingitore et al., 2013) showed that customers' privacy concerns remain at a high level, while their mistrust of online data collectors continues to grow. In the United States, customers' personal information can be shared among companies if the companies state their intentions in their privacy policy. In the European Union (EU), the privacy laws are much stricter, which can have a significant impact on targeting customers. The General Data Protection Regulation (GDPR) (European Council and Parliament, 2016) is a regulation on data protection and privacy for all individuals within the EU which aims to give control to citizens and residents over their personal data, which is defined as 'any information relating to an individual, whether it relates to his or her private, professional or public life. It can be anything from a name, a home address, a photo, an email address, bank details, posts on social networking websites, medical information, or a computer's IP address.' GDPR establishes the following principles:

- **Lawful basis for processing.** Data subjects (i.e., you and me) must provide *informed consent* for the processing of that data and personal data may not be processed if there is not at least one legal reason to do so. Consent must be specific, freely given, plainly worded, and unambiguous. Marketers can process personal data for direct marketing purposes as it is a legitimate activity. Data subjects can withdraw their consent at any time.
- **Responsibility and accountability.** A 'data controller' should be specifically named. It is their responsibility to create and follow effective *protection measures*. When data is collected subjects must be clearly informed about how much is collected, why it is being collected, and how long it will be kept.
- **Data protection by design and by default** requires data protection to be designed into the development of *business processes* for products and services. Encryption and decryption operations must be carried out locally. Outsourced cloud data storage is safe so long as only the data controller holds the decryption keys.
- **Pseudonymisation** should be used to ensure that data *cannot be attributed* to a specific subject without the use of the necessary decryption keys, which will be kept separately from the original data.
- **Right of access** by citizens to their personal data and details of how this *personal data is being processed*. A data controller must provide the categories of data that are being processed, as well as a copy of the actual data.
- **Right to erasure.** The data subject has the right to request *erasure* of personal data related to them if the interests of the controller fall short of the interests of the subject.
- **Data breaches.** The data controller is under a legal obligation to notify data subjects *within 72 hours* of becoming aware of the breach if it is likely to result in a risk to the subjects.
- **Sanctions.** In the worst case the organisation could be fined up to *€20 million or up to 4 per cent of the annual worldwide turnover* of the preceding financial year, whichever is greater.

The scope for ethical discussion regarding the production, ownership, use, and reward for data is vast, and beyond the scope of this integrated and practical guide. Excellent publications that take a political economy perspective on this specialist area include Christian Fuchs' (2014) work on information as a commodity and Shoshana Zuboff's (2019) work on surveillance capitalism.

CHAPTER SUMMARY

This chapter explores the richness and challenges of digital data. We reveal that despite the massive volume of data that is available in real time from multiple data points, this complexity slows us down due to imperfect and subjective processes that support its interpretation. When we can understand our strengths and accommodate our weaknesses, maybe then we can begin to make good decisions. But in whose best interests do we make those decisions? By the very act of using customers' data, we may be destroying the relationship that as marketers we are sworn to protect – that between the market and the organisation.

DIGITAL INSIGHT 2.2 Online: From a Leap of Faith to Being Wholly Reliable

One of the major barriers to the adoption of e-commerce platforms in the early days was the issue of trust. Since the process of buying online is quite different from buying through a physical outlet such as a shop or warehouse, customers were rightly concerned that goods they had paid for would arrive. Then, if they arrived and were not as advertised, or unsuitable for the intended use, could they be returned for a full refund? Then, would personal data and payment details remain secure throughout the transaction? On the issue of financial security, banks and credit card companies continue to improve fraud prevention and detection measures, using multi-level security measures to ensure access for only those authorised to do so. Complex algorithms detect abnormal activity and block access pending confirmation from the registered user. Data laws protect our information. Trading regulations protect our right to return goods if they are not as promised. However, it is market reputation that companies work hard to develop and maintain since this can be a major differentiator when presented with multiple alternative products and suppliers. How is it protected? Web 2.0 has enabled customer-to-customer feedback in the form of quantitative rankings (stars, ticks, etc.) and qualitative commentary. This too can be broken down based on the role in the transaction, whether it is product feedback (e.g., Amazon), seller feedback (e.g., eBay), or both (e.g., Uber, Airbnb). Business-to-consumer interactions are a slightly murkier area of the trust business, in terms of their openness to bias and questionable rigour. There are websites that will quantify the trustworthiness of businesses within certain sectors (e.g., TripAdvisor or Rated People) but efforts to establish a single reliable review of the trustworthiness of an organisation have not been popular among businesses and consumers – that is, until the arrival of Trustpilot which, according to Peter Holten Mühlmann (founder and CEO) (Trustpilot, 2018) is 'More than just a rating, Trustpilot stars signify that a company has nothing to hide, loves its customers and shares our mission to create ever-improving experiences for everyone.'

Review Questions

- How reliable are cookies in helping a business to identify and prioritise the needs of customers?
- How could behavioural tracking differentiate customers based on their loyalty?
- What are the arguments for and against the unlimited collection, retention, and use of customer data by businesses?
- What factors influence how long specific customer data will be usable?
- What are the arguments for and against whether business regulators should measure the trust of businesses, and if they fall below a certain level remove their legal right to trade?

END-OF-CHAPTER CASE: THE 2016 US PRESIDENTIAL ELECTION CAMPAIGN

Emergence of Social Media as a Democratic Mechanism

At the time of Barack Obama's election in 2008, the major social media channels of Web 2.0 were in their infancy. Facebook had recently celebrated its fourth birthday and boasted 100 million users. Twitter was just two years old, with 6 million users. In the year of the election of his successor, the 45th

President of the United States of America, these audiences stood at 1.86 billion and 319 million users, respectively – a sizeable and powerful 'captive' audience of reference groups, with their incumbent opinion leaders and followers. It was at this point that social media became a pivotal electoral platform to both understand and influence public opinion. This is no mystery since from the late 1990s marketers have understood the potential of the Internet as a communications channel offering easy, instant, and cheap access to vast markets that are conveniently networked. The question was whether the same strategies for moving breakfast cereal and fizzy drinks could and should be utilised in the rather more sensitive and risky tasks of shaping national public opinion and forming governments.

Media Strategies and More

So how did his campaign team and other supporters 'sell' Donald J. Trump to the US electorate? First, we should consider where the candidates put their money. Over the course of the election cycle, Trump's campaign invested $90 million towards digital advertising, the majority of which went to Facebook over any other platform. Hilary Clinton's team took a different approach, opting for the traditional broadcast-type channel of TV advertising, spending more than $200 million, where Trump spent less than half that (Lapowsky, 2016). Because Trump was not spending as much on television, it seemed that his team was not investing in changing anyone's minds. But they were: they were just doing it online. Next, we should consider the channel objectives of the respective candidates. Besides the communication of clear and compelling messages, whether of responsibility and hope or fear and victimisation common in any political campaign, there was a subtle difference in what other uses these digital channels might serve. In this respect, according to President-elect Donald Trump's digital director Brad Parscale, Facebook was massively influential because it also helped generate the bulk of the campaign's $250 million in online fundraising. 'Facebook and Twitter were the reason we won this thing', he says. 'Twitter for Mr. Trump. And Facebook for fundraising.'

Social Media as a Tool for Talking, Listening, and Retelling

Working with huge sample sizes, sophisticated analytics, 'real-time' responses, and the ability to refine and retest messages (and their impact) made Facebook an essential campaign and polling tool for the Trump team. 'They have an advantage of a platform that has users that are conditioned to click and engage and give you feedback', says Gary Coby, director of advertising at the Republican National Committee (RNC), who worked on

Trump's campaign (Lapowsky, 2016). 'Their platform is built to inform you about what people like and dislike.' Such was the potential to perform massive tests with its advertisements on Facebook that the Trump campaign was running 40,000–50,000 variants, testing how they performed in different formats, with subtitles and without, and static versus video, among other small differences. On the day of the third presidential debate in October the team ran 175,000 variations. Coby calls this approach 'A/B testing on steroids' (Bell and Owen, 2017). This dynamic approach was in stark contrast to the Clinton campaign, which invested $30 million in digital advertisements, principally using rapid-response videos that channelled respondents to a customer service team to help people with their voting questions (Lapowsky, 2016).

Fake News

Candidate Trump, as in his business and media careers beforehand, never missed an opportunity to share challenging opinions freely and confidently. His use of Twitter to access a populist support base operated outside the traditional moderating influences of the press and broadcast media, party communications chiefs, and government diplomatic channels. This freedom to connect directly with a customer base (or electorate) gave nuance to President Lincoln's promise in the Gettysburg Address of 'government of the people, by the people, for the people' some 150 years before Trump's campaign. Trump justified his desire to operate outside these channels to present 'the truth' to his audience in contradiction of the 'fake news' he insisted was perpetrated by media outlets, colleagues (current and former), individuals, and organisations who held contradictory views to his own. This assertion tapped directly into concerns common since the emergence of Web 2.0 that the democratisation of knowledge would indeed enable many voices to be heard. But which voices should we trust and how would this trust be established and tested?

Cambridge Analytica

None of the techniques described above are illegal. However, the scandal over Cambridge Analytica's acquisition of the personal data of Facebook users has revealed the working practices of an industry that has learned how to closely track the online footprint and daily lives of US voters. It emerged that in 2013 an academic in Britain built a questionnaire app for Facebook users, which 270,000 people answered. They in turn had 50 million Facebook friends. Data on all these people then ended up with Cambridge Analytica. During the Trump campaign the firm used this data to build a system that could profile individual voters and target them with personalised political advertisements to influence their choices at the ballot box. Facebook confirmed that by late 2015 the company had found out that information had been harvested on an unprecedented scale. However, at the time it failed to alert users and took only limited steps to recover and secure the private information of individuals. When claims of data misuse were made public, Mark Zuckerberg, CEO of Facebook, conceded that Facebook had lets its users down in the past but seemed not to have grasped that its business faced a wider crisis of confidence. At the time of writing (July 2018) Cambridge Analytica has ceased to trade (but its owners and directors are facing legal action) and Facebook has faced questions from US lawmakers, has been fined for data misuse, and has been issued with a fine by the UK Information Commissioner's Office. Public concern over data misuse continues to be a major PR issue for Facebook and similar firms, so much so that Facebook has changed its practices relating to data permissions and transparency over what it holds, going to great lengths to communicate this with its global customer base.

Russia and the Mueller Investigation

Misuse of data to enable political parties to target individual voters to gain an advantage for their candidates is one thing. The potential implication of a foreign power aiming to skew voting patterns within a sovereign nation is another. In early 2017 Facebook dismissed the idea that fake news had influenced the election as 'pretty crazy'. In September Facebook said Kremlin-linked firms had spent a mere $100,000 to buy 3,000 adverts on its platform, failing at first to mention that 150 million users had seen free posts by Russian operatives (*Economist*, 2018). As rumour spread as to potential malign interference in the democratic process, the Trump administration appointed Robert Mueller, former director of the US Federal Bureau of Investigation, to head an inquiry into the parties to the accusations.

Wider Implications

The victims of perceived untruthfulness, in this case, do not solely sit in legal, administrative, and political institutions. The ramifications of growing mistrust spread throughout society and the economy, leading to radically changed behaviours and relationships. The degree to which this case and other related factors may have affected the reputation of the United States as a nation is measured most recently in the Edelman Trust Barometer (2018), which saw the United States' perceived trustworthiness plummet. While no immediate sanctions came into play because of this perception, it is reasonable to assume that future commercial, legal, and political relationships will be conducted very differently to compensate for questionable opening positions, concerns over 'lack of good faith', or in retaliation for past misdeeds.

DISCUSSION QUESTIONS

- How much of an issue is 'trust' in online communication and transactions?
- What type of personal information about yourself would you be prepared to share publicly with complete strangers?
- Is the risk of identity or financial fraud a risk worth taking for the choices and efficiencies we get from the digital marketplace?
- How should digital platforms be regulated beyond the scope of the current regulations for the personal data of individuals? Present your cases for and against.

Develop Your Skills

What Is the Skill?

Analytical skills refer to the ability to collect and analyse information, problem-solve, make decisions, and develop solutions. In the big data environment huge amounts of data are available to the organisation from multiple sources. Since this data is dynamic (i.e., it is gathered and fed to the organisation in real time) we need to develop effective systems to interpret and respond to it in a timely manner, in turn monitoring the effects of our actions to capitalise on an opportunity or reduce the risk from an emerging threat.

Why Is It Important?

By way of example, consider how our bodily senses of sight, touch, hearing, smell, and taste feed into our brain, which uses established criteria to alert us to changes in our physical environment which may trigger a 'fight' or 'flight' response. In a business context this skill can help solve a company's prob-lems and improve upon its overall productivity and success. It gives us visibility of our market environment so that we may respond accordingly, usually by reallocating the resources of skills, effort, money, materials, and equipment within the business. Analytical skills are in demand in many industries and are commonly listed requirements in job descriptions.

How to Develop It

For this exercise you will need to open a Google Analytics Demo account. The data in the Google Analytics Demo account is from the Google Merchandise Store, an e-commerce site that sells Google-branded merchandise. The data in the account is typical of what you would see for an e-commerce site, and includes the following kinds of information:

- traffic source data about where website users originate – this includes information about organic traffic, paid search traffic, and display traffic;
- content data about the behaviour of users on the site – this includes the URLs of pages that users look at and how they interact with page content; and
- transaction data about the transactions that occur on the Google Merchandise Store website.

You are to explore the functionality of the site, experimenting with different settings. Areas to explore include categories of data, customers' dimensions, goals, reporting, search console, AdWords, and site search. Discuss the patterns and trends within your team.

How to Apply It

Make a brief verbal presentation to the management of the Google Merchandise Store that highlights which reports you accessed, how you interpreted the information, and where marketing action may need to be taken within the organisation. You can use the eight drivers of digital marketing as your framework for these recommendations.

References

Bart, Y., Shankar, V., Sultan, F., and Urban, G. (2005). Are the drivers and role of online trust the same for all web sites and consumers? A large-scale exploratory empirical study. *Journal of Marketing*, 69(4): 133–152.

Bartl, M., Kannan, V. K., and Stockinger, H. (2016). A review and analysis of literature on netnography research. *International Journal of Technology Marketing*, 11(2): 165–196.

Bell, E., and Owen, T. (2017). The platform press: how Silicon Valley reengineered journalism [online]. Available from: www.cjr.org/tow_center_reports/platform-press-how-silicon-valley-reengineered-journalism.php [Accessed 11 April 2019].

Blumberg, A., and Eckersley, P. (2009). On locational privacy, and how to avoid losing it forever. Electronic Frontier Foundation. November. Available from: www.eff.org/wp/locational-privacy [Accessed 20 August 2018].

Botsman, R. (2017). Big data meets big brother. *Wired*. November. Available from: www.wired.co.uk/article/chinese-government-social-credit-score-privacy-inva sion [Accessed 2 August 2018].

Chen, H., Chiang, R., and Storey, V. (2012). Business intelligence and analytics: from big data to big impact, *MIS Quarterly*, 36(4): 1165–1188.

Chui, M., Löffler, M., and Roberts, R. (2010), The Internet of Things. *McKinsey Quarterly*, 2: 70–79.

Economist (2018). Facebook faces a reputational meltdown [online]. Available from: www.economist.com/leaders/2018/03/22/facebook-faces-a-reputational-melt down [Accessed 11 April 2019].

Edelman. (2018). Edelman trust barometer global report [online]. Available from: https://cms.edelman.com/sites/default/files/2018-01/2018%20Edelman% 20Trust%20Barometer%20Global%20Report.pdf [Accessed 25 August 2018].

European Council and Parliament (2016). General Data Protection Regulation on the protection of natural persons with regard to the processing of personal data and on the free movement of such data. (EU 2016/679).

Fuchs, C. (2014). *Digital Labour and Karl Marx*. London: Routledge.

Greene, K. (2008). Reality mining. *MIT Technology Review*. [online]. Available from: www.technologyreview.com/read_article.aspx?id=20247&ch=specialsections& sc=emerging08&pg=1 [Accessed 20 August 2018].

Heaton, R. (2017). How does online tracking actually work? [online]. Available from: https://robertheaton.com/2017/11/20/how-does-online-tracking-actually-work/ [Accessed 13 August 2018].

Henke, N., Bughin, J., Chui, M., et al. (2016). The age of analytics: competing in a data driven world. McKinsey Global Institute.

Hildebrandt, M. (2006). Profiling: from data to knowledge. *DuD: Datenschutz und Datensicherheit* 30(9): 548–552.

Kozinets, R. V. (1998). On netnography: initial reflections on consumer research investigations of cyberculture, *Advances in Consumer Research*, 25(1): 366–371.

Kozinets, R. V. (2015). *Netnography: Redefined*. London: Sage.

Krishnamurthy, B., and Wills, C. (2009). Privacy diffusion on the web: a longitudinal perspective. *Proceedings of the 18th International Conference on World Wide Web*. Madrid: ACM.

Lapowsky, I. (2016). Here's how Facebook actually won Trump the presidency [online]. Available from: www.wired.com/2016/11/facebook-won-trump-elec tion-not-just-fake-news/ [Accessed 5 July 2018].

Pingitore, G., Meyers, J., Clancy, M., and Cavallaro, K. (2013). Consumer concerns about data privacy rising: what can business do? J. D. Power report.

Tactical Technology Collective (2017). How does browser tracking work? [online]. Available from: https://myshadow.org/browser-tracking [Accessed 13 August 2018].

Trustpilot (2018). Ever improving experiences and the new era of trust: introducing Trustpilot's new brand [online]. Available from: https://uk.business.trustpilot .com/reviews/inside-trustpilot/ever-improving-experiences-and-the-new-era-of-trust-introducing [Accessed 13 August 2018].

Twain, M. (1906). *Chapters from My Autobiography: North American Review*. Salt Lake City, UT: Project Gutenberg.

Wedel, M., and Kannan, P. (2016). Marketing analytics for data-rich environments. *Journal of Marketing*, 80(6): 97–121.

Zuboff, S. (2019). *The Age of Surveillance Capitalism: The Fight for a Human Future at the New Frontier of Power*. London: Profile Books.

3

The Big Picture
Strategy, Innovation, and Value

Introduction

This chapter considers the strategy development process in the context of the radical and disruptive effects of digital technologies. In an uncertain and dynamic environment many organisations question whether it is appropriate to fashion a strategy at all, or whether they should simply respond to events as they occur. This dynamic approach, if professionally managed, allows for the rapid testing of the tactical tools of *product* and *price* to boost customer engagement, and develops actionable intelligence for the organisation, enabling it to adapt, manoeuvre, and dominate its chosen markets.

Learning Objectives

- Evaluate how approaches to strategic planning, execution, and evaluation have changed in response to digital technologies.
- Appraise strategic choices and their digital implications.
- Consider the digital implications for the core and extended product.
- Evaluate the factors impacting upon alternative online pricing tools.

CASE INSIGHT: CRYPTOCURRENCIES: FAD, FRAUD, OR FUTURE?

Cryptocurrencies are a form of money (Bitcoin and Ether are examples) used in transactions which are recorded on a public blockchain ledger. The allure of blockchain technologies has been too much to resist for those who wish to challenge the dominance of the international banking sector. Traditionally, financial institutions rely upon their hard-won reputations and considerable security infrastructure to protect your money, both in its physical form (i.e., cash) and its virtual form (i.e., monitoring balances and recording transactions). Banks also earn considerable income from the funds that they hold for you by lending it out for personal and business investment, and from the charges that they make for credit cards, transfers, and exchanges. As the retail banking and insurance sectors have both been hard hit by digitisation, automation, and disintermediation, it is now the turn of the currencies in our pockets (both physical and virtual) to be similarly challenged. The challenge to governments and banks is clear, but it remains to be seen whether markets will widely adopt this new ledger-based technology, and what its role will be. With the ease of launching a cryptocurrency (otherwise known as an initial coin offering, or ICO), and varying levels of demand, market confidence is volatile. Speculators seeking strong early positions are investing heavily in resourcing and promoting their ICO, with many taking significant losses as they have failed to establish themselves with investors or users. As with any new technology, it will take time for the dominant version to emerge and in so doing many suitable (and potentially preferable) alternatives will perish, with substantial losses for owners and users.

Questions

- List the potential opportunities and threats posed to organisations by cryptocurrencies.
- In what way do you think governments and banks will respond to the threat of cryptocurrencies?
- How do you feel about surrendering the security of your national currency (or an internationally recognised alternative such as the euro, British pound, or US dollar) to instead be paid in a cryptocurrency such as Bitcoin or Ether?

3.1   What Is Strategy?

Since this book is a practical guide, it is important to examine not just what strategy *is*, but also what it *does*. A good strategy will simplify and clarify the approaches that the organisation should take to increase its competitive advantage. This is fine in a predictable world, but not all customers, consumers, and competitors respond in the ways that we expect since we are all subject to a range of external forces that are out of our control (e.g., politics, the economy, social attitudes). Chandler (1963) defines strategy as 'the determination of the long-run goals and objectives of an enterprise and the adoption of courses of action and the allocation of resources necessary for carrying out these goals'. Let us unpack these terms:

- **What is the 'long-run' timeframe?** We have already discussed the accelerating pace of change, so the duration of the 'long run' is determined by a combination of internal planning cycles (e.g., tax year, annual reports, capital expenditure programmes), changes in customer needs, or the speed at which competitors overtake us by doing things more efficiently and effectively. Given the speed and scale of change of digital technologies, the 'long run' for a given product or service might be truly short indeed. For instance, in the development and distribution of computer games the rate of change, as driven by competition and consumer tastes, is so rapid that the follow-up version is being planned before the preceding version has gone to market. Analytics helps developers to receive feedback on the preceding version to inform their design choices for the following version. Thus, digital marketers need to feel the urgency of the challenge while at the same time having the tools at hand to gather and interpret data to make timely decisions.
- **What are goals and objectives?** These relate to the *mission* of the organisation, which will explain its purpose for existing – beyond the generation of profit to be sustainable or provide maximum financial returns for investors – which may refer to specific industries or segments). You will also hear mention of the organisation's 'vision', which is essentially a question of 'what does success look like?' which forces us to be specific about what we are trying to achieve and by when – in objective terms that are unambiguous and clear to all. Measures may relate to sales, growth, profit, or innovation. Large data sets from multiple reliable sources that are interrogated by sophisticated algorithms in real time give us closer to perfect market knowledge than has ever previously been available to assist marketers to set their goals and objectives.
- **Courses of action** relates to determined paths that we will take to reach our objective. While a single overarching approach may work (such as the launch of a new app), strategy-in-practice often involves a subtle interweaving of different approaches across the eight drivers of digital marketing. We may choose to boost some activities and reduce others, dependent upon the insights from complex analytics programmes. Experienced digital marketing teams will keep meticulous records of past campaigns, understanding the issues, drivers, and timing of marketing activity to generate a tangible result. These benchmarking activities can be used to overlay similar current and future campaigns to anticipate

responses, checking and refining their understanding of the main actors in the market.

• **Allocation of resources.** Digital marketers not only have a deep understanding of the market and customers in general, but also the marketing assets within their organisation. To deploy a sustainable marketing campaign we also need to understand the cost implications, what media and personnel we have at our disposal to build relationships, and who our partners are and what their roles are. Planning and co-ordinating these factors has become increasingly challenging in dynamic global markets for any business with a range of customers and products offerings. Digital is critical to monitoring, measuring, and managing this process to maximise effectiveness and efficiency.

RESEARCH INSIGHT 3.1 Why Digital Strategies Fail

Bughin, J., Catlin, T., Hirt, M., and Willmott, P. (2018). Why digital strategies fail. *McKinsey Quarterly*, 1: 61.

The exponential processing power of the smartphones that connect us have become intertwined with our lives in countless ways. Few of us get around without the help of ridesharing and navigation apps such as Lyft and Waze. This article examines the principal issues with digital strategy as we currently understand it, with the authors explaining why each of the issues doom any digital strategy to failure.

3.2 How Does 'Digital' Strategy Differ from 'Traditional' Strategy?

The constant disruptive effect of digital technologies (see Chapter 1) forces us to reframe the strategy process to be relevant to weather the constant storm of radical and rapid change in the marketplace. The key factors at play in this reimagining are:

• **Hyperscale platforms** incorporating a common operating language and multi-device connectivity create network effects that significantly reduce the time and resources previously required by the organisation to secure market awareness, reputation, and capacity on a global scale. The threat posed to incumbents by new competitors and new technologies may lead to them being overtaken, and sometimes rendered obsolete, by start-ups within a matter of a few years.

- **Low-cost technologies** such as software as a service, sensors, smart devices, and cloud computing have become commodities, offering extremely low barriers to market entry and low switching costs for customers. Consequently, customer loyalty must be earned daily and customer 'lock in', either through technology or commercial actions, is virtually impossible.

- **New ways of doing business,** such as dispersed networks, create new digital ecosystems (e.g., cloud computing). Gig working, crowdsourcing, blockchain encryption, customer self-service, mobile computing, and the changing role of retail have all challenged the ways in which businesses organise and present themselves to their markets.

- **The role of the human agent.** Algorithms that use machine learning to stimulate customer purchases, and the artificially intelligent chatbots that service our aftersales needs, negate the role for human intervention in some processes. However, the issue of decision oversight (i.e., the level of decisions that are made by humans and not machines) is a moving target for many organisations seeking consistency and efficiency, on one hand, yet meaningful person-to-person contact and the understanding of emerging/unmet customer needs, on the other. At an individual level it is becoming increasingly challenging for organisations that invest in state-of-the-art digital technologies to recruit personnel skilled and experienced enough in using it to its full potential. This skills gap is both a challenge and an opportunity for educational institutions of all levels as they increase their efforts to embed cross-curricular digital literacies into teaching, training, recruitment, and promotion schemes.

- **The near-zero marginal cost** potential of digital technologies has resulted in many previously 'paid for' services, such as news and entertainment, now being given away for free. For businesses to sustain they must at some point move beyond this 'freemium' model to a place where customers will pay for a service to generate revenue that the organisation can pay to its investors, suppliers, employees, etc. This remains a significant challenge for organisations and is a key driver in customers' promiscuous buying behaviours.

- **Big data** can be both a blessing and a curse. Which information should the organisation regard highly and which should it disregard? Access to real-time data insights that are available because of the network effects of integrated global communications and production facilities creates added pressure and complexity for the digital strategist. Global marketplaces with fast-moving competitors make it difficult to anticipate threats and reorient the organisation in a timely manner.

- **Empowered customers** have developed escalating expectations due to digital personalisation at scale and are becoming increasingly engaged in product/service co-creation, and the influencing of other customers.

3.3   The Digital Strategy Process

Strategy can be a messy and vague activity. Whether is it practised on a small or large scale over the short or long term, it is nevertheless a process with deliberate steps to ensure that effective and efficient actions are taken to safeguard the sustainability of the organisation. It is important to remember that as marketers our views and priorities may be at odds with others in the organisation. This is because we habitually take a 'market-driven' view, which is essentially external in focus, looking to build relationships with customers and networks with intermediaries to access more, and higher value, customers. This approach challenges the organisation to be what its customers want it to be, despite its current capabilities, creating tensions with other functions that may take a more 'resource-driven' view which prioritises the internal organisation and the resources and skills that it currently has. This tension between what the organisation **is** and what it **wants to be** is heightened for the digital marketer seeking the smart and timely deployment of the organisation's capabilities to succeed in a rapidly changing and increasingly competitive market.

3.4   Setting Objectives

We start by making a clear differentiation between where the organisation currently is and where it aspires to be with respect to its performance at a defined point in the future. The organisation's objectives may be expressed with such measures as:

- the **markets** it serves (i.e., customer groups, industries, countries, regions). For example, we may choose to target the teenage fashion market in China, beach resort holidays for customers aged over 60 in Argentina, or sports coaching for children aged under 10 in Australia;
- the **products** that it provides (e.g., vintage products such as rock band T-shirts, refurbished/resale products such as older smartphones, current mass-produced products, new product development and innovation);
- its scale of **operation** (i.e., a small team within the organisation working on a targeted opportunity, or a larger multifunctional operation across the organisation to develop a global opportunity);

- its **stakeholders** (e.g., investors, employees, community, regulators);
- its **value chain** (e.g., whether it wants to move upstream, closer to supply, or downstream, closer to the end-user; outsourcing vs in-house production; alliances and partnerships); and
- its **financial** situation (e.g., profitability, debt–equity mix, solvency/breakeven).

The important step here is to describe a future in terms of objective measures, understood by all, that relate to both the desired outcomes and the time window within which we intend to achieve them. This provides clarity for all concerned and sets a 'future' to which we all aspire.

3.5   Understanding the Market Macro-Environment

This section looks at factors that impact upon on all markets. PESTEL (Thomas, 2007) factors (political, economic, social, technological, ecological, legal) are most effectively analysed in a specific place since factors may vary by country and region. While this tool can be broad in nature, it does draw out themes that require our attention and builds an essential understanding of the drivers that may affect the organisation's future competitiveness. Here are some *general* factors where digital technologies have had an impact. However, the macro-environmental analysis should be undertaken based on the specific *context* of the organisation.

Political

1. Pressure to regulate social media channels either as a tool for state censorship or to eliminate extreme content.
2. Pressure to regulate multinational technology firms by domestic or foreign governments, for political (influence) or economic (sales tax), or legal (employee rights) motives.
3. Pressure to increase the online monitoring of groups and individuals (as a method of state control or as a crime-fighting measure) versus the right to individual privacy and identity integrity.

Economic

1. Blockchain technology is creating new currencies, free from statutory regulation, taxation, and intermediaries. This avoids the national treasuries' control over sovereign currencies and challenges the role of the banking system.
2. The reach and dominance of global digital companies, and inadequate international tax laws and policies, make it difficult to monitor trading

activity and generate tax receipts, in turn disrupting national treasuries and jeopardising public investment.

3. Despite the dot-com bubble of the late 1990s (Malmsten et al., 2011), technology investors are still taking significant gambles on businesses with tenuous earnings models. While some investors do generate significant returns, many will lose massive sums.

Social

1. Changing purchase behaviour as a result of digital stimuli and multiple channels (e.g., you might have connected with promotional material from the publisher for this book, but you might not have bought it from the publisher or even the university bookshop, instead opting for a generic online platform or even buying a used copy).
2. Changing work patterns to more flexible models. The rise of the gig economy (Prassl, 2018) creates access to self-employment for many workers. However, as with blockchain, this is currently unregulated and is therefore open to abuse by employers seeking high-quality employees at low cost.
3. We are beginning to see the effects of all the above on individuals' mental health, with social pressure, work pressure, and a relentless stream of data from the Internet across multiple platforms leaving many struggling to cope with the perceived demands upon them.

Technological

1. The gap in the human–computer interface will lessen as more decisions are made automatically on our behalf (informed by intelligent algorithms that are themselves informed by data from our past behaviours). This may free up our time and resources for more fulfilling uses of our time or condemn us to static behaviours.
2. As with any dominant technological innovation there will be customers who adopt the new technology in its early stages and those who resist, and a wide distribution in between (Rogers, 2003). These multiple audiences provide a significant technological challenge for organisations seeking efficiency.
3. The rate of technological change will also cause a complexity problem as multiple generations of the same product require hardware, software, and service support.

Ecological

1. Sensors and algorithms can lead to better use of natural resources, for example in farming (arable and livestock), fisheries, mining, and forestry.
2. Cameras and algorithms can reduce pollution, congestion, and delays in transport systems with automated active traffic management.

3. Remote working could reduce the ecological damage caused by the construction, operation, and maintenance of workplaces, commuting from home to work, and the duplication of equipment and facilities.
4. Inadequate recycling of the rare metals that go into producing devices and the massive increase in electricity consumption accelerate environment damage.

Legal

1. Workers' rights globally will come into question with the rise of the gig economy. Fair trade pressure groups will also seek to protect those at risk from digital exploitation.
2. Ethical issues relating to data privacy will need to regulated and policed. For example, when does consumer research turn into surveillance? Also, will we always consider the interests of the individual to be superior to those of a company, the government, or society at large?
3. Cybercrime and the private/public bodies that counteract it will see significant growth as the scale and complexity of the Internet, and our reliance upon it, grows at exponential rates.

3.6 Understanding the Micro-Environment

At the industry/market level we can consider our environmental opportunities and threats through the lens of the five forces of competition (Porter, 2008). Again, these are some **general** factors where digital technologies have had an impact. However, the micro-environmental analysis should be undertaken based on the **specific** context of the organisation.

Bargaining Power of Buyers

1. This is significant, given a substantial range of choices and number of alternative suppliers from the global digital supply chain.
2. Purchase decisions and transactions can be completed quickly, with a high degree of traceability.
3. New supply relationships can be formed quickly, but the need for fast and quick delivery has the potential to lead to increased levels of fraud and supply chain disruption.

Bargaining Power of Sellers

1. Sellers have access to global markets through multiple intermediaries, and can also access many resale networks. This could represent a significant opportunity or a significant threat, depending upon the readiness of the organisation.

2. Market and customer data offer the opportunity for a significant increase both in sales revenue and sales volume using dynamic pricing (more on this later in this chapter)
3. The capacity to innovate in response to (or in anticipation of) changing customer needs using digital technologies will be a key determinant of the long-term sustainable success of organisations.

Threat of New Entrants

1. Many companies fear not only their established competitors, but also those who have yet to emerge. Digital technologies allow rapid and scalable innovation; coupled with the freedom of an entrepreneurial mindset this can disrupt whole industries (see the Blockbuster/Netflix case study in Chapter 1).
2. Scalable digital innovators can come from anywhere in the world, rapidly changing the locus of an established industry and its supply chain. It is often the case that customers are more mobile, whereas supply chains are less easy to reconfigure at scale at short notice.
3. With the rise of intellectual property theft and the inconsistency in levels of legal protection, the incidence of production imitation or subversion is a significant threat for technology-intensive organisations.

Threat of Substitutes

1. Chapter 1 deals at length with the disruptive effects of digital technologies which radically reshape established markets by taking a customer-centred approach.
2. The rise of the sharing economy (Sundararajan, 2017) and the ecologically sustainable need to reduce, re-use, and recycle means that products are staying in use for longer than many organisations might hope, potentially stifling the organisation's opportunity to innovate whereby it would create new income streams and a sustainable competitive advantage.
3. Augmented reality and virtual reality technologies are bringing new user experiences which are highly interactive. They can be used to complement or replace existing physical offerings. They can also be consumed on-site or remotely as required by the consumer.

Competitive Rivalry

1. The collection and harvesting of user data by online marketplaces not only enables the data to be used by the seller; it can also be reasonably re-used by the platform provider to develop their own marketing mix (e.g., to inform what products are sold, when, and at what price), as well as those of other sellers.

2. While the use of multiple channels might seem to be an effective distri-
    bution strategy to grow global sales, there might also be instances when
    the same channels compete with one another, with the effect of reducing
    sales margins. We also need to carefully consider the role of online
    intermediaries and whether they add or divert value from the in-
    house offering.
3. Data is king. Along with cybersecurity there are few corporate initiatives
    where investment in money, equipment, software, and personnel is
    growing at a faster rate.

3.7   Considering Options and Making Choices

While many strategy choice tools exist, it is the product–market growth
matrix (Ansoff, 1988) that I prefer to provide simplicity and clarity of
approach. You should be mindful that it is often not one single choice for
the whole organisation, for ever, but instead an intricate weaving of product
mixes and customer groups across vast geographies and diverse competitive
landscapes within varying timescales.

3.7.1 Existing Products to Existing Market

Also referred to as *market penetration*, this involves providing a greater share
of the products that the customer regularly buys. So, whereas a customer
might go to multiple providers for products (e.g., grocery stores), how can we
persuade them to buy from just us? This philosophy was the driving force
behind loyalty schemes, but has also driven process innovation where the
reasons for customer promiscuity might not be to do with the product or the
price, but might be driven by convenience (e.g., 24/7 opening, online
ordering, home delivery). Digital helps us to understand these patterns of
behaviour so that we might effectively pre-empt a customer purchase, maybe
by texting a voucher for a discount on a bottle of wine which it notices that
you frequently buy early each Friday evening, perhaps after a challenging
week at work!

3.7.2 New Products to Existing Markets

Once we have the largest feasible share of a customer's purchase, we might
seek opportunities to further grow our income, or fight off a competitor's
interest, by innovating new products and processes. This approach helps to
meet emerging customer needs which could provide long-term competitive
advantage for the organisation. Digital can help by co-ordinating and

monitoring test marketing programmes which target large-scale loyal users to try new products which are built with their interests in mind. Think about computer games, whether on dedicated consoles or as apps, where you receive pop up advertisements for other games that you might like to try.

3.7.3 Existing Products to New Markets

Not all customer markets in the world are at the same stage of development. For a range of economic, social, political, and cultural reasons, markets will develop at different times and at different speeds. This creates an opportunity for marketers in countries where demand might be slowing in market A, perhaps due to customer saturation or competitor activity, yet the organisation's ongoing macro- or micro-environment scanning activity has identified that market B is showing signs of growth that might make it an attractive target for future growth. Think about how Uber developed its ride-hailing app in the United States then moved to China, where it developed quickly only to be outgrown and acquired by DiDi.

3.7.4 New Products to New Markets

Also referred to as *diversification*, this activity relies on the organisation's rich knowledge of how to create new products, enter new markets, and retain customers through excellent processes. All these skills are deployed to fight against new competitors in new marketplaces. On the other hand, as with many diversified companies such as Virgin, Amazon, and Alphabet, they might rely upon brand awareness, superior data, and financial heft to create entirely new markets. Diversification is not solely the purview of major companies. Many start-ups take a diversification approach where they take significant risks on entering emerging markets, many of which are fast-growth and technology-driven.

3.8 Tactical Deployment

Effective marketing is a highly integrated organisational philosophy and discipline. As this book progresses, we will explore how every business function is affected by the eight drivers of digital marketing, as seen in the overview in Table 3.1.

The importance of developing an integrated digital marketing plan cannot be understated. The scope, scale, and speed of technological change have significantly impacted upon every aspect of marketing practice, rather than just a few isolated innovative practices in select areas. Also, the connectivity, reporting, and analysis of multiple business functions in real time make it essential that we

Table 3.1 Key organisational functions and the eight drivers of digital marketing

Key organisational functions	Driver of digital marketing							
	Product	Price	Place	Promotion	People	Processes	Physical experience	Partnerships
Innovation: the development and manufacture of a product or service	X	X			X			X
Logistics: the acquisition of raw materials and distribution of the finished article		X	X	X				X
Infrastructure: contracts, people, land, buildings, equipment, information, communications		X			X	X		X
Sales: acquiring, building, and exploiting commercial relationships			X	X			X	X
Finance: the acquisition, management, and distribution of money	X	X				X	X	

understand and respond to changes inside and outside the organisation. Having an integrated approach across the marketing mix enables us to:

- have effective customer-facing operations which provide the right product in the right place at the right time;
- respond to competitor actions by either challenging them directly with a price discounting and market saturation approach, or by creating new market strengths where we are clearly differentiated from their offering;
- configure our internal operations to optimise how we invest money and time into products and services. This will prioritise the offerings with greatest potential and either retire or reinvigorate offerings that have declined in popularity; and
- have a detailed understanding of current and emerging customer needs so that we can serve our chosen markets better than our competitors.

Choice inevitably involves the risk of pursuing the 'wrong' avenue for development, with the sacrifice of valuable time, resources, and skills that might have been better invested elsewhere. To validate these choices we can use the SAF criteria (Johnson et al., 2019) of *suitability* for the set goals, *acceptability* to stakeholders, and *feasibility* given the current resource and time limitations. This is a helpful final check to determine whether the new strategy is 'fit for purpose'.

RESEARCH INSIGHT 3.2 Digital Value Creation

Pagani, M. (2013). Digital business strategy and value creation: framing the dynamic cycle of control points. *MIS Quarterly*, 37(2): 617–632.

This paper provides insight into the dynamic cycle of value creation within the context of changing digitally supported networks. Set against the backdrop of the European and US broadcasting industry, this article explains the transformative effect that incremental innovations have by enabling a move from static, vertically integrated networks to more loosely coupled networks. This looser arrangement may also precipitate cross-boundary industry disruptions.

3.9 The Digital Product Mix

For the purposes of simplicity, we will consider both products and services as being the same thing in the eyes of the customer – that is, anything that is capable of satisfying customer needs. However, the essential differentiation in traditional marketing literature is that products are more tangible (i.e., you can touch and store them) whereas services are more intangible (i.e., you cannot touch or store them). In this book we treat them as the same thing because digital technologies have blurred the boundaries between the definitions. Take movies, for example. Until a few years ago many people solely owned DVDs or Blu-ray discs. However, when we watch a movie we may only own a physical copy of it in as much as the code is held on the hard drive of our phone, tablet, PC, games console, TV box, or in a personal cloud storage account. With the rise of streaming (i.e., accessing digital content online, on demand) we can also view the content directly from the supplier's cloud server without the coded files ever being retained on our viewing device (e.g., Netflix, Amazon Prime, and BBC iPlayer).

With the rise in the sharing economy that has grown on a global scale due to digital platforms, our focus moves away from controlling a physical product. For example, in using Uber (a ride-hailing service) or Airbnb (an accommodation rental site), we at no time control the vehicles or properties. Thus, the sharing economy sees us moving to purchase services or experiences where we spend valuable time away from our daily/weekly routine to learn, rest, have fun, and grow as individuals. As such, the sharing economy is driving a fundamental reconsideration about:

- how we think about work (e.g., the gig economy as discussed earlier);
- whether there is a need for us to own physical things (e.g., music, movies); and
- the challenge of finding just the right thing that we want, rather than relying on companies to package together products and services which they think we may need (e.g., the traditional package holiday).

Digital products have several distinctive characteristics that are available to use by virtue of Web 2.0, the Internet of Things (IoT) and big data:

- **They are customisable.** Products from cars to pizza delivery to apparel are customisable within a wide (but not infinite) range of features. Unsure whether the new car would look better with the four-spoke alloy wheels in red or the six-spoke alloy wheels in blue? Then visit the manufacturer's website and you can render many more design variants than any car showroom can accommodate. Do you like those trainers that you saw in the sports shop but want to stand out from the crowd? Using a service like Nike ID you can specify the colour palette of the entire shoe. The ability to host design software at scale online and allow customers to specify their requirements in a flexible manufacturing system supports the growing phenomenon of personalisation (which, on a global scale in real time, is referred to as mass customisation). The emergence of 3D printing as an additive manufacturing technique has enabled bespoke products to be manufactured. Although currently at a niche scale, this technology has the potential to produce on an industrial scale that would massively disrupt existing industrial supply chains, offering savings and choice for customers.

- **They are trackable.** Through websites and apps we are encouraged to create user accounts, which helps organisations to track our behaviours using cookies, to interpret this data (see Chapter 2), and to enhance our user experience. The things that we buy, in what combinations and with which frequency/what timing, helps the organisation's algorithms to understand our behaviours and predict/suggest potential future purchases to retain our loyalty by prompting us to buy, even before we have a clear understanding of our potential needs. This visibility creates a sense of anticipation and trust with the consumer, as does the ease of arranging order changes, rescheduling deliveries, making cancellations, and returning unwanted goods.

- **They are networkable.**
  - Synchronicity within software and across multiple devices allows a seamless user experience. For example, more short-duration passive tasks such as browsing or reviewing news updates might take place via a smartphone, whereas medium-duration interactions, such as gaming or movie viewing, are more likely to be via gaming console, smart TV, or tablet. Alternatively, where more complex work or leisure tasks are concerned, perhaps needing access to multiple sources of information, then a PC is more likely to be used. As organisations try to offer more digitally enhanced services it is important that these platforms connect and update in real time.
  - More complex consumer items, such as home entertainment systems, cars, and kitchen appliances, although bought separately, all offer the capability to network wirelessly with third parties and with each other to provide a more integrated and seamless user experience. Examples of this 'digital ecosystem' include:
    - Samsung's smart refrigerator, which communicates with your online groceries account, monitoring your products and your level of usage, and proactively reorders replacements before you run out;

- Mercedes-Benz's Car-to-X technology, which enables the autonomous exchange of information with vehicles to identify and track potential service issues before they become a problem, booking an appointment with a service station and arranging a replacement courtesy car while repairs take place.
  - It is highly likely that customers will share their experiences, knowledge, and opinions within online communities, either as customer feedback on the organisation's website, or more likely through social media platforms, potentially within specialist communities. These contacts will open further opportunities for online or offline collaboration between producers and consumers, in effect vastly extending the product features and support open to users (though not entirely from the organisation itself). We will explore user communities further in Chapter 4.
- **They are packageable.** The development of digital products that complement one another, and the tracking technology that models consumer behaviour, means that companies can tailor product offerings into dedicated packages; for example, a Sky TV package that is dedicated to your entertainment needs. This process is automated based on behavioural data. Algorithms will suggest alternatives and complementary products which they will package into unique bundles of products, potentially with a saving on the cost of the larger purchase.

3.10   Core and Extended Products

Digital technologies offer significant opportunities to enhance the core and extended product in both online and offline environments. By way of example, let us consider LEGO, a company which has diversified its product offering beyond generic bricks into more specialist sets designed internally or linked to movie tie-in licensing arrangements. Supporting this development has been a wide range of digital technologies which have developed online purchases, grown customer loyalty, and built a global online community which is embraced by LEGO not only to make even higher levels of sales, but also to engage enthusiasts to develop and test new product ideas. Table 3.2 shows that despite LEGO being predominantly a physical product, it offers a valuable digital user experience by connecting the LEGO brand with user communities.

Table 3.2 Core and extended product of LEGO

Classification	Product	Technology
Core product	Generic bricks (e.g., Duplo)	Online purchase and returns; order tracking; building instructions; ordering of replacement parts. LEGO® Life app
	Themed sets (e.g., City, Ninjago, Friends, Architecture)	Apps; movies; video games; web games
	Tie-in sets (e.g., Toy Story, Star Wars, Harry Potter, Avengers, Marvel)	Apps; movies; video games; web games
	Educational sets (e.g., Boost, Technic, Creator, Mindstorms)	LEGO Education website; coding
Extended product	Original movies and TV (e.g., LEGO movie, Ninjago)	Broadcast, DVD, Blu-ray, download and streaming
	Tie-in movies and TV (e.g., Batman, Avengers, Guardians of the Galaxy)	Broadcast, DVD, Blu-ray, download and streaming
	Attractions (e.g., house, parks, and discovery centres)	Online booking; bundling of products; pre-booking for rides; special offers
	Apparel and merchandise	Direct and third-party online retailers
	Customer service	Email; online chat; customer reviews (third-party online retailers)
	Social media channels (e.g., Facebook, Instagram, YouTube, Twitter, Snapchat)	Groups, discussions, suggestions, design competitions.

DIGITAL INSIGHT 3.1 Measuring the Organisation's Digital Quotient

Based upon an in-depth diagnostic survey of 150 companies around the world, McKinsey has developed a Digital Quotient benchmarking tool which correlates digital activities and financial performance. The measure assesses maturity across four business disciplines comprising 18 management practices (see Figure 3.1) and can be measured by a single metric representing its Digital Quotient, or DQ.

Once the DQ methodology was established, specific assessments were made of the digital maturity of some large organisations.

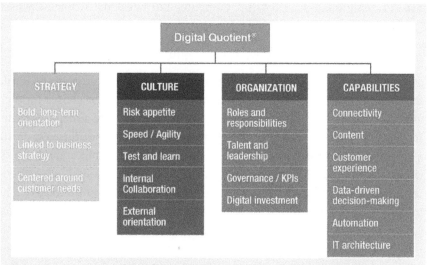

Figure 3.1 Components of the Digital Quotient metric (Catlin et al., 2015). Exhibit from 'Raise your Digital Quotient', June 2015, McKinsey Quarterly, www.mckinsey.com. Copyright © 2022 McKinsey & Company. All rights reserved. Reprinted by permission.

3.11   The Product Lifecycle

The product lifecycle considers the financial performance of a product during its lifetime. This approach is also helpful for us to understand the role of digital marketing in facilitating an efficient and effective journey for the customer and for the organisation.

3.11.1 Product Development Stage

The role of digital at this stage will principally be that of market research (both into customers and competitors) with the intention of:

- spotting trends to expand upon previous offerings (perhaps with enhanced product functionality); and
- exploring new and more radical directions.

If the latter is the desired course of action, marketers will be involved in prototype design, piloting to 'lead users' (more about them in Chapter 5) and market testing through 'soft' launches. This activity will refine the marketing proposal with relation to product form, target audience, and initial pricing levels. Digital manufacturing technologies, potentially 3D printing, may be used to create small-scale batches. Computer aided design (CAD) may be used to visualise the look and utility of the product.

3.11.2 Introduction Stage

Digital promotion plays a key role in developing product awareness and media 'buzz' during the launch. Key retailers and distributors will be chosen for their ability to provide market access along with valuable and timely customer feedback from the initial users. Social media channels will be utilised to create awareness of the product and to monitor customer interactions and responses. Organisations will also be monitoring social media for early signs of competitor responses, particularly if the new product is significantly different from its predecessors or competitors' existing products. Sponsorship and other campaigns through third-party channels (e.g., Amazon) and search engine optimisation (SEO; more in Chapter 7) will be designed to gain awareness of the new product and to build momentum for sales growth.

3.11.3 Growth Stage

It is at this point that the pressure upon the supply chain to radically adapt is at its highest. At an organisational level the intelligent interpretation of data is crucial to predicting demand for individual products, and potentially a range of products within the digital ecosystem. This rapid growth in demand may impact upon organisational responsiveness, so it is important to manage expectations through delivery updates (perhaps app, text, or email notifications) and customer service chats (potentially with AI chatbots). As market awareness builds, so will the interest from intermediaries – such as brokers, agents, and resellers – seeking to secure supply, so it is important that these organisations are effectively integrated into the wider distribution network. At the growth stage it may also become apparent which of the organisation's products are showing the greatest potential. To minimise waste and maximise customer response, data-driven strategic decisions will determine those products in which we should invest and those products which may have reached or passed their peak and should be retired.

3.11.4 Maturity Stage

It is here where the pricing and promotional pressure will be at its highest. Product shake-out, where weaker competitors leave the market, may have occurred in the growth stage, leaving a few dominant products/suppliers to fight it out for market share ahead of the eventual decline in demand. Product saturation – that is, where all potential markets are served and there is no more potential for growth of the current product offering – is occurring and new products from the organisation and/or its competitors are entering the market at the introduction stage. Organisations will be eager to promote customer loyalty for replacement products, or for other ecosystem or complementary products supplied by the organisation. An example of this might be where a smartphone maker will ask you to upgrade to the newest version, or where you will be encouraged to buy products such as cases, speakers, or earphones to help you to get more benefit from your existing device before replacing it.

3.11.5 Decline Stage

Organisations will be seeking a managed retreat from the market at this point. There will be a requirement to support customers who choose to stick with their legacy products, making ongoing support essential to avoid alienating existing customers. An example of this might be to provide ongoing software updates and product repairs for older version smartphones. There will also be a growth in the market for used products. Vendors will seek to extend this period to run down the supply chain. Finally, there will be a drive to create new markets for old products, either in different geographies or in different customer segments, so market intelligence and promotional expertise are again to the fore.

RESEARCH INSIGHT 3.3 Innovations and Technological Comebacks

Foucart, R., Wan, C., and Wang, S. (2018) Innovations and technological comebacks. *International Journal of Research in Marketing*, 35(1): 1–14.

Few markets have been more disrupted by the emergence of digital technologies than the music industry. Initially creating new opportunities for music creators and publishers to create higher-quality and more durable products (i.e., compact discs (CDs) and digital versatile discs (DVDs)), as opposed to vinyl records, which are easier to damage and more difficult to store and transport, purchases soon moved from the physical to the digital, necessitating a complete change in the current supply chain, but also changing the entire ecosystem by removing the need for dedicated devices such as record players and tape players with the introduction of integrated hardware devices that performed multiple functions (i.e., phones, tablets, and laptops). So, what does this mean for the market for legacy products, such as vinyl? This article explores the idea that the success of a third-generation technology (digital music) can have adverse effects on the second generation (CDs) but positive effects on the first one (vinyl), with ongoing implications for product positioning and product design.

3.12   Value

Pricing is an important tool in the traditional marketing mix since it serves several functions. Its principal role is to generate sufficient income to cover costs and generate a profit that is retained and reinvested or paid out to shareholders in the hope that the earning potential of the organisation makes it an attractive prospect for further investment. Pricing also serves the role of being the principal signal of the product's value and its target audience – think about the motivation behind discounts (as will be explored more in a moment), imitations, and premium brands. However, the headline or 'list' price is only part of the story when it comes to the final cost to the customer. Behind this may sit a range of other price-based incentives:

•   Discounts for preferred or loyal customers may be available in return for registering with the organisation's website or app, which provides valuable behavioural data and potentially develops the loyalty of convenience of buying from an organisation that already knows you (in terms of order history, stored payment details for purchases and returns, and delivery preferences). Discounts may also be offered in return for bundling the principal purchase with other complementary products as suggested by the vendor. Free postage for non-priority shipping will also offer a saving for many customers.
•   A choice of payment methods which may include paying by smartphone/smartwatch, contactless, credit/debit cards, cash, cryptocurrency, international currencies, online services such as PayPal, or extended credit terms which help customers to plan their cashflow.
•   Other transactional protections such as guarantees and warranties which will carry a commitment to repair or replace the product free of charge within a given period after purchase. At a standard level these may be included in the purchase price, but for extended cover an extra charge will be made. Order cancellation terms and refund policies are good practice for organisations that rely upon ongoing customer relationships, but in some countries they are a legal requirement of consumer protection regulations given the potential for misrepresentation or misunderstanding of goods bought online, where is it difficult to gain a clear understanding of their physical properties and thus their fitness for purpose.

At the time of the emergence of the World Wide Web its biggest benefit to consumers was seen to be that it offered perfect transparency of price and access to a global supply base. This freely available information soon pre-cipitated the demise of intermediaries, such as brokers and agents (covered in more detail in Chapter 6), since their market knowledge was replaced by publicly and permanently available databases. This process is known as **disintermediation** and will be covered in more detail in Chapter 4. However, the situation that emerged was a great deal more complicated as the true implications of the Internet became known due to significant growth in information available to suppliers and buyers alike. This took the form of downward and upward pressures, which will be explored more in the following sections.

3.13   Downward Pressures on Price

The following factors offer operational cost savings to the organisation because of the digital marketing mix:

- **Order processing.** This is the automated capture of digital data which can then be transmitted via wireless devices and sensors, globally and in real time. Automated processing can also remove human error on the buyer's side (e.g., mis-stating their order preferences or requesting goods that are out of stock) and on the vendor's side (e.g., lost orders, order fulfilment errors, or invoicing errors).
- **Just-in-time inventory.** Goods in the supply chain can be closely moni-tored through an amalgamation of supply, stock, manufacturing, and sales data. By working in a 'lean' manner (that is, not carrying excess resources but only those that are required to fulfil the required tasks), organisations are able to maximise their cashflows and reduce their working capital and maintenance costs.
- **Overheads.** The costs of running the organisation include support ser-vices such as management, administration, security, and data. Many of these functions rely upon the management of data to provide infor-mation which requires decisions that then need to be communicated to where they are implemented. The extent to which data is collected, transmitted, interpreted, and communicated is the core function of the Internet and the World Wide Web. This inevitably leads to a streamlining of activity as some processes and job roles are rendered redundant as a result of automation.
- **Customer service.** With transaction and order progress data becoming fully visible, and the ability to provide proactive updates to customers via digital messaging services, the role of the customer service agent is

diminishing. Additionally, global telephony services have allowed out-sourcing of human customer service operations to lower-cost economies. The rise of chatbots (i.e., automated online assistants that are essentially algorithms with intelligent language capabilities) has further reduced the expense of maintaining customer service operations.

- **Printing and mailing.** Digital document transfer, either by email or via cloud-based storage links for larger files, reduces the need for expensive copies that need to be printed, mailed, and stored. Digital signatures allow for legal copies of key documents to be held on file and accessed on demand.

- **Digital product distribution.** Product digitisation allows for goods to be manufactured and distributed at almost zero marginal cost. Products such as music, films, software, books, and news no longer need to be physically manufactured, distributed, and stored. Avoidance of these costs represents significant savings to organisations.

3.14   Upward Pressures on Price

The following factors incur additional operational costs for the organisation as a result of the digital marketing mix:

- **Online customer service.** Considerable scaling-up opportunities for businesses will also require a similarly scaled customer support infrastructure that helps around the clock and around the globe. This will require multilingual operatives – including chatbot and website versions – that can be accessed via a range of technology platforms from simple dial-up telephone lines to fully integrated online apps. Likewise, an internationalised audience (regardless of the country of origin or their current location) will expect a consistent level of service. Where an organisation is more localised in its international organisation it will need to ensure that local systems integrate with global ones to ensure seamless service and consistency with the organisation's brand values.

- **Distribution.** Again, a scaled-up market requires a scaled-up supply chain that will combine products made in different parts of the world, which through the digitisation and globalisation processes can create location advantages for the organisation (Porter, 1990). These complex and vulnerable global supply chains require careful integration, so development can be expensive and time-consuming. The organisation will need to make careful choices as to whether to supply local needs from local, regional, or international hubs. It will also need to take into consideration the associated time delays and transportation costs that each supply hub might incur.

- **Affiliate programmes.** We will discuss partnership and alliance structures further in Chapter 6. Affiliate programmes seek to exploit the network effects (McIntyre and Subramaniam, 2009; Shapiro and Varian, 2013) of the World Wide Web by gaining revenue from a merchant or a key online influencer (e.g., fashion bloggers Gabi Gregg, Lisa Gachet, and Wendy Nguyen) when they refer traffic. The incentive for this arrangement is a commission based on a proportion of the sale or a fixed amount. Such credible referrals reduce promotional expenditure and increase the rate at which enquiries are converted into purchases.

- **Site development.** Product, language, cultural, and technological complexities demand ever-higher website capabilities. The need to make these improvements with service outages (i.e., delays of cessation of service) for an always-on global audience requires significant investment in hardware infrastructure, supporting software systems (such as cloud services), and a growing army of web developers and security specialists who might be directly employed or independent contractors brought in on an ad hoc basis.

- **Customer acquisition costs.** The global capability of the World Wide Web also exposes the organisation to increased levels of competition. This may require significant increases in expenditure to expand and defend a domestic market. Additionally, many offline promotional costs will be incurred through sponsorship, local sales forces (or representative agents), and print and display advertising – all of which will need to be designed with local language, culture, preferences, and buying behaviours in mind.

3.15 Digital Pricing Strategies

The ability to profile audience behaviour, target them, and measure the results gives the marketer a rich and varied selection of pricing approaches. These can be broadly classified as content-based, market-based, demographic, and behavioural.

Content-Based Pricing

- Flat-rate subscriptions, such as Netflix, are simple to administer as repeat processes, offering ongoing income to the organisation which is not reliant upon customers' changing consumption habits. Where the product has a zero marginal cost of production (i.e., no more cost is incurred to supply two versions of the product instead of one) this is a highly efficient strategy.

- As previously mentioned, organisations may seek to bundle packages of products together based upon customers' tastes and needs. These products are often complementary and offer a rich experience for the customer. It may be the case that part of the package may never be used by individual customers, but there is still a perception of added value when the cost of the package is lower than the sum of its individual parts.

- 'Freemium' deals offer a basic version of digital products for free, but with enhanced versions carrying a fee. Additional credit can be purchased as required. Well-known monetisation strategies include:
  - advertising (via banner, video, native ad, interstitial ad, incentivised ad);
  - referral marketing (Amazon);
  - in-app purchase and freemium model (PokemonGO);
  - subscription model (*Wall Street Journal*);
  - sponsorship (Weather Channel);
  - crowdfunding (Hello Earth);
  - email marketing (*New York Times*); and
  - app merchandise and e-commerce (Angry Birds).

Market-Based Pricing

- Competitor-oriented pricing will be designed for offensive or defensive purposes. In the case where a strong competitor market presence is detected, an organisation will be motivated to offer lower prices to undermine the existing market leader's dominance. Where new products are being introduced against very little direct or indirect competition, then a higher level 'skimming' strategy could be used to maximise profits.

- Demand-oriented pricing adapts to surges or lags in demand. Prices will rise at high-demand times to take account of the scarcity of supply, but also to get customers to self-regulate their demand to 'smooth' the market to avoid disruptions of service from excess demand. Likewise, in periods where sales levels drop, organisations will offer discounts to stimulate demand.

- Dynamic pricing offers frequent changes based on data that reflect the timeliness of customers' purchasing behaviour and the relative prices of close competitors. Figure 3.2 is a worked example showing how the price level for a common product changed over time from a range of online and offline retailers. This approach is, in effect, an intelligent combination of competitor, demographic, and behavioural pricing strategies.

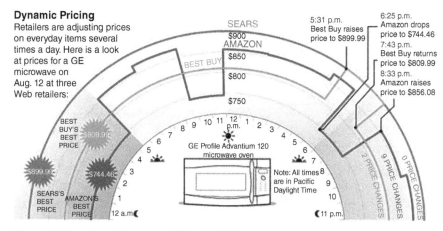

Figure 3.2 Dynamic pricing example (Uresin, 2019).

Demographic Pricing

- Gender, age, location, and socio-economic classifications are relatively easy to profile given existing data-mining techniques which source information from a wide range of social media platforms, apps, and subscriber databases. This data can track trends in purchasing behaviour and connect them to pricing levels, which determines customers' price sensitivity, openness to discounted price offerings, and lifetime earning potential (more about this in Chapter 5). Data is easily collected and interpreted from these aspects, but its value in anticipating needs is low.

Behavioural Pricing

- Negotiated pricing exploits the full interactive potential of Web 2.0, which enables two-way communication between buyers and sellers. These frequently take the form of auctions, where a seller states a reserve price then those who are interested submit incremental bids within a given timescale, and at the end of the process the highest bidder achieves the purchase. Reverse auction sites such as marketdojo.com utilise the same technology but allow buyers to request bids from potential suppliers for a specified range and quantity of products over a fixed timescale, with the lowest bid winning the auction. This process operates predominantly in business-to-business and on rare occasions consumer-to-business interactions.
- Lifestyle, interest, value, and relationship data across social media platforms offers insights into existing and potential consumer behaviours by tracking online activities, which will in turn indicate beliefs and attitudes. Messages can be tailored to influence these audiences in a timely manner. Such activity can affect the value, volume, and frequency of purchases over time and can significantly influence customers' lifetime financial value to the organisation.

RESEARCH INSIGHT 3.4 Digital Piracy

Chang, Y., and Walter, J. (2015). Digital piracy: price–quality competition between legal firms and P2P network hosts. *Information Economics and Policy*, 31(C): 22–32.

This paper explores the disruptive effect of the World Wide Web in relation to the removal of traditional intermediaries (in this case legal practitioners) and their replacement by either automation or peer-to-peer (P2P) provision, which potentially has significant product and cost implications. The paper develops a model in which a legal firm determines the price for its product and a P2P host site decides on its investment to improve the quality and accessibility of its product, which is free to download.

3.16   Ethical Issues in Digital Pricing

You would be right to think that the digital pricing techniques described above are principally designed to maximise returns from the customer for the organisation. You may think that this is fair, given the level of pricing transparency from the World Wide Web, that suppliers should utilise the same technologies to ensure a balanced relationship. However, ethical concerns regarding the exploitation of consumer data, and the market dominance potential because of network effects, leave the following questions over the fairness of these approaches:

- **Price fixing** occurs when networks of suppliers collaborate to keep the price of a good artificially high, potentially through the restriction of supply to create scarcity, or artificially low to deter new entrants who may bring more innovative high-quality products. This distorting effect is an unfair abuse of market power and acts to the detriment of the consumer, who is faced with excessively high prices or continually poor products.
- **Predatory pricing** seeks to unfairly exploit physically or financially vulnerable customers to pay over the odds in situations where demand is at its highest (also known as 'price gouging').
- **Deceptive pricing** can occur when entry-level prices are not made clear as such and additional products are charged for. Some organisations make introductory pricing offers to win new custom only to introduce accelerating price increases with no corresponding increase in quality.

- **Price discrimination** occurs when different individuals or groups are charged different prices for the same product. Although this approach is integral to the marketing discipline of market segmentation, if there is no meaningful difference in the quality of the product this practice is unfair.
- **Product dumping** occurs where excess supply in a home market cannot be sold. Globalisation and digitisation allow for this product to be moved to other markets where it might be sold, potentially to the benefit of consumers who are likely to achieve lower prices, but most certainly to the detriment of incumbent/domestic suppliers who will see a significant disruption of their market share, potentially leading to a damaging financial loss and shrinkage of the organisation.

DIGITAL INSIGHT 3.2 **The Price of Free**

Video games such as PokemonGO are a happy pastime for many children and adults, and are one of the most common products distributed for free by global media companies. *Free* in the respect that the most basic, pared-down, ad-heavy version is free at the point of download. However, media companies make a great deal of money from selling subsequent upgrades, perhaps in the form of advanced features such as playing with other users online, or by accessing extra capabilities such as weapons in combat-based adventures. They also generate significant advertising revenues from pitching directly to their captive audience, who are rarely given the opportunity to skip the ad content to continue with their play. As a result, parents and regulators are becoming increasingly concerned over the addictive qualities of these games, which can lead to the financial exploitation of users. This 'freemium' business model seemed to share all that was good about the Internet, particularly the benefits of the zero marginal cost of producing many digital goods that could be shared free of charge with customers. Now it is a cause for ethical concern for marketers.

CHAPTER SUMMARY

This chapter considers the factors that influence digital strategy, particularly within the changing wider market environment in which the organisation interacts with its customers and competitors. Digital technologies allow the tailoring of product and pricing packages to meet the identified needs of target customers. This agility helps to determine the long-term sustainability of the organisation.

Review Questions

- How have approaches to strategic planning, execution, and evaluation changed in response to digital technologies?
- At a corporate or business unit level, what digitally enhanced strategic choices does the organisation have and what are their implications?
- How has the distinction between products and services changed with the emergence of digital technologies?
- What role have digital technologies played in how organisations manage facets of the core and extended product?
- What factors influence digital pricing strategies and what are their ethical implications?

END-OF-CHAPTER CASE: ADDITIVE MANUFACTURING

Background

Additive manufacturing is a long-established technique where materials are built up, layer by layer, to create products. Many assembly-based industries bring together different components for their function, weight, and strength, through binding processes such as welding to create an effective and efficient end product. This contrasts with methods such as stamping or carving, which are subtractive processes (i.e., they create substantial amounts of waste as a proportion of the base material will be discarded). Materials technology engineering advances in areas such as 3D printing and advanced CAD software programs have enabled new manufactured products not only to be rendered visually, but also manufactured to create a physical model or prototype for further testing. On a certain scale this is not news. However, a range of complementary digital technologies have created a convergence that allows for the wider application of additive manufacturing, and for it to be offered on a larger scale. Mass connectivity of devices (the IoT), common coding capabilities that allow for the ease of transmission of data and instructions between them (Web 2.0 and big data), and the software to interpret and act upon these instructions (machine learning and robotics) have led to strategy, product, and price implications for the organisation.

Technologies

The process whereby wafer-thin materials are overlaid to inductively create more substantial parts comprising plastics, metals, and carbon fibre has been available for some time. However, the philosophy of additive manufacturing is not simply restricted to making things out of metal and plastic. The technology itself is evolving from simply adding layers of material to using more sophisticated methods where software-controlled chemical reactions are used to grow parts, again building layer upon layer.

Applications

- Adidas, a sports good manufacturer, 3D prints components for its running shoes in highly automated domestic factories instead of producing them in low-cost countries in Asia. The firm will thus be able to bring its shoes to market faster and keep up with fashion trends. This reduces product development lead times from months to days.
- Caterpillar and John Deere, agricultural and construction equipment manufacturers, are moving their warehouses to the online cloud, allowing digital designs of components to be accessed remotely and printed on demand.
- GE, a manufacturer of power systems, has invested $50 million in a new factory to print fuel nozzles for its new LEAP jet engine.
- GKN Aerospace is developing new ways to print large structural aircraft parts in titanium, reducing waste material by 90 per cent and halving assembly times.
- Johnson & Johnson, a US healthcare company, is working to print parts of the human knee known as the meniscuses, cartilage pads that separate the femur from the tibia, which act as shock absorbers – a role that causes significant wear and tear over time, occasionally requiring surgery to alleviate pain and restore mobility.
- The medical industry has identified four potential applications of additive manufacturing:
  1. Millions of individually sculpted dental implants and hearing-aid shells are now printed, as are a growing number of other devices such as orthopaedic implants.
  2. Researchers are already using bioprinters to make cartilage, skin, ears, bones, and muscles. These have been successfully tested on animals, with human testing and roll-out imminent. Currently, skin grafts for burn victims are a lengthy, painful, and unpredictable process. It may

soon be possible to print new skin of the same colour and texture as that of the recipient, directly onto the affected area.

3. With a reducing supply of donor organs for transplant (as a result of safer cars and more effective first aid) researchers are addressing the question of how to build organs, such as kidneys, from scratch. This is a significantly more challenging task, given the need for the networks of blood vessels needed to keep body parts alive.

4. Researchers have also used additive manufacturing to ensure medical efficacy of treatments. For example, it is possible to replicate a patient's own cells to print multiple versions of a cancerous tumour, allowing a range of interventions to be tested to ensure effective and efficient treatment of the illness.

Implications

This technological convergence has the potential to radically disrupt:

- traditional large-scale product offerings by enabling on-demand mass customisation;
- established global supply chains by reducing the need for complex networks of suppliers; and
- costing and pricing structures as easy-to-change software means 3D printing on an industrial scale can turn out one-off items with the same equipment and materials needed to make thousands.

Also,

- storage, transport, and fuel costs will reduce as products are lighter and stronger than those made by traditional manufacturing methods;
- environmental costs can be minimised as waste is eliminated and fuel costs reduced; and
- ethical issues in medical testing can be addressed as the need for animal testing will be eliminated. This will also please companies who would prefer to test on human skin, albeit the manufactured variety, instead.

DISCUSSION QUESTIONS

- How does additive manufacturing impact directly and indirectly upon the strategy-making process?
- What are the opportunities for new, enhanced, and extended products?
- How will approaches to pricing change in response to this disruptive technology?

Develop Your Skills
· ·

What Is the Skill?

Gaining insight into what the future holds is notoriously difficult. The scenario thinking process (Wilkinson and Kupers, 2014; Wright and Cairns, 2011) offers a systematic approach to build up a view of the potential future market environments that might provide challenges or opportunities to our organisation. It requires an understanding of the macro-environment drivers (i.e., political, economic, social, technological, ecological, and legal) that are likely to impact upon us over a given timeframe, their degree of predictability, and their potential impact (positive or negative) upon the organisation. Taken to its natural conclusion of recommending changes to the marketing mix to be 'future-proof', the process moves into 'scenario planning' for the organisation.

Why Is It Important?

If there is one thing that we can be certain of it, is that change will occur. That change will have an impact upon our organisation, but we simply do not know *which* change will happen, *how* it will happen, *where* it will happen, and *when* it will happen. The scale and scope of change, and the required organisational responses, are matters for our consideration that will subsequently determine the long-term sustainability of the organisation. The scenario thinking process gives us some insight into potential futures, but offers no guarantees or certainty as to the form and function of that change.

How to Develop It

Scenario thinking builds upon the rudimentary market and organisational strategic analysis tools of PESTEL, which considers relevant factors in the market environment, and strengths, weaknesses, opportunities, and threats (SWOT) analysis, which determines the level of 'strategic fit' that the organisation achieves. In other words, is the current marketing mix what the market requires, thereby achieving 'strategic fit', or should our efforts be targeted elsewhere, at other markets, or indeed by changing our current marketing mix to better serve our existing customers, thus addressing 'strategic misfit'?

How to Apply It

Take an organisation of your choice and work through the following scenario thinking process.

Step 1: Define the Timeline

This needs to be far away in order to create time for changes that might need to be made to the organisation, but close enough that we can realistically project future changes, rather than completely guessing them and thereby undermining the entire process. More dynamic industries will naturally have shorter 'long terms' (e.g., computer games which may be only two years) with less dynamic industries having longer 'long terms' (e.g., aerospace which may be around 15 years).

Step 2: Generate the Factors of Uncertainty

The PESTEL framework in Section 3.5 will guide you here. Aim to generate a list of around 20–30 factors which are balanced across the PESTEL framework (i.e., don't concentrate on some categories at the expense of others) as this will give you a more rounded view. It is important that these factors do not include numbers, since then they will be predictions and as such reduce the flexibility of the process when we come to step 4. For example, if in Economic you think that average salaries will increase (as opposed to decreasing), then state it as such rather than 'average salaries will increase by 4 per cent'. There will be no definitive version of this analysis since there will be many differing views across the organisation, so at this stage it is not necessary to look for consensus.

Step 3: Prioritise the Factors

It will quickly become clear that we cannot plan for all eventualities. Indeed, some factors may be contradictory. In order to prioritise the key factors, we should rank the factors based on their importance (i.e., those which will have the most positive or negative impact upon the organisation) and their uncertainty (i.e., how predictable they are). Figure 3.3 shows how the most important and least certain factors are selected as a basis for our planning.

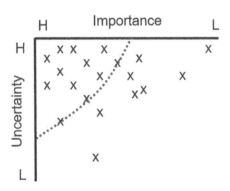

Figure 3.3 Prioritising factors in the scenario thinking process.

Step 4: Developing Scenarios

Using either the most dominant uncertainties or a cluster of interrelated uncertainties you should aim to identify three scenarios to sum up the market environment that is anticipated at the timeline you stated in step 1. They should be simply stated with two or three short sentences. For example:

European Decline: Europe's power and influence are decreasing; so is its currency and the image of its products. Unemployment in Europe is increasing and there is little European funding for research and development. At the same time, emerging markets (e.g., China and India) are now mature markets, with growing levels of gross domestic product.

Cutting-Edge Technology: After a long period of prosperity, lots of funds, both from governments and companies, are spent on cutting-edge technology development. New materials and fuels have been developed.

The Urban World: The world population is concentrated in cities, increasing their density. New trends in living standards have emerged with public transport, working from home, and personal space being reduced.

The three scenarios should not be linked to represent a 'good' environment, a 'bad' environment, and something in the middle. Once developed these scenarios can be used to assess the current resources and competencies of the organisation in the context of the future market environment, possibly by using SWOT analysis. Any mismatches can be addressed from the market side or from the organisation side so as to achieve strategic fit.

References

Ansoff, H. I. (1988). *Corporate Strategy*. London: Penguin.

Bughin, J., Catlin, T., Hirt, M., and Willmott, P. (2018). Why digital strategies fail. *McKinsey Quarterly*, 1: 61.

Catlin, T., Scanlan, J., and Willmott, P. (2015). Raising your Digital Quotient. *McKinsey Quarterly*, 3: 30.

Chandler, A. D. (1963). *Strategy and Structure: Chapters in the History of American Enterprise*. Cambridge, MA: MIT Press.

Chang, Y., and Walter, J. (2015). Digital piracy: price–quality competition between legal firms and P2P network hosts. *Information Economics and Policy*, 31(C): 22–32.

Foucart, R., Wan, C., and Wang, S. (2018) Innovations and technological comebacks. *International Journal of Research in Marketing*, 35(1): 1–14.

Johnson, G., Whittington, R., Scholes, K., Angwin, D., and Regnér, P. (2019) *Exploring Strategy: Text and Cases*, 12th ed. Harlow: Pearson.

Malmsten, E., Portanger, E., and Drazin, C. (2011) *Boo Hoo: A Dot.Com Story from Concept to Catastrophe.* London: Cornerstone Digital.

McIntyre, D. P., and Subramaniam, M. (2009). Strategy in network industries: a review and research agenda. *Journal of Management.* 35(6): 1494–1517.

Pagani, M. (2013). Digital business strategy and value creation: framing the dynamic cycle of control points. *MIS Quarterly*, 37(2): 617–632.

Porter, M. E. (1990). *The Competitive Advantage of Nations.* New York: Free Press.

Porter, M. E. (2008). The five competitive forces that shape strategy. *Harvard Business Review*, 86(1): 58–77.

Prassl, J. (2018). *Humans as a Service: The Promise and Perils of Work in the Gig Economy.* Oxford: Oxford University Press.

Rogers, E. M. (2003). *Diffusion of Innovations*, 5th ed. New York: Free Press.

Shapiro, C., and Varian, H. R. (2013). *Information Rules: A Strategic Guide to the Network Economy.* Cambridge, MA: Harvard Business Review Press.

Sundararajan, A. (2017). *The Sharing Economy: The End of Employment and the Rise of Crowd-Based Capitalism.* Cambridge, MA: MIT Press.

Thomas, H. (2007). An analysis of the environment and competitive dynamics of management education. *Journal of Management Development*, 26(1): 9–21.

Wilkinson, A., and Kupers, R. (2014). *The Essence of Scenarios: Learning from the Shell Experience.* Amsterdam: Amsterdam University Press.

Wright, G., and Cairns, G. (2011). *Scenario Thinking: Practical Approaches to the Future.* Basingstoke: Palgrave Macmillan.

4 The Digital Customer
Attitudes and Behaviours

Introduction

This chapter considers why and how customers make decisions, so that we can understand, anticipate, and influence their needs in a way that makes it easy for them to engage in a positive manner. Customer attitudes can be identified within subgroups of individuals or organisations with common needs, known to marketers as segments. These groups have a role to play in agreeing, articulating, sharing, and promoting the needs of the group and offer an efficient research and communication channel for any organisation seeking to market to it. However, there is a dark side to digital marketing, and here we consider the motivations and means of customer misbehaviour and the need to ensure the digital wellbeing of all the organisation's audiences.

Learning Objectives

- Consider how digital technologies impact upon the customer decision-making process.
- Evaluate the role of online communities in the relationship between buyers and sellers.
- Summarise what factors affect engagement and disengagement with digital customers.
- Appraise misuse and misbehaviour in online communities.
- Recommend approaches by buyers and sellers to ensure wellbeing.

CASE INSIGHT: CHANGES IN CONSUMER BEHAVIOUR – EVOLUTION OR REVOLUTION?

As recently as 10 years ago we mostly bought our goods from physical shops, paying with physical money and then physically having to carry them home with us. The only price comparison tools we had were to visit different shops selling the same product, or to speak to a friend or relative who had, and only expected a discount on retail prices if we bought from the trade counter in volume. This linear, retail-focused model concentrates upon providing a stimulus of point-of-sale advertising which drives the customer towards a product display in a retail outlet (the 'first moment of truth') which persuades them to buy and experience the product (the 'second moment of truth') and subsequently become loyal to the brand. With the advent of online retailers, smartphones, and a massive range of product options, this relationship has been stretched since we are now more likely to search online with broad product descriptors that reflect our needs than we are to travel to a store to see their displays. This is the 'zero moment of truth' (Google, 2011). Additionally, the enormous amount of decision power and information unlocked by smartphones and the Internet means that customers no longer interact with a single company in a linear manner. Instead, the modern customer's decision process is much more iterative as they skip between different stages of the traditional decision-making process, exploring and learning from a range of alternative products and suppliers as they go, to potentially make a purchase decision, eventually. This behaviour has come to be recognised as the 'customer decision journey' (Court et al., 2009). However, the increasing speed and volume of digital technologies is evolving this behaviour into 'the accelerated loyalty journey', which places a premium on hyper-speed targeting, delivering information in the shortest amount of time to the most targeted customer segments, pushing that information aggressively in front of the customers at the exact moment their needs are generated to get these customers to take immediate action and convert.

Questions

- Which digital technologies have driven these changes?
- What have been the positive/negative implications for businesses?
- What have been the positive/negative implications for customers?

4.1   The Role of Digital Technologies in Customer Behaviour

The study of customer behaviour seeks to understand why individuals act in certain ways. This helps us as marketers to understand what motivates individuals and organisations to buy, what attributes appeal to them the most, how to develop and project a message through a range of media to gain and retain their attention, and importantly how customers subsequently reflect on their purchase and consumption experience, deciding whether to buy from the organisation again (thereby developing a loyalty) or to recommend it to others within their social or professional groups. Digital, through its ubiquity, integration, and richness has significant positive and negative impacts upon customer behaviours. In profiling our search and consumption habits it aims to increase our satisfaction by pre-emptively offering purchases that algorithms consider appealing to us. On the other hand, it can make us complacent conformists, following similar patterns trodden by other buyers, taking away from us the richness and the randomness of choice open to us from exploring the wonders of the World Wide Web. Post-purchase, the constant request for feedback on our levels of satisfaction leads to survey fatigue and may actively reduce response rates and deter customers from further purchases from 'nuisance' organisations.,Lastly, our willingness to share the minutiae of our lives via social media only spurs on organisations to build closer relationships with us at a personal level to be integrated within our online identity and highly visible to others within our virtual and physical networks.

Digital, through the interactive nature of Web 2.0, has also created a fundamental power shift in the customer–supplier relationship. Co-ordinated media pre-Web 2.0, such as print, display, TV, radio, cinema, and the early Internet took a broadcast approach where a small number of general messages were transmitted to a mass audience. If organisations wanted a more targeted approach to specific groups of customers or segments, then direct mail and sales activity (e.g., speculative telephone calls or impromptu visits) would be the preferred approach. These are resource-intensive activities requiring time, materials, and expert skills, and regularly incur a high attrition rate to achieve the desired sales outcome. However, the emergence of Web 2.0 allowed for a more tailored and interactive approach to customer relationships. Enhancement of search engine technologies, cookie tracking, and social media flipped the relationship by empowering customers to dictate the terms of business in a way that sellers could not ignore. While significantly reducing customer acquisition costs for organisations, this development also increased risk through the emergence of competition on a global scale, and interaction with customers who were not lacking in confidence when it came to specifying the product they wanted and the price they were prepared to pay for it.

DIGITAL INSIGHT 4.1 **Is the Internet Making Us Less Productive?**

Throughout the 1990s and 2000s industrial productivity surged because of improvements in information technology that have helped us to locate, share, and store information. At the time employers were sometimes

> ## DIGITAL INSIGHT 4.1 (cont.)
>
> reluctant to allow employees access to the Internet for the fear of allowing distractions and possibly misuse that might bring the organisation into disrepute. In time their attitudes softened due to the staggering efficiencies offered by such connectivity. More recently levels of productivity have been dipping, and many believe this is due to the distractive qualities of the Internet and social media. Studies tell us that we use our smartphones between every 30 seconds and 7 minutes. Conducting tasks while receiving emails and phone calls reduces a worker's IQ by about 10 points relative to working in uninterrupted quiet. By one estimate it takes nearly 30 minutes to recover focus fully for the task in hand after an interruption. Besides dips in the productivity of individuals, distracted workers also tend to be less empathetic and less satisfied.

4.2   Types of Decisions

The complexity and scope of customer decisions have a significant impact upon their purchasing behaviour (Figure 4.1).

- **Routine decisions** are largely habitual in nature and mainly occur at a subconscious level. For example, what we might choose to eat for breakfast or lunch, or even which news outlets we tend to use. If marketers can successfully connect the required conditioned response (e.g., the specific brand of soft drink that we want customers to buy) and connect this to a conditioned stimulus (e.g., a colour, image, sound, or smell) then it is possible to automate customer decisions.

Routine	Limited problem solving	Extended problem solving
Low-cost products	⟵────────────────⟶	More expensive products
Frequent purchasing	⟵────────────────⟶	Infrequent purchasing
Low consumer involvement	⟵────────────────⟶	High consumer involvement
Familiar product class/benefits	⟵────────────────⟶	Unfamiliar product class/brands
Little thought, search, or time given to purchase		Extensive thought, search, and time given to purchase

Figure 4.1 A continuum of decision behaviour.

- **Limited problem solving** considers a relatively small number of alternative choices. For example, whether we travel to our place of work by car, taxi, tram, bus, train, or on foot. There will be a small number of variables to consider, such as route suitability and cost (if travelling by bus or tram), the cost versus convenience (if travelling by train or taxi), the availability of parking (if travelling by car), the weather (if travelling by bicycle or on foot). Digital platforms such as apps offer public transport information, weather information, maps to locate car parks, car or bicycle hire from a dealership, or scheduling of private car hire via Uber or Lyft.
- **Extended problem solving** is required for complex products with the potential to come in many alternative forms, have high significance to us, and are expensive and seldom purchased. Customers will take time and effort to make this decision; they may often not make the decision on their own but will seek an independent view from comparison websites or trust-based platforms such as TripAdvisor or Trustpilot. They also seek input from opinion leaders in reference groups with which they identify, such as preferred social media platforms.

4.3 The Customer Decision-Making Process

To understand the stages and drivers of customer decision-making, Blackwell et al. (2001) provide a linear model (Figure 4.2).

4.3.1 Need Recognition

As the initiator of the process, we should first understand what initially makes the customer aware of a dissatisfaction which drives them to find a solution. Maslow (1943) posited that we are motivated to achieve several ordered states, beginning with the **physiological** requirement to survive (e.g., air, food, drink, shelter, clothing, warmth, sex, sleep), then **safety** (e.g., protection from the elements, security, order, law), **belongingness** (e.g., togetherness, family, friends, work, love), **esteem** (e.g., achievement, mastery, status, prestige), and finally **self-actualisation**, which encompasses our desire to reach our full potential. McGuire (in Hawkins et al., 2007) identifies our drives and motives as **biogenic** (e.g., the physiological needs of hunger and thirst), **psychogenic** (i.e., to achieve social and cultural status), **cognitive** (i.e., achieving a sense of meaning), and **affective** (i.e., love). Awareness of these personal triggers assists marketers to develop suitable marketing mixes to either address an identified need or to artificially stimulate a new need by

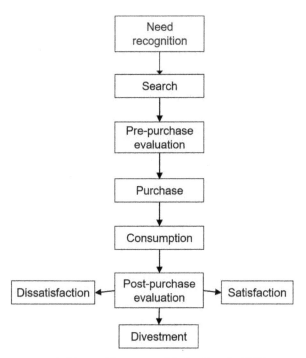

Figure 4.2 The customer decision-making process (Blackwell et al., 2001).

identifying areas of aspiration or dissatisfaction that might prompt an engagement. The complex use of keywords, meta-tags, algorithms, and machine learning in the research process helps organisations to spot purchase combinations which are common for certain customer segments, which they can then use to propose new product purchases for selected customers.

4.3.2 Search

The customer will search for information on how best to satisfy the identified need (Court et al., 2009). This information might have been accrued internally in our memory over time as a result of exposure to previous marketing efforts or if the buyer feels that this information is inadequate; or if there is a creeping dissatisfaction with their usual purchase, they may seek additional external information from their peers (e.g., via social media), trusted sources (e.g., user reviews or consumer protection websites), or directly from the supplier (e.g., via app, website, chatbot, comparison site, or third-party intermediary). Customers will be exposed to information through a range of devices (e.g., PC, TV, tablet, phone) that will include 'push' messages such as advertisements and tailored suggestions, or 'pull' messages such as search engine queries and social media reviews.

4.3.3 Evaluation of Alternatives

The search phase will end when the customer feels they have enough information to make a good decision. This information will be categorised into a set of criteria that will be used to evaluate alternatives. Many suppliers of more complex high-involvement purchases use their websites, apps, and notification services for the user to specify the criteria and search parameters, which simplifies an otherwise time-consuming and frustrating search experience, to present the customer with feasible options that are based on their requirements. For example:

- accommodation: rent/share/buy, price, location, number of bedrooms, parking, configuration (e.g., apartment, terraced, detached, number of floors, size of internal areas, size of external areas);
- holiday: location, accessibility, duration, availability, amenities, cost, climate, culture, language, activities, entertainment;
- computer equipment: brand, style, size, weight, speed, memory, printing, Bluetooth, Wi-Fi, storage, cases, printer, accessories.

4.3.4 Purchase and Consumption

Certain digital products (e.g., books, movies, music, games) can be purchased and consumed or stored instantaneously. However, in many cases the time between these two phases can be considerable and unpredictable. This is where the tracking and communication potential of digital technologies can create significantly higher levels of perceived customer service quality by keeping the customer updated and not eroding their experience through the frustration caused by waiting.

4.3.5 Post-Purchase Evaluation: Customer Satisfaction

Once the product has been consumed it creates a user experience which the customer will compare to the level of satisfaction that was anticipated at the *evaluation of alternatives* stage. In a transactional sense the supplier will drive for high levels of customer satisfaction to minimise complaints or returns and to maximise repeat purchases and the desire for complementary products. In a relational sense, whether they are satisfied or dissatisfied, customers are highly likely to share their experiences with their online community, such as a social media platform, via the process of electronic word-of-mouth (eWOM), which will be covered later in this chapter.

4.3.6 Divestment

Once customers have no further use for a physical product, they may consider throwing it away, recycling, selling/swapping, or donating it. This might be because they need to make room for new products. It may also be because technological advancements have led to shortened lifecycles for some products (e.g., mobile phones, computers, printers), which along with a desire to buy the latest model puts extra pressure on consumers to dispose of their old products. Many online services have emerged to resell or donate used products. As a sustainability approach to re-use or recycle products from a seller point of view there may be an impact upon the pricing of existing products or the development of new products. From a customer perspective this reduces the cost of purchasing and the subsequent ecological damage from unsafe disposal (e.g., roadside dumping), pollution caused from the landfill or burning of a product, and the overuse of natural resources by the constant creation of new products.

4.4 Customer Groups

As marketers you will be familiar with the practice of segmentation, where we try to group customers based on common interests and needs to tailor our marketing mix to achieve the most effective and efficient outcome for both sellers and buyers alike. The connectivity and data capabilities of the World Wide Web enable this to be a hyper-efficient activity. While the Internet carries rich socio-economic data on users, such as age, location, job, and income, this only helps us to identify customers by what they are today. As marketers we are interested in customers' emerging interests and needs both as individuals and as members of wider social and professional networks. It is here where we consider the behavioural factors that help us to build sustainable relationships with customers, and the role digital technologies play in building those relationships.

4.5 Attitudes to Technology

Rogers (2003) wrote on the rate of technology adoption, with a focus upon the role played by the attitudes that customers hold towards innovation. The model suggests five customer classifications that each have distinct characteristics.

- **Innovators** are eager to take risks and try new ideas and need little persuasion to do so. They tend to be younger and have higher status and education. They have a broad range of interests and are socially mobile. The approval of this audience is crucial for the later stages of adoption as, by the nature of their technical/product expertise, they will act as a reference point for those seeking to further investigate the potential of the technology. In the early days of new product development, their feedback, directly to the supplier or indirectly within their community (e.g., via a blog), will influence the organisation's decisions regarding the technology and its variants. These users may form focus groups or lead user enquiries during the supplier's market research activities.

- **Early adopters** are often in leadership roles (giving them high status), highly respected in local societies, and are often asked for their opinions and advice. Given their influential social and expert status with social groupings, marketers may sponsor social media influencers who are opinion leaders within their online communities – for example, fashion bloggers or gaming vloggers – to promote the product on their behalf.
- The **early majority** will deliberate over adoption decisions. They may be older and less technically literate but are open to suggestion from peers that they consider having similar interests but being better informed. These customers form the core of 'followers' within a social group, being prepared to be guided by opinion leaders.
- The **late majority** are sceptical and can be reluctant to change and will only consider it feasible when they see others like themselves using it. They are most likely to adopt when they perceive little risk. This group are most likely to adopt when the product has gone through several development iterations, eliminating any glitches, perhaps simplifying its operation and reducing the cost.
- **Laggards** are bound in tradition, may not seek out new information or experiences and may be socially isolated. They tend to be older and from lower socio-economic groups. Despite their reticence they tend to be loyal, low-maintenance, light users, and resilient.

4.6   Age Subcultures

Many authors have written of the experiences and attitudes of successive generations of customers with a view to understanding their motivations and preferences. This can be helpful for the digital marketer to understand the terminological shortcuts, but comes with the same 'health warning' for anyone attempting to extrapolate future behaviour based on socio-economic data. Nevertheless, Table 4.1 outlines the broad classifications and drivers.

This overview summarises the challenge for marketers to address broad, complex, and diverse audiences, on a global scale. The opportunity of big data, artificial intelligence (AI), and integrated (and automated) global supply

Table 4.1 Digital generations

	Born	Attitude towards technology	Communication media	Market characteristics
Silent Generation	Pre-1946	Largely disengaged	Letter	Satisfy their needs through younger generations
Baby Boomers	1946–1964	Early IT adopters	Telephone	Large and affluent segment
Generation X	1964–1980	Digital immigrants	Email and text message	Smaller families with larger purchasing power
Millennials/ Generation Y	1981–2000	Digital natives	Text or social media	Smaller numbers that are highly networked
Generation Z	2000–2010	Technoholics with a limited grasp of alternatives	Hand-held communication devices	Fully mobile
Generation Alpha	Post-2010	Emotional connection to AI devices	Augmented reality	Multiple market identities which are impossible to generalise

chains can bring massive returns for organisations with brave and ambitious leadership supported by significant funds to invest. For the rest of us a smarter approach, along with many social targeting mechanisms, helps us to target our selected groups of customers effectively and efficiently.

DIGITAL INSIGHT 4.2 Take Your Pick: 'New' News or 'Old' News?

According to a survey by Brodeur Partners (2019), generational approaches to a generic news product vary considerably, evidencing quite different customer values, attitudes, and behaviours across the age groups:

- Baby Boomers consider social media to be insignificant and strongly prefer their news via newspapers and magazines.
- Generation X prefer newspapers and magazines but will access some news via social media.
- Millennials/Generation Y are more balanced in their approach, with social media edging it.
- Generation Z strongly prefer social media.

The study also found that entertainment and engagement are increasingly important to consumers of news and journalism. It showed that the younger you are, the more you consider the journalism you consume daily as 'entertainment'. Thus, the confluence of the genres of entertainment and information, termed 'infotainment', has led to a significant reduction in attention windows (i.e., the exposure time to our focal attention to retain interest) to as little as 8 seconds. As a result, marketers need to continue to adapt the way they package and deliver their messages in a more sensory way.

4.7   Online Communities

So far in this chapter we have considered the behaviours of individuals and how these can be broadly defined to create meaningful and valuable segments at whom our marketing mix can be pitched. For us to understand how these groups identify themselves, organise, and behave we need to understand the role of reference groups in mediating social behaviour. Reference groups comprise individuals who have a sense of relatedness because of their interactions at any given time. Being part of a reference group brings with it a pressure to conform to collective norms and expectations, often subjugating the individual's own judgements, beliefs, and behaviours. There are a range of reference group types that may represent our culture (e.g., nationality, ethnicity, religion), our history (e.g., family, friends), our hobbies and interests (e.g., sports, entertainment, politics, learning sets), and our profession (e.g., a formal membership organisation, such as a professional body, or an informal grouping, such as a community of practice). Muniz and O'Guinn (2001) made clear that for online communities to be recognisable and to perform a meaningful role in providing tools, content, and information for their members, the following key attributes were required:

- consciousness of kind – which recognises shared beliefs, values, attitudes, and ambitions;
- moral responsibility towards the group – the need to act in the interests of the group and not individuals or external bodies; and
- presence of shared rituals and traditions – recognising common symbols and ways of getting things done.

4.8 Influencing

When groups form they bring together a collective benefit which exerts influence over other groups, but also upon individuals within the group. This power takes many forms and influences the activities of the group, and the behaviour of individuals, in a range of positive and negative ways:

- **Reward power** can manifest in the gaining of resources (e.g., increased income from career progression, or savings from negotiated discounts) or experiences (e.g., entertainment, vacations). The strength of the power increases with the size of the reward.
- **Coercive power** is the opposite of *reward power* and involves punishment via withholding of rewards, or the denial of group acceptance from non-admission (in the case of associative groups which we aspire to join) or group ridicule from groups we wish to please (e.g., cyberbullying).
- **Legitimate power** arises when individuals perceive that the group has a legitimate right to influence them (e.g., family, friends, education, professional body).
- **Expert power** occurs where the individual seeks information from a more knowledgeable group.
- **Referent power** arises from the feeling of identification that the person has with the group and will occur when the individual joins the group to achieve wider recognition, or whose progress within the group helps them to achieve greater status because of the group's legitimacy in the eyes of members and non-members alike.

For us to make good use of the potency of word-of-mouth within online communities we need to understand the role of opinion leaders (Song et al., 2017), identifying and targeting them as we would a market segment.

RESEARCH INSIGHT 4.1 Social Value

Manchanda, P., Packard, G., and Pattabhiramaiah, A. (2015). Social dollars: the economic impact of customer participation in a firm-sponsored online customer community. *Marketing Science*, 34(3): 367–387.

This research explores the relationship between online communities and financial benefits to the firm, and is guided by the belief that customers who join an online community which is moderated by the firm will consequently become more engaged with the firm and/or its products, resulting in increased levels of purchases. The authors describe this benefit to the firm as 'social dollars'. The results confirm this relationship and more specifically found that financial benefit accrued principally via online channels.

Commentators with a strong social media following are an example of this. For many years, advertisers have used celebrities to endorse their products (e.g., sports, arts, or just those people who are famous for being famous). The followings that these celebrities have are easy to determine from their YouTube channel, Twitter feed, Facebook likes, or Instagram followers. So, just as a traditional advertiser would employ the services of famous people to reach a wider audience through promotional campaigns, so a social media marketer will pursue the recommendation of specialist contributors (e.g., cosmetics, fashion, home improvement, gaming) who may have built a following from their followers' perceptions of honest and unbiased product reviews. They will send free products to the opinion leader in the hope that a positive review will follow. For the opinion leader this can lead to an erosion of their legitimacy in the eyes of their followers and a potential drop-off of attention. Such activity needs to fall short of paid advertising as this can be a deterrent to followers who choose to search for information in this manner precisely because it is seen as honest and unbiased.

The individual roles within online communities have been a focus for the research of Colayco and Davis (2003), who found that members generally performed several distinct functions as determined by their seniority, experience, community-mindedness, and aspirations. Table 4.2 outlines approaches to boosting individual engagement with online communities.

Table 4.2 Approaches to boosting individual engagement with online communities.		
Category	Level of the individual's involvement	Objectives for the organisation
Visitor	Will be an occasional (or one-off) participant with a highly specific need. At this point they do not consider themselves to be part of the community in either a passive or active capacity.	Ensure that answers to the visitor's enquiry are easily available, possibly in the form of a frequently asked questions (FAQ) section. The benefits of membership should be clearly defined on the homepage. There should be a call to action to join (i.e., an introductory discount or free trial membership period).
Novice	A recognised member who is largely passive. Spends time in the group observing activities and consuming content. Begins to learn the culture and starts to identify areas of interest.	Build trust by showing caring (e.g., through a welcome message, special discussion, explanation guide, offers of dedicated support through a human or chatbot link). The emphasis is upon the organisation, through its senior members, to reach out to new members. For users who aren't quite ready to engage more fully it is important to have an easy interface which might include a site map with a search bar.

Table 4.2 (*cont.*)

Category	Level of the individual's involvement	Objectives for the organisation
Regular	Participates in others' discussions (with likes, shares, or brief comments) but rarely starts their own topics.	Promote discovery and involvement by invitation to join discussions and special-interest groups. Differentiate individuals through membership scales or by special awards in recognition of their contribution, boosting their status and encouraging others to follow.
Leader	These may comprise volunteer members or salaried staff. They will be committed to the group and will create most of the topics for development.	Leadership of the group is an important part of their identity in terms of the kudos it brings and the opportunity to further the development of a cause that they hold dear. Besides formal leadership they may also take roles which include mentor, guide, or adviser. They will value a record of achievement and will appreciate thanks upon membership anniversaries.
Elder	These will be highly respected members who were previously highly active and are now seeking an easier role where they can pass along their knowledge and experience.	Try to prevent losing them by making the process for engagement easy. Utilise their profile to gain external impact. They will act in a senior advisory capacity, as ambassadors for the organisation, or simply as storytellers seeking to continue the group's rich history and perpetuate its achievements.

4.9 Why Do Organisations Care?

Due to the efficiency (i.e., several individuals with common objectives) and effectiveness (i.e., they tend to be driven to achieve certain distinct goals) of online communities, the organisations that are marketing to them have several clear benefits from engaging at a digital level. Please note that this does not simply mean through social media channels (more in Chapter 7), but includes a broad engagement across the eight drivers of digital marketing:

- **Awareness** of the organisation, its brands, and their activities leads to further discussion, and the formation of hopefully positive attitudes in the minds of its customers. This may develop loyalty and could result in customers acting as advocates for the organisation.

- **Influence** comes from developing the image of being a leader in the organisation's chosen field. This credibility sets the standard within the industry and can impact upon the behaviour of competitors. In turn we can learn from the messages of our competitors and respond appropriately through the eight drivers of digital marketing.
- **Increased web traffic** can be achieved from well-designed and timely messages which can be shared online. This creates significant positive impacts upon the organisation's budget as fewer resources may be required or it may enable the existing levels of resource to reach larger audiences and create greater profitability.
- **Customers' experiences** are enhanced as they are linked to like-minded individuals with similar interests. The organisation might also choose to pilot ideas for new products within the community by offering discounts or additional benefits to members in return for their feedback.
- **Brand relationships** create a recognisable short-cut in the promotional activities of an organisation, which enables stakeholders to quickly identify and relate to its offering based on experience or anticipated future use (particularly for aspirational brands such as the luxury sector). The concept of brand community has been used to understand how consumers create value around brands online, and the work of Arvidsson and Caliandro (2016) explores how brand publics – social formations that are not based on interaction but on a continuous focus of interest, such as a product or organisation – mobilise an individual or collective affect in social media-based consumer culture, where publicity rather than identity has become a core value.

4.10 Why Do Customers Care?

Our exploration of group power, group roles, and online purchasing behaviours brings us to a deeper examination of how customers gain value from online communities. Again, the work of Colayco and Davis (2003) guides us to understand that the relationship is not merely the idle exchange of gossip but contains substantial benefits to meet a range of customer needs. This insight drives us to create richer experiences, rather than simply just selling opportunities, to appeal to deeper needs that create lasting positive benefits for the customer, their community, and the organisation.

- **Informational value (i.e., knowing).** Potential customers will be interested in gaining insight regarding which products or configurations might best suit their intended purpose. Existing customers may seek opinions on whether to switch products to another supplier or may seek answers to usability questions that may not be covered by the FAQ sections of the supplier's website. Suppliers can use this information to identify potential product defects which would be addressed by designing-out the identified flaw in future versions, or proactively offering free repair or replacement (building substantial customer and community goodwill in the process).

- **Social value (i.e., sharing).** User communities benefit from the participants' need for a connection to others with a common interest. The shared language, knowledge, experience, and goals lead to rich and mutually beneficial communications in an era where digital technologies are used by many organisations to eliminate or reduce the human elements of customer service. This can lead to a great deal of frustration and delay when trying to address a non-standard query that is not covered by the FAQ section of the website or recognised by the AI virtual customer service agent, or chatbot. It's not all about complaints and queries. Many people get real joy from products that make their lives easier and are happy to share their joy via social media posts.
- **Hedonic value (i.e., feeling).** We like to feel. To be joyful. To laugh. To cry. To be angry. Love, humour, sadness, and anger play an enduring role in our individual lives and in how the advertising industry seeks to gain our attention and transform it by using our emotions and associations to create powerful bonds with their brands and products. Web 2.0 is rich in multimedia to present to the user in multiple formats, allowing customers to interact, guide, and inform the relationship. Online content can provide opportunities to dodge boredom and have fun. Companies benefit greatly from providing entertaining content which has no explicit sales purpose. Customers begin to feel that a relationship is developing which goes beyond the short-term requirements of a financial transaction. Additionally, very good-quality content that is well designed and well produced also has a much higher chance of being shared online, creating even higher levels of free exposure for the organisation. Bad content also gets shared, but perhaps we don't want to focus upon this route as it rarely creates positive brand relationships.
- **Transformative value (i.e., changing).** The open and democratic nature of the World Wide Web has enabled many people to contribute to global discussions which have changed their own experiences and perspectives – for example, through online learning programmes and apps. It has also given the opportunity to contribute to local, national, and global political discussions either directly through evaluation of political candidates putting themselves forward for election, through pressure groups

(e.g., climate change), and in supporting the work of charitable organisations through online donations, petitions, sharing of messages, discussions, and the organisation of physical protests. The Internet has been a key enabler for global citizenship.

- **Practice value (i.e., doing).** Online communities, because they are driven by people and organisations, give us many opportunities for enhanced engagement with the offline world to practise our hobbies, interests, and professions. Events, meetings, networks, and projects offer significant opportunities for social sharing which will lead in expected and unexpected directions as participants explore more broadly and deeply their specific areas of interest. These opportunities for practice also lead to deeper levels of experience and reflection which subsequently lead to understanding and competence.

4.11   The Transfer of Value within an Online Community

In summary, online communities exist to support their members to achieve their goals. For this to become an extensive and sustainable activity the value transferring activity needs to be clear and balanced. We are familiar with the dynamic of users sharing value with each other, but this process also requires an administrator function to ensure that the form and function of the community serves its users to best effect.

4.11.1 User to User

Users support one another through the sharing of information and content through conversations that are started, occasionally through the proactive sharing of ideas or content, or added to by users contributing their thoughts, ideas, and suggestions to an existing open conversation. These conversations are largely supportive, but the occasional 'rogue actor' may seek to undermine a user or a conversation for malicious reasons, which may cause the administrator to intervene at the behest of other users who find the rogue input to be unhelpful.

Users can also galvanise fellow users into collective action to achieve an objective to effectively 'crowdsource' (Brabham, 2013) a solution to a problem instead of relying on traditional routes or established organisations. This platform for co-operation also allows users to sell to each other, to share products within the community, and to co-create new products. This phenomenon is known as *prosuming* (Sioshansi, 2019) and will be discussed further in Chapter 6.

4.11.2 Administrator to User

The key initial role of the administrator is to provide a clear and reliable online forum for interaction, and may also be to support offline activities such as events, visits, and celebrations. Standards of behaviour between users will be overseen by the administrator, which may take the form of an explicit agreement upon joining or as part of the later curation/moderation/mediation role. Occasionally there will be a 'no soliciting' rule, but most groups are open to commercial messages if they are not overly intrusive with regard to the declared interests of the group. Indeed, some communities rely heavily upon commercial sponsorship to deliver enhanced resources and activities to their users, but the level of this involvement will be for each community to agree.

Administrators will also act as the responsible person to ensure compliance with data protection regulations, and may perform an externally focused ambassadorial role in order to recruit new members, participants, and other supporters (e.g., sponsors, guest contributors, professional advisers) to enable the needs of the users to be met.

4.11.3 User to Administrator

Users play the key role in making a community a compelling place to be by the volume and valence of their interactions. This rich engagement from a broad audience creates communications traffic which potentially has value for all concerned with the goals of the community. Without this, the administrator would have no activity to support and organise, finding their external recruitment task to be a challenging one.

The financial benefit gain directly from users includes subscription fees, fees for access to specialist third-party content, commission on user-to-user sales made via the community, and entrance fees for offline visits and events. Indirectly the administrator will provide selective access to the community through either advertising or sponsorship revenues, or discounts for users.

RESEARCH INSIGHT 4.2 Why Do People Contribute Content to Twitter?

Toubia, O., and Stephen, A.T. (2013). Intrinsic vs. image-related utility in social media: why do people contribute content to Twitter? *Marketing Science*, 32(3): 368–392.

Seeking to understand the motivations for user contributions on social media, this research distinguishes between intrinsic utility as the direct effect of posting content, and image-related utility which is derived from the perception of others. These two types of utility can be empirically distinguished because the former depends on posting behaviour whereas the latter only relates to the number of followers a person has on the social network. They found the intrinsic utility outweighed image-related utility when Twitter users had fewer followers, whereas image-related utility became more dominant as they gathered more followers.

4.12   Customer Misbehaviour

While we welcome positive word-of-mouth for its promotional and relational potential, there is always a risk that the customer experience (more in Chapter 5) will be a dissatisfying one, potentially leading to negative word-of-mouth, allowing customers to release their anger, regain control over a bad situation, and gain sympathy from others. This behaviour constitutes an act of customer misbehaviour which Fullerton and Punj (2004) define as 'behavioural acts by consumers which violate the generally accepted norms of conduct in consumption situations and thus disrupt the consumption order'. These acts of misbehaviour are usually motivated by a dissatisfying experience whereby customers attribute the blame to someone else and where they feel that there is a greater chance of redress from the organisation. The World Wide Web provides an easy and accessible platform for customer complaints which can be made by direct (i.e., privately to the organisation or individual concerned) or indirect (i.e., via an alternative channel such as consumer media, regulatory bodies, or social media) actions.

Misbehaviour in online communities is not limited to complaining alone. Hoyer et al. (2012) give an overview of the typologies:

- **Abnormal behaviour** includes excessive buying to compensate for psychological problems. This may be exhibited through compulsive purchases to compensate for a bad day at work. This is easily done through the plethora of retail apps that we carry in our smart devices. Since they record and predict our search and purchase history it is not too demanding a task for them to make suggestions that might interest us, directly via messaging or email services. From there we are only one or two taps/clicks away from making a purchase. This highly intuitive, proactive, and convenient service means that we often spend little time deliberating a purchase, but instead make it instinctively. In excess this can lead to us overstretching our financial resources, leading to credit default or bankruptcy.

- **Illegal behaviour** includes the misuse or theft of personal data and payment information. Within third-party reseller sites the counterfeiting of brands also qualifies. Given the 'no quibble' returns policies of online retailers in response to various distance-selling regulations designed to protect the rights of consumers, there are cases of customers taking delivery of a product, using it, then returning it for a full refund (e.g., premium fashion pieces and accessories). In more serious cases illegal behaviour could refer to the buying of illegal products (such as weapons, drugs, and sex-related products). While the Internet that we access every day is fairly well moderated by users and platforms alike, there is a developing body of literature regarding the dark net (Bartlett, 2015) which comprises sites that are accessible only through heavily encrypted networks which prevent the identities and locations of dark net users from being traced. The principal services are *The Onion Routing* project (TOR), which focuses on providing anonymous access to the Internet, and *Invisible Internet Project* (I2P), which specialises in allowing the anonymous hosting of websites. This level of protection makes it attractive for those with an interest in illegal activities.

- **Misinformation** through the wilful submission of inaccurate or misleading feedback responses, reviews, or social media commentary/engagement is a complex phenomenon where several actors, with their differing intentions, could be at play:
  - Suppliers could submit fabricated 'independent' reviews to infer higher levels of customer satisfaction and recommendations with the expectation of increased levels of business.
  - Competitors could similarly submit reviews to infer customer dissatisfaction to restrict the capability of the target organisation to retain and grow custom.
  - Customers who are dissatisfied with the organisation's product, or perceive an inadequate response to their concerns, may inflate their dissatisfaction which they will share across a wide range of social media platforms, either in an altruistic effort to prevent other customers being similarly mistreated, or to punish an organisation they feel to be to blame for the experience. The intent here would be to deter other customers.

- **Boycotts** occur where customers co-ordinate their actions to withhold business from organisations who have been seen to act against their interests. This may be in response to the unacceptable personal (e.g., workplace harassment) or professional (e.g., inappropriate comments or misleading of regulatory bodies) behaviour of senior individuals. It could also be attributable to behaviour at a corporate level, such as the exploitation of vulnerable communities when sourcing globally, a poor record on worker and product safety, or using unsustainable and environmentally damaging practices (e.g., excessive pollution or waste due to inefficient processes and inappropriate product disposal). An opposite effect could occur where an organisation aligns itself to the interests of a pressure group, sponsoring its activities to gain global exposure through 'friendly' social media activity.

DIGITAL INSIGHT 4.3 The Costs of Digital Piracy

Since the emergence of the Internet, piracy of digital content has been rife. The easy transferability of digital files, including music, movies, books, artwork, and software, coupled with basic security standards mean a 'wild west' approach to policing and regulation have had a significant effect upon the industry. It is a significant barrier to growth, with annual losses estimated to rise to $52 billion by 2022 according to Digital TV Research. In addition, piracy negatively affects every single person working in these industries and their supply chains. There is less money to invest in new software, developing music artists, and creating movies. There is less work for developers, testers, sound engineers, videographers, actors, scriptwriters, musicians, assistants, set designers, security guards, stores, salespeople, website developers, and every other person who goes into creating, packaging, advertising, distributing, supporting, promoting, or reviewing these products and services. For the user of pirated content there can be significant costs too, since the content carries a significant risk of malware which may corrupt their operating system and data, and access confidential information such as contacts, passwords, and banking and employment details, opening them up to identify theft and fraud. The malware could also turn the computer into a part of a criminal botnet.

4.13 Digital Wellbeing

While customers may gain the most from the information and choice given via the World Wide Web, it is also they who could potentially suffer the most from the misbehaviours of governments, companies, criminals, and their peers. It may be appealing to have a digital assistant that recognises your voice, understands what you say, knows your preferences, and holds your key data, thus saving you the trouble of re-entering codes time and time again. However, this information in the wrong hands can lead to criminal behaviour. Additionally, the 'always on' nature of the Internet can lead to addictive behaviours. One such case is the fear of missing out (FOMO) phenomenon as discussed by Blackwell et al. (2017), which is epitomised by the desire to interact across multiple forums and the perceived pressure to post remarkable content on social media accounts to win and retain the admiration of our friends, and to constantly interact with friends' posts, which can place impossible demands upon the wellbeing of users. There is also evidence that extreme use of digital tools may create mental health risks (OECD, 2019).

Many governments, charities, and businesses make it their mission to improve people's lives. But how can they know whether they are succeeding? The purpose of measuring wellbeing is to help understand whether life is getting better for people – so that, ultimately, we might better identify what drives positive and negative changes in people's lives. To understand and tackle this issue, the Organisation for Economic Co-operation and Development (OECD, 2019) utilises their Wellbeing Framework (Figure 4.3)

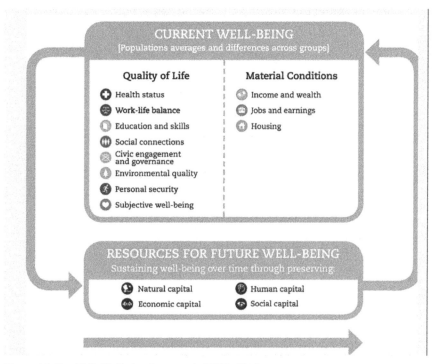

Figure 4.3 The OECD Wellbeing Framework (OECD, 2019).

to assess the risks posed by digital technologies to individual wellbeing, with the main risks identified as:

- **digital divide:** the disparity of access to technology, networks and software, paucity of usage, and digital skills;
- **digital illiteracy:** as a mix of cognitive and emotional skills that is necessary to sort out information quality, self-control digital involvement, and avoid mental health problems; and
- **digital insecurity:** data privacy, hacking, cyberbullying.

Based on this framework, their subsequent report (OECD, 2019) creates assessments at a national level of digital risks and opportunities. The Digital Wellbeing Wheel distinguishes between risks (in yellow) and opportunities (in dark blue) of digital transformation. Blank areas identify where no data is available to make an objective assessment. By way of example, Figure 4.4 shows the assessment for Hungary.

Compared to other OECD countries, Hungary is highly exposed to the risks of the digital transformation, while only experiencing limited benefits from its opportunities. Hungary has a very high level of inequality of Internet uses. Despite limited use of Internet, Hungary is in the top three of OECD countries in

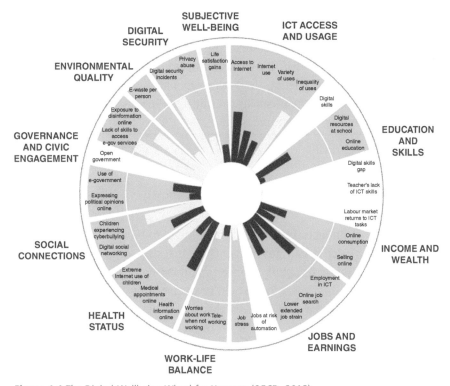

Figure 4.4 The Digital Wellbeing Wheel for Hungary (OECD, 2019).

the share of people reporting digital security incidents. While there is no data on digital skills, Hungary is the country with the highest share of people reporting lack of skills as a reason not to use e-government services. However, national data show that 29% of Hungarian people have submitted completed forms to public authorities' websites, which is in line with the EU average. The Internet is not widely used for key economic activities such as online consumption and finding jobs online, although the share of information industries in employment is well above the OECD average. While comparatively few people use the Internet to express political opinions, many people report having been exposed to disinformation. Furthermore, children are particularly affected by online risks: the share of extreme Internet users among children is above the OECD average and Hungary ranks second in terms of children reporting cyberbullying.

(OECD, 2019)

RESEARCH INSIGHT 4.3 Children and Digital Wellbeing

Nansen, B., Chakraborty, K., Gibbs, L., Macdougall, C., and Vetere, F. (2012). Children and digital wellbeing in Australia: online regulation, conduct and competence. *Journal of Children and Media*, 6(2): 237–254.

This article explores children's online use, experience, and regulation. It examines the use of technology by children and their families in the contexts of everyday and home Internet use, focusing upon mediation, conduct, and competence. Age-related gaps in the literature on children's online risks are identified. By contributing to our understanding of the concept of digital wellbeing, the authors emphasise the need to educate children to be active, ethical, and critical online users, alongside the existing parental protection measures.

4.14   What Is the Role of Digital Marketers?

Public outcry at data security failures by a range of banks and social media companies have led some governments to investigate how regulation or legislation can improve customer protection, potentially creating a new duty of care towards online users that would be overseen by independent regulators. Given the scale of social media this would have a significant impact upon digital marketing practices, given the scale of the changes that would be required to improve oversight. Gourlay and Butler (2019) report that it would take over 2,000 years to watch all the content uploaded to YouTube based upon the resources needed to filter the 500 hours of new video content uploaded every minute. However, the threat of social media regulation jeopardises its key reason for being, which is the free exchange of unregulated ideas and opinions.

The marketing industry has begun to respond with the launch of the Global Alliance for Responsible Media (World Federation of Advertisers, 2019), a global collaboration with agencies, media companies and platforms, and industry associations to rapidly improve digital safety by recognising the role that advertisers can play in collectively pushing to address harmful and misleading media environments. The Alliance comprises support from:

- **advertisers**, including Adidas, Bayer, BP, Danone, Diageo, General Mills, GSK Consumer Healthcare, LVMH, Mars, Incorporated, Mastercard, Mondelēz International, NBCUniversal, Nestlé, Procter & Gamble, Shell, Unilever, and Vodafone;
- **agencies**, including Dentsu, GroupM, IPG, Publicis Media, and Omnicom Media Group;
- **media companies**, including Facebook, Google/YouTube, Teads, TRUSTX, Twitter, Unruly, and Verizon Media; and
- **industry associations**, including ANA, 4A's, Interactive Advertising Bureau, ISBA, Mobile Marketing Association, Coalition for Better Ads, Effie Worldwide, and WFA.

4.15 Digital Wellbeing Tools

At a macro-level, the OECD framework and assessments provide a useful overview, but as marketers what practical actions can we take to protect the wellbeing of our customers on a day-to-day basis? Drawing upon the principles of positive psychology described as 'the scientific study of what makes life most worth living' (Peterson, 2006), this process focuses on topics such as character strengths, resilience, and happiness. The Seligman (2011) PERMA model helps to explain the five measurable elements of wellbeing as *positive emotion, engagement, relationships, meaning*, and *achievement*. Since digital wellbeing is often defined in terms of the capabilities and skills that an individual requires to successfully make use of digital technologies, the PERMA model formed the basis for the JISC (2015) research, which contextualised the definition of digital wellbeing as 'the capacity to look after personal health, safety, relationships and work–life balance in digital settings'. Subsequently their Six Elements of Digital Literacy framework identifies the following individual capabilities:

- use digital tools to pursue personal goals for health and fitness;
- use digital tools to participate in social and community activities;
- act safely and responsibly in digital environments;

- negotiate and resolve conflict;
- manage digital workload, overload, and distraction; and
- act with concern for the human and natural environment when using digital tools.

We will consider the practical application of this framework, as both a wellbeing and an employability tool, in Chapter 10.

At a practical level Google is leading in this area with their Digital Wellbeing app, which helps users to place limits on when and how Google Home devices are used (Google, 2019). Users can specify downtime for digital devices to avoid addictive behaviours and create time for offline activities, such as outdoor play, family time, meeting with friends, or to ensure a good night's sleep. Additionally, users can choose the filters to determine who will be protected (i.e., individually or collectively) and the specific content to which access is controlled, which includes:

- video – to only play videos from YouTube Restricted Mode, YouTube TV Filtered Mode, and YouTube Kids; users can also block all video content or allow all video services without any filtering;
- music – whether to block explicit music, all music, or no music; remember that when it comes to explicit lyrics no filter is foolproof;
- calls and messages; and
- Assistant answers – limits Assistant answers to basic subjects like weather.

4.16   Digital Detox

Beyond the managed approaches to digital engagement there is a growing movement of psychologists championing the need for a simpler approach to digital technologies to gain a sense of balance leading to improved mental health. Snow (2017) proposes the following practical steps for creating a better relationship with technology:

- **Remove unnecessary distractions,** such as alerts and notifications (except for voicemails for emergencies) to focus upon interactions with family, friends, health, and work.
- **Don't glamorise busyness** as it creates a barrier to taking time to pursue what would really make us happy. By doing the latter, you can start to think more clearly about how you are choosing to spend your time.
- **Always ask 'why' when you pull out your phone** so that it is a purposeful act rather than simply a distraction.
- **Divide your life into thirds** – 8 hours for work, 8 hours for sleep, and 8 hours free. Working more does not make us more productive. Working

smart and keeping time free allows our minds to wander in ways that make the hours we do work more effective.

- **Periodically, fast from electronics.** This forces you to connect with others and with yourself, leading to rich and fulfilling experiences. The concept of digital minimalism is further explored by Newport (2019), who encourages users to rethink their relationship with social media, prioritise 'high bandwidth' conversations over low-quality text chains, and to consciously rediscover the pleasures of the offline world.

CHAPTER SUMMARY

In this chapter we considered digital technologies from the perspective of the consumer. We looked at how interactive technologies have changed the dynamic of the buyer–seller relationship in both positive ways (i.e., increased choice and convenience; reduced waiting times and costs) and negative ways (i.e., the pressure caused by a deluge of information that is pushed upon us and which we insatiably search for, causing stress and anxiety). One cannot write about the decision-making processes of individuals without considering the influences of groups upon what we perceive our needs to be. The rise of influencer marketing has taken off from where opinion leadership left off, with digital technologies such as social media amplifying the good and bad effects of powerful individuals with strongly held beliefs. Being part of online communities gives enormous potential to widen our social scope, leading to rich and diverse experiences, but sometimes relationships sour, leading to misbehaviours. This, along with our addiction to digital devices, requires marketers and individuals alike to take positive measures to limit our digital exposure, making it efficient and meaningful, so that we can live a balanced life as grounded individuals with a strong sense of wellbeing.

Review Questions

- Discuss the ways in which digital technologies have changed the ways that customers evaluate and act upon their needs. Has this change been largely for the better or the worse?
- Communities can create good and bad experiences for individual members. Which membership roles are more likely to ensure a healthy environment and how do they ensure it?

- Anonymous and distant digital channels make good mouthpieces for angry and disaffected individuals and groups. How well do you think companies and governments are ensuring responsible online behaviours without curtailing the free speech principles of the Internet?

END-OF-CHAPTER CASE: IN WHOM WE TRUST?

Since the inception of the Internet and the World Wide Web, trust has been a significant issue. In the early days of the intrepid pioneers who were connected with each other over closed networks within a tight-knit community with shared values (e.g., government officials and academics), trust was assumed and freely given. Once this network became open it had a global audience and the issue of trust became considerably more nebulous and paradoxical.

The key characteristics of the Internet create significant benefits but are also perceived as its biggest vulnerabilities to malicious action:

- *Access by anyone, anywhere, anyhow, anytime.* These multiple 'front doors' make the creation of a safe and secure online environment next to impossible to achieve. There are cases to be made where some sections of the community would benefit from more moderated access, such as where children may have their access limited due to parental controls that might be activated on their devices, which protects them from upsetting content and exploitative contact. Also, in some parts of the world, aspects of the global Internet might be made inaccessible by a government seeking to exercise political control though the restriction of local internet service providers. Older citizens and those with physical or learning impairments also benefit from a wide range of technologies which enable two-way audio interaction, motion sensing, or large print/large keys to navigate content. However, the semi-anonymity offered by online interactions mean that anyone could misrepresent themselves and their intentions in order to access and exploit vulnerable audiences.
- *The death of distance.* With online communication being such a narrow medium it is difficult to gather and interpret complex social cues that we might normally use to decide how we feel about an item, a person, or a situation. When buying domestically we will be protected by whatever consumer protection measures are in place. When buying remotely from other countries and regions the scope to make returns or receive refunds or replacements may not be so generous. The physical cost of returning the product might also make this a wasteful exercise. Distance in personal

relationships can also cause ambiguity. When we make friends, we typically do this after observing another person in a range of situations, interacting with a range of different types of people. Online, however, individuals can carefully cultivate their image, which to a degree is admirable but can develop to a point where their 'online self' is unrecognisable from their 'offline self'. This is common in dating apps and has been evidenced in child protection cases where adult males may represent themselves as being the peers of children they are interacting with online, which is a deeply questionable behaviour.

- *Volume of user-generated content.* The sheer mass and complexity of content that is posted on a daily basis far exceeds any capacity for employees, contractors, and volunteers to moderate it. Additionally, the lack of commonly agreed standards for what is acceptable and unacceptable content significantly reduces the potential effectiveness of AI detection systems to recognise, block, and remove content. The ease with which new identities can be set up largely renders obsolete any recognised policing approaches we may take to serial offenders.

- *Education in programming and networking technologies.* Given improving educational standards and widely available self-learning material made available by learning institutions and peers online, it is relatively cheap, easy, and quick to gain new skills in systems development and manipulation. Such is the threat of digital hackers and cybercriminals that many digital companies hire ex-hackers through formal competitions and events such as 'hackathons'. Any cybersecurity expert will tell you that no system is 100 per cent secure if it is connected to the Internet as it will be vulnerable to external hackers, whereas closed systems will be vulnerable to disgruntled employees deliberately sabotaging systems, or inadvertently importing malware through email and external drives.

- *Lack of regulatory oversight.* Given the multinational activities of digital companies and technologies, it is often difficult to determine which financial or legal jurisdiction takes precedence. Internet-based companies have exploited this for many years as they seek to claim that the majority of their income-generating activities take place in a low-tax destination so as to reduce their financial liabilities. However, a flurry of large-scale data breaches of banks, online retailers, and social media companies has mobilised citizens to hold their politicians to account for their lack of protection. For some time companies have attempted to self-regulate only to fail again and cause their customers to lose patience at their assumed reticence to act, fearing a drop in advertiser or user income. We may soon see co-ordinated action across multiple judicial systems to regulate the Internet.

DISCUSSION QUESTIONS

- How do you think customers will respond to increasing levels of threat from fraud, identity theft, cyberbullying, loss of privacy, and extreme and upsetting content?
- Which parties should accept responsibilities for addressing trust issues?
- What should they do? This answer should include specific responses detailing who should do what and when to understand the resources required.
- What should be the penalties for failure?

Develop Your Skills

What Is the Skill?

Influencer marketing utilises the credibility of powerful individuals to persuade those who follow them to engage with products that they recommend, in turn creating social ROI (return on investment) for the organisation. This can occur across a range of social media platforms (more on this in Chapter 7) and thus can be a timely, expensive, and frustrating activity. But get this right and the organisation can leverage significant exposure and gains in return for little effort and expense. However, this relies upon the intelligent design, execution, and measurement of specific promotional campaigns, often in collaboration with other digital and offline marketing activities.

Why Is It Important?

Social Media Today (2017) cite five statistics to consider:

- 70 per cent of teenage YouTube subscribers trust influencer opinion as opposed to traditional celebrities;
- for every $1 spent on influencer marketing, a business makes $6.85, an ROI that is 11 times higher than traditional methods of digital marketing;
- 46 per cent of people rely on recommendations from influencers when making a purchase;
- Twitter users report a 5.2 times increase in purchase intent when exposed to promotional content from influencers; and
- 40 per cent of people have purchased an item online after seeing it used by an influencer on social platforms.

How to Develop It

There is a wide range of free tools available through a search engine query. Some are simple selling exercises undertaken by advertising consultancies, but there are some genuinely useful established free tools, and new ones emerge on a regular basis. There is no 'standard' in this respect, with many offering different functionalities and levels of integration with the analytics capabilities of different social platforms. Experiment and explore this dynamic environment to maintain the currency of your digital marketing practice.

How to Apply It

Search for and identify five different influencer-scoring tools:

- How do they differ in their objectives and approaches?
- How is their scope defined (i.e., which platforms do they include/exclude)?
- Using your own personal social media accounts, what feedback do you get on your level of influence?
- Using a product with which you are familiar, compare the social media activity of three competing brands. What can you tell from the effectiveness of their different approaches?

References

Arvidsson, A., and Caliandro, A. (2016). Brand public. *Journal of Consumer Research*, 42(5): 727.

Bartlett, J. (2015). *The Dark Net*. London: Windmill Books.

Blackwell, D., Leanman, C., Tramposch, R., et al. (2017). Extraversion, neuroticism, attachment style and fear of missing out as predictors of social media use and addiction. *Personality and Individual Differences*, 116: 69–72.

Blackwell, R. D., Miniard, P. W., and Engel, J. F. (2001). *Consumer Behaviour*, 9th ed. Mason, OH: Southwestern.

Brabham, D. C. (2013). *Crowdsourcing*. Cambridge, MA: MIT Press.

Brodeur Partners (2019). Generation Z's preference for sensory journalism [online]. Available from: www.brodeur.com/new-study-by-brodeur-partners-shows-generational-shifts-in-how-news-is-consumed/ [Accessed 27 June 2019].

Colayco, J., and Davis, J. (2003). Community. In R. A. Mohammed (ed.), *Internet Marketing: Building Advantage in the Networked Economy*, pp. 391–441. London: McGraw-Hill.

Court, D., Elzinga, D., Mulder, S., and Vetvik, O. J. (2009). The consumer decision journey [online]. *McKinsey Quarterly* (June). Available from: www.mckinsey

.com/insights/marketing_sales/the_consumer_decision_journey   [Accessed 25 June 2019].

Fullerton, R. A., and Punj, G. (2004). Shoplifting as moral insanity: historical perspectives on kleptomania. *Journal of Macromarketing.* 24(1): 8–16.

Google (2011). Winning the zero moment of truth [online]. Available from: www .thinkwithgoogle.com/marketing-resources/micro-moments/2011-winning-zmot-ebook/ [Accessed 26 June 2019].

Google (2019). Set up digital wellbeing [online]. Available from: https://support .google.com/googlenest/answer/9141219?hl=en [Accessed 26 June 2019].

Gourlay, T., and Butler, G. (2019). Marketers must lead the digital detox [online]. Available from: https://exchange.cim.co.uk/blog/news-exchange-marketers-must-lead-the-digital-detox/?_cldee=YW5kcmV3LmNvcmNvcmFuQGJssdWViZ XJyeXRyYWluaW5nLmNvbQ%3d%3d&recipientid=contact-c993e856f1f4e411 80fec4346bad624c-01465d9593834d9093e5abd368e22404&utm_source=Click Dimensions&utm_medium=email&utm_campaign=Exchange&tesid=4709b1f7–2197-e911-b815-0050568966f8 [Accessed 26 June 2019].

Hawkins, D., Mothersbaugh, D., and Best, R. (2007). *Consumer Behavior: Building Marketing Strategy.* New York: McGraw-Hill.

Hoyer, W. D., MacInnis, D. J., and Pieters, R. (2012). *Consumer Behavior*, 6th ed. Boston, MA: Cengage Learning.

Joint Information Systems Committee (2015). Building digital capabilities: the six elements defined [online]. Available from: http://repository.jisc.ac.uk/6611/1/ JFL0066F_DIGIGAP_MOD_IND_FRAME.PDF [Accessed 22 July 2020].

Manchanda, P., Packard, G., and Pattabhiramaiah, A. (2015). Social dollars: the economic impact of customer participation in a firm-sponsored online customer community. *Marketing Science*, 34(3): 367–387.

Maslow, A. H. (1943). A theory of human motivation. *Psychological Review*, 50(4), 370–396.

Muniz, A. M., and O'Guinn, T. C. (2001). Brand community. *Journal of Consumer Research*, 27(4): 412–432.

Nansen, B., Chakraborty, K., Gibbs, L., Macdougall, C., and Vetere, F. (2012). Children and digital wellbeing in Australia: online regulation, conduct and competence. *Journal of Children and Media*, 6(2): 237–254.

Newport, C. (2019). *Digital Minimalism: On Living Better with Less Technology.* London: Portfolio Penguin.

OECD (2019). *How's Life in the Digital Age? Opportunities and Risks of the Digital Transformation for People's Well-Being.* Paris: OECD Publishing.

Peterson, P. (2006). *A Primer in Positive Psychology.* Oxford: Oxford University Press.

Rogers, E. M. (2003). *Diffusion of Innovations*, 5th ed. New York: Free Press.

Seligman, M. (2011) *Flourish: A New Understanding of Happiness and Well-Being – and How to Achieve Them.* London: NB Publishing.

Sioshansi, F. P. (ed.) (2019) *Consumer, Prosumer, Prosumager: How Service Innovations Will Disrupt the Utility Business Model.* New York: Academic Press.

Snow, B. (2017). *Log Off: How to Stay Connected after Disconnecting.* Independently published.

Social Media Today (2017). 5 free tools to research and find social influencers [online]. Available from: www.socialmediatoday.com/social-business/5-free-tools-research-and-find-social-influencers [Accessed 27 June 2019].

Song, S. Y., Cho, E., and Kim, Y. (2017). Personality factors and flow affecting opinion leadership in social media. *Personality and Individual Differences*, 114: 16–23.

Toubia, O., and Stephen, A. T. (2013). Intrinsic vs. image-related utility in social media: why do people contribute content to Twitter? *Marketing Science*, 32(3): 368–392.

World Federation of Advertisers (2019). Global Alliance for Responsible Media launches to address digital safety [online]. Available from: www.wfanet.org/news-centre/global-alliance-for-responsible-media-launches-to-address-digital-safety/ [Accessed 26 June 2019].

5 Digital Relationships and the Customer Experience

Introduction

This chapter considers the mechanics of how customers and suppliers interact online to deliver a high-quality experience for the customer and an efficient sales operation for the supplier. It connects principally with Chapter 4, where we considered customer interests and priorities, one of which was for close communication. It also links to the customer service elements of Chapter 3 and the analytics that are used to track and provide information on these interactions as discussed in Chapter 2. We will explore the 'bigger picture' of the processes for customer relationships and how these develop and progress over time. We will also consider the detail of individual transactions and how these can be identified and improved to create a 'frictionless' experience for customers.

Learning Objectives

- Differentiate between the development stages of the customer relationship lifecycle.
- Summarise the key design principles for enhancing the customer experience.
- Appraise online service quality.
- Consider the causes for online attrition.
- Summarise good practices for the collection and evaluation of metrics.

CASE INSIGHT: SEE IT, FIND IT, BUY IT, LIKE IT

Consumer culture, with its plethora of product choice and multiple communications channels to sellers, distributors, and other consumers, has extended the buying cycle from merely buying and using the product to an extended dance of relationship building, satisfaction, loyalty, and recommendation. These complex dynamics require careful handling through the customer-facing internal processes of the organisation. Rarely now do disgruntled consumers merely slink off quietly to next time buy a different product from a different supplier. With social media, the merest slight, such as poor customer service or a product delivered later than promised, can lead to public complaints that are outside the organisation's control. If there are multiple complaints and they are not dealt with sympathetically or promptly, the situation can further deteriorate, leading to a reduction in sales, and in the worst case of customer dissatisfaction, retailer withdrawal.

The 'see it, find it, buy it, like it' mantra encapsulates the complex consumer relationship that marketers have with their audiences. This is further complicated with the frequent arrival of even more choices, which creates customer promiscuity and disloyalty, despite the rich array of data, analytics, and behavioural profiling and targeting made possible by the Internet. Consider your own purchasing behaviour here.

- When was the last time you were stimulated by a social media post (either a paid advertisement or a 'share' by a friend) for a product you had no idea that you needed until someone suggested it?
- How easy was the purchase link to find – that is, was there a link to follow? Did this helpfully connect to a retailer who already had your login data or was a new account easy to set up instantly with just an email address, password, postal address, and possibly email verification?
- Did the retailer accept a range of online payment methods in your home currency, including credit/debit cards, PayPal, and Apple Pay?
- Once you had completed the purchase, were you offered the opportunity so 'share' the news of your purchase on social media?
- How soon afterwards were you asked to provide an online review of the product and customer service that you received?
- Approximately how many messages have you subsequently received from the company for products that you are not interested in?
- Have you tried to 'unsubscribe' from their promotional messages, or is it easier to ignore/delete them instead?

Reflecting upon your own purchasing activity will give you a strong insight into the importance of processes and physical experiences in the eight drivers of digital marketing.

Questions

- When was the last time you acted upon a recommendation to purchase from a friend that was received over social media?

- What products/brand do you actively avoid because of adverse social media coverage even though you have no personal experience of using that brand in the past?
- What are the advantages and disadvantages to you as a consumer of following the online subjective recommendations of your friends versus your own objective assessment of how well the product/organisation may meet your needs?

5.1   Digital Customer Relationships

The needs of digital customers differ little from the needs of customers buying offline, in absolute terms. However, digital technologies alter the dynamics of the marketing relationship in four important respects. There is a heightened customer experience due to the significant **choice** available, which can often involve complex decision-making processes due to the greater range and depth of variables there are for us to evaluate. Additionally, the instant market accessibility creates an expectation of the **immediacy** of our needs being met. Depending upon your disposition (and the reliability of the supplier information) this can lead to feelings of reassurance or anxiety. The technologies also provide us with **visibility** of our transactions and usage, empowering us as customers, as returning/exchanging/refunding purchases can become significantly easier, and the supplier gains a greater understanding of our interests and needs and can therefore stimulate our purchase behaviour by making timely suggestions, perhaps with the added incentive of a special offer to buy from them. Whether we have queries regarding an item or a purchase or are ready to express our satisfaction (or dissatisfaction), there are multiple opportunities for **engagement** with the organisation, our online community, or with the wider market via electronic word-of-mouth (eWOM) to share our feelings. This can lead to feelings of pride (or catharsis), but also provides feedback for the company and other potential buyers. These factors combine to give us a platform for the customer experience, which potentially meets their needs because it is:

- *easy* based on the facility given by cookies to track and remember our activity, which enables websites and apps to behave more as personal shopping assistants than just a place to view and buy products. Cross-platform (i.e., phone/tablet/PC) integration can also create a seamless purchase experience.
- *reliable* largely in the respect of the 'always on' nature of the Internet, but also in that suppliers can be responsive about their supply capability (in volume and timing), enabling the customer to make better decisions.

- *consistent* in its presentation of product and transaction information, with apps creating a more tailored user experience. Any changes or deviations from this 'promise' can be notified automatically.
- *personal*, from when you are welcomed by name when you log in or receive a promotional text/email to suggest a trade-up or additional purchase that may be beneficial to you based on your (and others') past purchase behaviour and feedback.
- *trustworthy*, as inferred by the visibility of individual transactions, and the plethora of usernames, passwords, identity checks that confirm you are human (i.e., not a malware program), and security compatibility confirmations that suggest that your personal data is kept private.
- *good value*, as represented by choice, priority shipping as standard, cost savings in the search phase (which would include both the ability to specify and precisely locate the required products, and pre-emptive suggestions by the organisation that might anticipate customer needs, thus saving search time), and discounts for purchases made directly with the manufacturer or a preferred intermediary.
- *relevant* due to the content being rendered being largely judged by the user's search history, cookie profile, and established preferences coupled with the online behaviour of similar users which could be used as a benchmark to predict further interests. This analytical approach should significantly increase the presentation of relevant content and reduce the irrelevant content that is made available to users.

The relational paradigm potential of the World Wide Web allows us to build, monitor, and manage highly detailed programmes of marketing activity that consider not only isolated customer interactions, such as one-off purchases, but also their longer-term evolving needs. Pre-Internet, the transactional approach of organisations was to offer a small range of products at a fixed price to passive customer segments via mass market broadcast media. Now a more relational approach offers personalised products at variable prices (taking account of the customer's lifetime value to the organisation), to highly engaged individuals who can in turn talk to us, and about us, at scale. True relational interaction can be mutually rewarding:

- Customers feel an affinity with the organisation beyond mere repeat purchase.
- Customers can feel 'known' to the organisation, not just as an anonymous consumer but akin to the personal interaction of restaurateur and regular consumer.

- Customers often receive special treatment and extra pampering by the organisation.
- Customers are likely to receive timely and relevant communications of offers that would be of interest to them at that moment.

RESEARCH INSIGHT 5.1 The Age of Analytics

McKinsey Global Institute (2016). *The Age of Analytics: Competing in a Data-Driven World*. London: McKinsey & Company.

This extensive and highly detailed report provides context for the effects of a recent leap forward in data and analytics capabilities as the volume of available data has grown exponentially, more sophisticated algorithms have been developed, and computational power and storage have steadily improved. This has led to significant disparities in how organisations are adapting to the emergence of greater transparency in the customer–firm relationship.

- Retail has generally grasped these new opportunities to great effect, but manufacturing, the public sector, and healthcare have captured less than 30 per cent of the potential value open to them for enhancing the customer experience.
- While data is relatively easy to come by, it is organisational barriers that are affecting how we extract insights and incorporate them into day-to-day business processes. This is largely due to the mismatch of data and business expertise.
- Data and analytics are changing the basis of competition. Leading companies are using their capabilities not only to improve their core operations due to faster and more evidence-based decision-making, but to launch entirely new business models since new analytical techniques can fuel discovery and innovation.

5.2   Customer Lifecycle Management

Relationships depend upon understanding, reciprocity, trust, and pride if they are to be positive and sustainable. Lacking any of these elements is not necessarily the end, but it will stall the potential deepening of the relationship. In the worst cases, for instance with a failure of trust, the relationship could be jeopardised to the point where only extraordinary action will recover it. The willingness to commit to this extraordinary action has the potential to strengthen the relationship beyond pre-existing levels just because the parties care enough to strive to find a happy solution that will enable the relationship to be maintained and improved. We will talk more of this later when we cover dimensions of service quality.

Since an organisation will hopefully have relationships with a range of customers to avoid over-dependency on a few, thus creating a strategic vulnerability, it is a good bet that these customers will behave differently in terms of the timing, type, scale, and scope of their requirements. Catering for these needs creates complexity within the organisation, which can be proactively managed where suitable if certain principles are considered. The customer lifecycle considers how the relationship between buyer and seller typically develops over time, progressing past a series of milestones that are easy to identify within the organisation to trigger the appropriate response aimed at maintaining and developing valuable relationships (Table 5.1). As with the customer decision-making process covered in Chapter 4, there are no guarantees that this linear process will always apply, as some steps will take a while, some may happen very quickly, and some may be bypassed altogether as they may not be relevant to the ongoing needs of the customer.

This evolving set of complex and dynamic relationships needs an operational structure to plan, target, execute, and evaluate the organisation's marketing effort. Besides planning the day-to-day detail of campaigns and transactions, **customer relationship management (CRM)** processes also help us to determine the role of customers in the context of the organisation's objectives. Broadly speaking, any organisation will have customers on whom they lose money and make money over time. It is simplistic to only focus upon money-making customers since for the reasons discussed in earlier chapters it takes time for customers to understand their changing needs and how they might be satisfied. From a scale and scope perspective it is also important to remember that not all customers buy the same product, for the same reasons, at the same time, and in the same volumes/combinations. So, for management purposes we need to categorise customers so that we can develop them with targeted action. If they cannot be further developed, then we need to manage their operational and financial impact upon the organisation, since with limited resources we may have to choose which customers to prioritise based on their lifetime value (Kumar et al., 2007) to the organisation. Peppers and Rogers (2002) offer the potential customer classifications shown in Table 5.2, based on past behaviour and perceived potential for the development of a deeper relationship.

It is relatively easy to monitor and manage relationships from within an organisation since the data is to hand and we have agreed processes for dealing with that information and the decisions that follow. The roles of individuals within the organisation are also defined as to their

Table 5.1 Customer relationship stages: opportunities and risks

Stage	As indicated by ...	Get it right and ...	Get it wrong and ...
Approach	Identification and communication with specific individuals or groups with whom we have insight into their needs and behaviours	Customer profiling and response monitoring will help us to target the right offer at the right decision-maker at the right time. Customers receive consistent messages across multiple channels and platforms and can quickly access the content that they need, requiring minimal additional site navigation.	Customers can feel overwhelmed by irrelevant contact. You may turn potential customers, who may have been ready to buy in time, into hostiles due to nuisance messages. Ambivalent customers will be put off exploring due to aggressive contacts. If the online response is faulty then a valuable opportunity has been missed.
Establish	Enquiry and/or purchase. The product is not returned.	Acquisition costs per customer (i.e., the sum of sales, advertising, and management effort put into the campaign) are minimised, enabling the efficient use of smaller budgets and larger impact from bigger budgets.	Promotional effort that ends once the customer is satisfied is wasteful since it is at this point that the customer is most likely to be positively influenced to buy again. If this feeling is allowed to fade, then the customer may feel unvalued after trusting you with their money.
Secure	A follow-up purchase within a reasonable period as determined by product lifecycle and customer usage behaviour. Typically, only one product type.	A deeper understanding of customer's needs can be gained from their searches, purchases, product combinations, and returns. The customer is more likely to create a dedicated account, online or via a mobile app, that will collect user analytics data. The full marketing mix can be tailored to suit. Customers receive timely and personalised customer care messages to enhance their experience. Service is of a consistently high quality.	Customers who make repeat visits may be frustrated at having to input login and payment details every time. Failure to remember the customer's usual purchases increases the onerous searches and may leave them feeling uncared for. Failure to anticipate and precipitate customer needs increases operational costs. Inconsistent service levels cause customers to doubt whether there is anything more than a transactional relationship.

Table 5.1 (cont.)			
Stage	As indicated by …	Get it right and …	Get it wrong and …
Expand	Purchase of a range of product types. Engagement with social media channels as brand and organisational loyalty grows through shared values.	Detailed customer analytics and profiling helps to fine-tune the marketing mix and experiment with offering new products and combinations. This can lead to exciting new discoveries and higher levels of trust between customer and supplier.	Customers receiving offers that they do not value or recognise can lead to estrangement from the supplier. If this is done frequently the customer may feel that they are being exploited rather than being nurtured.
Advocate	Frequently shares news of their purchases in social media. Responds positively to requests for user reviews. Contributes to online community discussions, often leading topics and giving extensive positive responses to the contributions of others.	Customers will act as ambassadors, promoting the products and the company itself. Lead users will be used in a marketing mix development capacity either to test new products or give feedback on pilot communications campaigns. May begin to act as prosumers.	Can become a powerfully negative voice within influential online forums. Their hostile messages will create discord within groups. Customer dissatisfaction should be dealt with fairly, consistently, and swiftly. Using honesty, politeness, and humour (without being disrespectful or patronising) can moderate the complaint before it gathers damaging momentum.

responsibilities and how they connect with one another to deliver the agreed goals. However, Web 2.0 has changed the balance of the customer–supplier relationship with interactive platforms that are owned by the organisations (such as email, message services, websites, and apps) and non-proprietary social media platforms where customers and other interested parties can freely discuss the strengths and weaknesses of the organisation and its products on globally accessible public forums. This phenomenon has given rise to the need for the process of **social customer relationship management (SCRM)** where the organisation seeks to operate in a non-stop globally dynamic environment that communicates instantly across multiple platforms and is almost entirely unmoderated – whereby anyone can post anything at any time about the company or its products, allowing other users to nuance or share the comment, which leads to its amplification. When comments are

Table 5.2 Prioritising customer groups (adapted from Peppers and Rogers, 2002)

Category	Purchase size (volume and value)	Purchase frequency	Product combinations	Contribution to organisation's profits	Proportion of organisation's total customer base	Recommended strategy
Below-zero customers (BZCs)	Small	Low	Few	Loss	Low to medium	Establish / secure
Most-growable customers (MGCs)	Medium	Medium	Some	Low to medium	Medium	Secure / expand
Most-valuable customers (MVCs)	Large	High	Many	High	Low	Expand / advocate

positive or neutral this is not a problem. When the comment is negative then the organisation needs to act quickly to try to prevent lasting public relationship damage (see Chapter 7).

5.3　Delivering a Satisfying Customer Experience

To understand the stimuli that trigger these public customer responses it is wise to explore the antecedents of satisfying customer experiences. We have already explored the customer decision-making process in Chapter 4 and can build upon that to explore the underlying principles that require our attention. Customer satisfaction has significant benefits for the organisation:

- Staff morale improves when negative behaviours are removed from the workplace. As good as we may all think that we are as actors, the fact is that if we are dealing with a 'difficult' customer, or have recently disappointed an established customer, then this frustration will be shared within the organisation. If left to fester this will lead to the departure of good people. Poor culture also pervades other organisational activities. For example, innovation may decline because colleagues either do not see the point of trying or are not prepared to collaborate and share their ideas.
- Operational efficiency may fall as a lack of motivation leads to wasteful behaviours, which in turn will increase costs and product lead times while reducing service responsiveness and product quality. The sense of apathy within an organisation that frequently disappoints its customers then requires employees to defend this failure for fear that losing the customer's business may jeopardise their own careers; this is a frustrating and anxious experience.
- Sales effectiveness drops since it becomes increasingly difficult to sell to customers who are frequently disappointed. Even special incentives given to compensate customers for the loss or inconvenience cause an additional financial drain on the organisation (in addition to the operational inefficiencies discussed above), and they may not be enough to forestall the inevitable loss of a loyal customer and potential advocate.
- Market reputation helps us to recruit new customers, new employees, and new investment. Lack of active referrals and poor customer feedback will erode the pool of potential new customers that may be open to offers. Recruiting and retaining new staff will be challenging when alternative healthier working environments are available. Investors may fear losing their capital in a wasteful and declining business, but from a

public relations perspective may not wish to have their own reputation tarnished by an association with an unpopular and disrespected organisation.

Having said all of this, we should not be unreasonable and expect that our organisation will never make mistakes. It will. The problem comes when we keep making the same or similar mistakes, not recognising the fact (or worse, recognising and ignoring it because of general malaise and negligence), and failing to take positive action to address it. One-off errors by a previously reliable supplier are forgivable so long as they are quickly identified, more than adequately corrected, and never repeated.

DIGITAL INSIGHT 5.1 'Contamination' of the Customer Experience

New technologies have rendered obsolete the market dominance of some established players in global industries. Previously the strength of incumbents has been developed over many years through the painstaking construction of market presence and customer reputation. Today, instant and interactive communication across multiple channels enables new entrants to challenge market leaders due to their entrepreneurial cultures, organisational agility, and the mastery of digital tools over traditional approaches. This transformation in the customer experience can have significant benefits; however, some industries are slow to spot this trend. In the United States, for instance, the banking sector is grappling with the impact of rapidly improving customer experiences in the retail industry, which directly impacts upon the expectations and perceptions of traditional branch banking. In retailing, customers expect to shop for products in a way that is convenient for them no matter what channel they choose. This expectation of convenience extends to product availability, customisation, 24-hour service, rapid delivery, and responsiveness. Customers are seeing significant changes in their newly customer-centric retail experience, yet their banking experience remains distinctly organisation-centric, with menus of products rather than tailored offerings, rigid access hours, and poor responsiveness. In short, this highlights how digital has forced a rethink about the point at which value is created for the customer. Traditional models have a focus upon sale-specific activity, but changing customer behaviours in response to the multiple points at which organisations may connect to customers have led to a consideration of the wider customer experience to create a richer, more productive, and enduring relationship.

To create a framework for understanding how better customer–supplier relationships are won and lost, we refer to the 10 principles behind great customer experiences (Watkinson, 2013) so that our marketing engagement activity should do the following:

1. *Strongly reflect the customer's identity*, acknowledging their beliefs and values so that we may understand how they view themselves in the context of the world at large. Our beliefs and values play a decisive role in our behaviour as customers. Those experiences that reinforce our self-image and resonate with our personal values leave us feeling good about our decisions, while those brands that clearly stand for something engender much stronger loyalty.

    Digital enablers: images, keywords, semantics, brand and reference group associations.

2. *Satisfy our higher objectives* by appealing directly to our wants, needs, and motivations. Since these are derivative, it is satisfying the higher objective behind them that is the foundation of a great experience.

    Digital enablers: product and customer service enhancement.

3. *Leave nothing to chance* by understanding the organisation touchpoints in the consumer decision-making process and the customer journey. Every interaction needs to be considered, planned, and designed. There is no detail that is too small to consider.

    Digital enablers: Internet of Things, big data, dynamic reporting, diagnostics, and analytics.

4. *Set and then meet expectations* at each stage of the operational and influencing process to create positive attitudes to the organisation and its products (e.g., information search, prepurchase consideration of alternatives, and post-purchase evaluation). Existing customer expectations, learned behaviours, and associations are the criteria that consumers use to judge an experience from the beginning. We should aim to exceed these expectations where desirable.

    Digital enablers: metrics and reporting, criteria for meaningful qualitative and quantitative customer feedback.

5. *Be effortless*, in the respect that dealing with us should be convenient and intuitive. Interactions that put the onus on the consumer, soaking up their time and energy, are quickly off-putting or replaced with those that are less demanding. Few things generate more goodwill and repeat business than being effortless to deal with.

    Digital enablers: automatic login, retained contact and payment details, minimal clicks between enquiry and purchase, pre-filtered results to search queries based on past search and purchase history.

6. *Be stress free* by eliminating confusion, uncertainty, and anxiety.

    Digital enablers: avoiding an excess or shortfall of choice by enabling customers to set their own needs/search parameters (e.g., car insurance), comparing similar products, ranking customer reviews by their usefulness, and providing full visibility of the process (e.g., delivery tracking using sensors and GPS).

7. *Indulge the senses*, typically through sight (e.g., illustration, animation, photos, video), sound, or touch (i.e., vibration). Appealing to multi-sensory inputs leads to a richer experience and avoids sensory overload that may occur, for instance due to too much text, which tests the user's attention span and risks them missing key messages or calls to action. Appealing to customers at a level where positive feelings can be stimulated is highly effective to achieve perception, attention, learning, and memory.

    Digital enablers: virtual reality, augmented reality, and immersive adventures triggered by a user's physical gestures (e.g., eye, head, limb movement) instead of keyboard input, mouse click, or button selection.

8. *Be socially engaging* since the importance of cultivating personal relationships with customers cannot be overstated. We more readily buy from a friend than from a stranger. However, our position within a social group is also a powerful and private motivator. Those experiences that elevate our status are often the most highly valued.

    Digital enablers: reference groups and opinion leaders, typically accessed via social media activity though online communities.

9. *Put the customer in control* by giving them choice in the product range available (which can be tailored if necessary), how the products are delivered (e.g., priority shipping or a timeslot arrangement), the right to change their mind and return unsuitable goods with no questions asked, how the relationship is maintained (i.e., contact preferences), and proactively keeping them informed of the progress of their order either to deliver on the agreed expectations or to set new expectations due to unforeseen difficulties.

    Digital enablers: mass customisation, despatch scheduling and tracking, progress reporting, user account preferences, simple automated refund procedures.

10. *Consider the emotions by being sensitive to changes in user and group behaviours that may represent a shift in attitude.* We are all slaves to our emotions, yet most see their customers from a purely rational perspective. Evaluating the emotional aspect of an experience brings often unconsidered issues to the surface and opens new ways to delight the customer.

Digital enablers: user review sentiment analysis, tracking and engaging with the zeitgeist via trending hashtags.

DIGITAL INSIGHT 5.2 Connecting the 'Virtual' and 'Physical' Customer Experience

The contribution of digital technologies to the customer experience is significant in its depth and scope. Customers expect the mobile experience to be deeply complementary to the physical 'in-store' experience. Many organisations are adapting to these needs by adopting a 'showrooming' approach where some products are on display to give an appreciation of the product, but the final product that the customer buys can be accessed or tailored online, allowing for significant cost savings in floor space and inventory with no discernible degradation of customer choice or service. Should the final physical product not meet the customer's expectations when it is received then extended protection is provided by flexible and convenient return arrangements. Social media as a distinct and non-proprietorial sales platform opens vendors to new market dynamics beyond their means for control of the sales process, as discussed in the section on SCRM. Personalisation of customer communication will be further discussed in Chapter 7.

5.4 Measuring Online Service Quality

As with any management discipline, it is important to understand how well we have deployed our resources and competencies to meet customer needs. Traditional service quality measurement considers one-time person-to-person interactions which occur at a specific stage in the purchasing cycle – for example, when enquiring, purchasing, or returning goods. Online service management brings additional complexity given how the customer–supplier relationship unfolds throughout purchasing cycles. Given the potential for a greater amount of time to pass between a product being purchased and its consumption, this gives rise to a **recency effect** during which time a customer's expectations and needs may change, thus rendering redundant the originally conceived criteria for satisfaction. To overcome this, many online retailers offer a time-limited (often 30 days) 'no quibble' return policy. This 'no quibble' policy also gives reassurance to customers when buying at distance since they have little opportunity to physically experience the product before buying it, which is a **proximity effect**. This is a distinct difference from traditional mail order returns policies which may only have been accepted if they were damaged or faulty in some way. The 'no quibble' approach maintains customer trust and encourages impulse buying, but at the same time has led to significant increases in shipping and finance costs due to increased levels of customer returns. The customer service function has also become more complex with the onset of multiple digital technologies, which often cause confusion with customers due to the use of generic answers, automation, and the difficulty in reaching a human operator, causing a negative **ownership effect**. Many companies offer an automated process for standard returns where a refund or replacement is required. In more complex cases of customer query, companies try to automate responses either by customer searching the frequently asked questions (FAQ) section or taking up the offer of a real-time online chat with a virtual assistant chatbot program. These programs use intelligent language-recognition software to connect to the user's account to categorise the enquiry, which in simple cases can be resolved by signposting back to the most appropriate FAQ section or in more complicated cases can pre-screen queries to be addressed by human operatives. This rise of multiple actors, channels, and media can cause frustration and confusion with customers who are seeking a similarly speedy response to their queries as they expect from their purchases. To deliver superior service quality, managers of companies with web presences must understand how customers perceive and evaluate online customer service; it is here that the work of Zeithaml et al. (2002) provides us with a framework to categorise and measure the key service relationships that impact upon satisfaction. The **E-SERVQUAL** dimensions (Zeithaml et al., 2002) are explained as follows.

Core factors represent the basic service expectation of all customers that should be offered as standard to online buyers:

- *Efficiency – the ability of customers to get to the site, search for information, or transact.* To achieve this the website or app should be intuitive to use and should make good use of customer data to proactively link with relevant information, which would include purchase history, preferences, and contact/delivery/payment information. Designers will seek to build an experience that requires the fewest user clicks between their arrival at the site and when their visit ends, which may be upon receiving a response to an inquiry, adding a purchase to the purchasing basket in anticipation of returning to complete a purchase, or the completion of a transaction.

- *Fulfilment – accuracy of service promises.* Data is used to set, maintain, and update realistic service expectations for each transaction. It is highly embarrassing for the organisation, frustrating for customers, and ultimately damaging for the brand in the long term if these promises – which may relate to the functionality, availability, or delivery of the product – are not kept.
- *Reliability – technical functioning of the site.* Ensure that the correct pages are hyperlinked, that they are 'live' on the system, and contain current information. It should be supported by hardware, connectivity, and back-up that minimises service outages or downtime. Since automated services only rely upon the information that they are provided with, it should be the ultimate responsibility of human oversight to check the reliability of the data, with timely intervention as required.
- *Privacy – shopping behaviour data are not shared.* It is a legal requirement in many jurisdictions to protect the financial data of consumers (i.e., bank account details and transaction histories) and their personal contact details (i.e., telephone, email, home or work address). However, with the complexity of profiling approaches customers should be allowed to decline providing socio-economic data (e.g., age, sex, religion, interests, location) that might lead to intrusive targeting through social media.

Recovery factors represent the enhanced online service expectation of customers having trouble, whether they made their original purchase through online, offline, or affiliate channels:

- *Responsiveness – the ability of online sellers to provide support information when requested.* Automated user guides that are made available via links to the customer's purchase record can help in some situations. However, customers are more likely to search for help in the product category of the FAQ section or in the generic site search bar. It is useful here if the activities of registered users are tracked in a way that recognises when customers may not be getting the answers they need (for example, by multiple similar, or repeat, searches). An automated system can then launch a chatbot to offer the user additional help, thereby escalating the level of customer service support in a proactive manner.
- *Compensation – return facilities.* The returns process should be as simple, intuitive, and connected as the purchasing process. Links to the customer's purchase history can allow for the immediate reporting of an intention to return, selecting the required response (i.e., direct replacement, replacement with an alternative, cash refund, refund on account). If the

customer feels that they have suffered an extraordinary inconvenience or loss because of a faulty product, then they should be able to claim additional compensation. Failure to do so could contravene consumer protection regulations and leave the organisation open to legal action.

- *Contact – the ability of customers to talk to a live service agent online or on the phone.* In the event of automated services proving to be inadequate, which may be as much to do with the complexity of the issue as it may be the increasing frustration of the customer, it is important that helpful human intervention is at hand. Ideally this should be connected to the online record of the user's issue so that the customer does not have to incur further delay by having to repeatedly restate their issue and required outcome.

DIGITAL INSIGHT 5.3 When Processes and Objectives Misalign

There is a high incidence of failure in customer experience transformations because leaders cannot show how these efforts create value. With the best intentions to 'delight' the customer on many levels, which creates a short-term 'bounce' in satisfaction and probably sales, the longer-term effect upon the business due to a disruptive configuration, retraining, hiring, and implementation of new systems and retirement of old ones creates more costs than wins, rapidly losing support from across the organisation. The most successful initiatives are self-funding since quick wins remove costs from the system and simplify the business, creating organisational motivation and funds to invest in longer-term initiatives that will radically change the trajectory of the customer experience. Thereafter, the organisation needs to create a clear understanding among its staff as to what constitutes 'value' (with clear, specific, and non-conflicting measures), prioritising investment in areas that will create the greatest benefit and providing a detailed plan about how early gains will be achieved and rolled forward to invest in further change.

5.5   Engagement and Interaction

For customers to create a meaningful two-way interaction which extends beyond relatively passive social media engagement, to an involvement in the value-generating activities of the organisation, they need to feel that such a connection should create benefits for them (see Chapter 4). Since this chapter relates to the processes by which we support these experiences and relationships, we need to plan, design, and deliver systems that deliver these varied relationships 24/7 and on a global scale. To highlight this challenge, consider the support requirements of differing levels of customer interaction:

- *Self-service (minimal interaction)* takes the form of online purchases through to in-store self-checkout facilities, offering the customer the opportunity to be in control of the convenience of their interaction with the supplier. The speed, reliability, simplicity, and repeatability of such transactions make them relatively easy to automate through product labelling and electronic payment. Such 'frictionless' interactions are easy and convenient for customers, thus creating the foundation for a relationship.
- *Gamification (medium interaction)* applies game-based thinking to engage and develop loyalty by stimulating the brain and releasing dopamine to create feelings of happiness. Such an approach is gaining in popularity and complexity and requires the development and execution of a strong creative concept to engage users to play the game, in the face of an extremely competitive gaming marketplace, and to communicate core brand messages. Good games design encourages users to continue playing, normally by awarding points, compiling leader boards, and offering increasingly more challenging levels of play. Games offer momentary fun-based distractions (for example at break time or when utilising spare time when travelling) but can also offer social interactions as friends compete among themselves and share their experiences, further increasing exposure for the brand.
- *Prosumers (significant interaction)* can engage with the organisation across multiple channels. The 'pro' part of the term has separately represented customers who are proactive in that they may offer positive suggestions to the organisation on how it can adapt its marketing mix. Such customers could contribute to feedback activities from surveys to focus groups. Some customers may take a more active role in developing specific product ideas, to include concept, design, prototyping, and testing. Customers will be active in promoting the organisation, in an opinion-leader or ambassadorial role (see Chapter 4). Whatever their level of engagement and interaction, the concept of the prosumer is providing for richer relationships between customers and suppliers due to the honest and reliable sharing of views that is the hallmark of a strong and enduring relationship.

RESEARCH INSIGHT 5.2 Categorising Digital Engagement Practices

Eigenraam, A. W., Eelen, J., van Lin, A., and Verlegh, P. W. J. (2018). A consumer-based taxonomy of digital customer engagement practices. *Journal of Interactive Marketing*, 44: 102–121.

Consumers can engage with brands online in a variety of ways, ranging from playing a branded game to writing a review or viewing branded content. This work presents a consumer-based taxonomy of these digital engagement practices that occur across different media formats and platforms. These levels of interaction are classified based on the relationship with the brand and the perceived value that is extracted from the relationship as: *for-fun practices, learning practices, customer feedback, work for a brand,* or *talk about a brand.*

5.6   Principles for Web Design

Once we have a clear understanding of customer needs and expectations, we can consider how to design the principal digital processes by which customers interact directly with the organisation. If you are starting with a legacy customer service system that has embedded organisational processes which are delivered by colleagues with traditional skillsets and attitudes, then a more structured change process will be required – more of that in Chapter 9. If we are in the lucky situation of having an organisation that is skilled, knowledgeable, and open to change then we make significant changes quickly. This section will cover some of the key considerations in configuring how our organisation interacts with its multiple stakeholders through complex and integrated services to deliver an effective and efficient marketing operation.

As a guiding philosophy for delivering high-quality online customer experiences, we should ask ourselves the following questions:

- *It is accessible?* No matter how clear and rigorous your market research, segmentation activity, and promotional planning, there is always a chance that interest will come in unexpected ways from unexpected places.
  - Your connectivity should assume that anyone in the world will need to access your customer-facing systems, at any time and by any means. This creates challenges for managing high levels of traffic to and through your site, ensuring that access requests can be handled in a reasonable period. At times of peak forecast demand many online

businesses bring in additional server capacity, potentially through a cloud services provider, to ensure system integrity (i.e., no crashes, outages, or downtime that will interrupt the customer experience, leading to frustration or a lack of trust which might open the door for one of your competitors).

– Users may access the site across multiple platforms (e.g., watch, phone, tablet, laptop, desktop) which requires the user experience to be consistent and seamless. Sometimes this use will be concurrent so it is important that the system can cope with this traffic, prioritising requests and providing updated information instantaneously. Be aware also that the hardware used to access your site might not always be of the highest quality. Processing speed and storage capacities may vary greatly, so think again when designing complex pages that require significant amounts of data to be downloaded to the user's device before they can be viewed. In this context, users will often be happy to view a simpler page that loads quickly rather than a complex page their device or network cannot cope with.

– Browser and search engine compatibility still plays a significant role in whether users can find and access online services. If potential customers are using a generic search, as opposed to searching for the name of your organisation/brand or going directly to your URL, then you will need to ensure that you can be 'found' via a search engine. We will talk more about search engine optimisation (SEO) in Chapter 7. For this to occur the search engine needs to categorise the data in your site through keywords and metatags. If some search engines do not 'see' your site, then for their users you will simply not exist. It is worth investing in professional SEO guidance to check that your content is visible across a range of platforms and that it is correctly categorised to appeal to your target customers.

• *Is it usable?*

– When designing the online experience, we should be clear about its audience and its purpose. This can get complicated and will lead to many navigation issues. For example, not all customers will visit the organisation's homepage. Instead, their needs may be better served elsewhere on the site. With data analytics, it is possible to use the visitor's history and search criteria to channel them directly to the most appropriate content. Good design will carefully assess the user experience, making decisions such as – in its simplest form – what information needs to be added (possibly indicated by customer feedback or where the visit terminates) and what information needs to be removed (again based on customer feedback or which pages are used the least).

Surplus content clutters the website, causes SEO confusion, and if not regularly updated can provide an inconsistent customer experience with different presentation and potentially contradictory information.

– Connections between websites for different organisations, potentially through affiliate programmes (more of this in Chapter 6) and social media platforms, and within the site through hyperlinks, are attractive to search engines as they indicate enhanced functionality, and also to users as they make it easier to access relevant content. Occasionally technical glitches occur because of poor programming, inconsistent administration, or browser problems meaning that these links may no longer work. Periodically the organisation should audit its links to ensure they are still functional and relevant.

– Given the global internet audience, there are significant differences in how we communicate. Culture and language may require different content and versions for different regions. Accommodating disabilities should also be a design consideration since it is the most isolated and vulnerable users who will benefit the most from the internet community. Variable print size and maximising the contrast of images accommodates the visually impaired; functionally simplified versions could assist those who experience sensory overload; audio versions for the hearing-impaired; larger keypads or motion control (e.g., head or eye movement) for those with physical disabilities. Simplification of language and great use of images and emojis could help younger users and those with learning difficulties.

• *Is it persuasive?* There is much debate regarding the addictive qualities of digital media (see the digital wellbeing section in Chapter 4). However, as a business function it is our role to stimulate and mediate the organisation's contact with its current and potential audiences. To do this responsibly we create a positive and compelling manner, and do not stray into negative and addictive relationships. Site analytics go some way to measuring the relationship between the stimulus that we offer through the eight drivers of digital marketing, and the subsequent effect this has upon the customer as demonstrated by the speed and extent to which they give the desired response.

5.7   Navigation

We begin planning the overall structure of the website by determining who the key audiences are, under what circumstances would they use the site, and what we anticipate their objectives to be. Articulating these needs and expectations will ensure that we build the content and functionality that help the visitor address this need, whether it is the immediate need to make a purchase, or a more leisurely exploration of what the organisation has to offer. From this insight, web designers will build the information architecture around a site map. This is a graphical depiction of the relationship between different groups of content on a website, which will be optimised to be as convenient and easy to use as possible. The resulting infrastructure may be 'broad and shallow' or 'narrow and deep' as designers will aim to have no more than three 'clicks' between where the user arrives at the website and their desired destination within it. Narrow and deep navigational designs tend to prevail for high-involvement purchases that require complex decision-making, but where the range of potential options is low. Broad and shallow navigational designs tend to prevail for low-involvement purchases that require habitual decision-making and where the range of potential options is high.

While many sites will offer a text search bar as the principal navigation mechanism for visitors, this mainly works well when visitors arrive knowing precisely what they want, which will make it easy for them to describe their needs in keywords, allowing easy recognition by the site for signposting to the required content. Visitors who arrive with a general interest, intending to explore the site as it relates to the organisation or its products, will value a more structured menu-based approach. The efficacy of how the different pages connect to give the desired outcome for each visitor is referred to as 'flow'. To enhance the flow of visitors through a site, leading to a pain free and satisfying experience, Rettie (2001) identifies the key design considerations which either inhibit or encourage flow (Table 5.3).

Table 5.3 Web design for flow (Rettie, 2001)	
Factors that inhibit flow	Factors that encourage flow
Long download time	Quick download time
Delays to download plug-ins	Alternative versions
Long registration forms	Auto-completion of forms
Limited stimulation	Opportunities for interactions
Slow responses	Rapid responses
Sites which are not intuitive	Navigation which creates choices
Navigation links that fail	Predictable navigation for control
Challenge greater than skill	Segment by internet experience
Irrelevant advertising	

5.8   Style

The style of the website, in terms of imagery, tone of voice, and graphical design, needs to be consistent across the corporate and product branding, both offline and online. Online this is represented most strongly in the design of website pages. A consistent style not only reinforces a brand's identity, increasing its familiarity and perceived ease of use for the visitor, but also provides a consistent online experience for customers as they can quickly locate key information and take the necessary action if it is rendered in the same format (e.g., image, colour, key terms, or on-screen location) across all similar pages. This is essential for 'high-traffic' pages such as search results or product details, but for non-standard low-demand pages such as company information or contact details there may be some variability on layout from page to page.

When first designing your own web pages there is a temptation to include as much as possible, both in terms of navigation options and content, in the hope that all types of visitors will be satisfied. This type of satisfaction is simply not possible and often leads to cluttered and confused designs. A search box and a simple menu bar help to stimulate the visitor to state their requirements. Note that this should be available on all pages so that the visitor does not have to suffer the inconvenience of having to return to the homepage every time they wish to start a new search. For the rest of the page we need clear and consistent guidelines as to the layout, often referred to as 'elements', which determine the amount of text and images to be used in proportion to one another. For example, there may be a word limit for each product description, or a limit of two images per product, to avoid overload-ing the visitor. In a more positive sense, many designers work to a ratio of content (i.e., images and text) to 'white space'. It may seem wasteful to have unused screen space, but this simplistic approach can have a calming effect on visitors, increasing dwell time on the page and drawing them in to make more detailed enquiries. Cluttering pages with an excess of detail can over-load the customer's processing ability, misleadingly giving them the impres-sion that the purchase decision is more complex than they perhaps originally thought it would be, and consequently deterring them from further enquiries.

As we discovered earlier, making your page accessible to many different types of users represents good design practice. However, it is not only users with a visual impairment who may wish to view the content, especially images and video, in greater detail. Resizing options allow users to appreciate the finer detail of the product to assess whether it may meet their needs. For example, the style and colour of an item of clothing or the shape and colour of a piece of furniture will help the visitor to see whether the item fits with their needs and existing complementary items. Resizing is also helpful when visitors access content on smaller devices, such as smartphones or tablets, to increase the user experience and allow better choices since it is possible to make a more detailed assessment of key variables such as style, shape, and colour; it can also reduce eye strain.

Many users still require a printing option for web pages in their browser. This may be the preferred way to compare alternatives, to access key information, to augment other printed material, or to make notes. From a cost and sustainability point of view users will want to minimise the amount that they print. This requires designers to be clear about which content the user needs to be on the web page, avoiding excessive and irrelevant information. Additionally, when printing directly from the screen the resulting hard copy can look clumsy as positions are changed and content is split across pages. It is good practice to offer users a printer-friendly version, perhaps as a PDF (portable document format) file, which retains the key information relating to the product being viewed without the superfluous screen layout items such as URL, menus, and search box. It also allows the organisation to maintain a consistent and professional look that is adaptable across multiple online and offline channels.

5.9   Responses

Once the user has been stimulated with a message, we need to be clear about what form the next step in the purchasing cycle will take. In this respect, when we are designing our message we need to make clear to ourselves what 'call to action' we want the user to receive and act upon. This next step seeks to make it easier and more instinctive for customers to buy, but it is also a crucial measure of the effectiveness of the message, the campaign, and the longer-term relationship which we will cover in the next section on metrics. Potential response options are as follows:

- *Click-through* from a general search into a specific product page, then subsequently to a purchase page which allows the user to add the product to a 'basket' and having the option to continue purchasing or to checkout and complete the transaction. This process is largely automated, with little need for human interaction with the customer.
- *Social media* referral for customers who want to seek opinions from their online community (who may also follow the organisation), or those who wish to share news of their purchase. This activity enhances the user's

standing within its reference group and may open them up to new ideas, recommendations, tips, and complementary products from the group. It could also be recognised by the organisation as incentivised as a sales referral activity.

- *Personal contact*, which may be supported by a chatbot program with intelligent language recognition, effectively offering a more user-friendly FAQ functionality. Alternatively, online chats are also supported by human customer service operators via SMS, other messaging services, email, or voice apps. This option offers reassurance for inexperienced online shoppers, and new or vulnerable users. Efforts to fully automate the customer service function in recent years have suffered a backlash due to the perceived lack of aftersales service, specifically in the case of disputes. The resulting frenzy of social media activity has forced many organisations to rethink their approach to dehumanising the customer experience.

- *Offline support* by ringing a customer service call centre run by the organisation or its local agent, postal enquiries (such as returns), or a store visit. This integration with the firm's physical activities could be a welcome last resort for customers who may be frustrated by the inability of the online system to recognise and resolve their issue from its standardised response set.

5.10   Metrics

We have already established that digital marketing gives us many opportunities to measure our actions and the potential to assess their effects. There is a data health warning here in that we cannot always guarantee a clear and exclusive link between cause and effect because marketing is a social science, so there may be many uncontrollable variables that influence how customers respond to stimuli. This may cause us to dismiss metrics, but we do so at our peril. Consider your own relationships. Are you still friends with everyone you went to school with or ever worked with? Did you lose contact with some and make friends in other work or social contexts? Perhaps there are people you only ever contact online, whom you will never physically meet, that you may feel you have formed a friendship with? It's the same in business and is referred to as 'churn'. This relates to the customers that we lose over time and customers that we gain from new marketing efforts. Losing customers is not always a bad thing. There are certain unavoidable events in the customer–business relationship that mean they can no longer work together; a customer's needs may change to an area not covered by the business, or the business may reposition itself to serve different market segments.

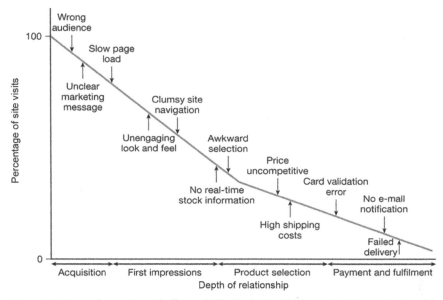

Figure 5.1 Causes for attrition (Chaffey and Ellis-Chadwick, 2019), reprinted by permission of Pearson Education Limited.

Competition will also play a significant part in testing an existing relationship: as we seek to win customers from our competitors, so they seek to persuade our customers to buy from them. A final consideration is the controllable actions of the organisation that might lead to an inadvertent loss of custom. Chaffey and Ellis-Chadwick (2019) illustrate this in their *causes for attrition* model (Figure 5.1).

5.11   Measuring Marketing Activities across the Customer Relationship Stages

With the plethora of data available it is easy to get to a stage of 'paralysis by analysis' as we pursue statistics on a want-to-know rather than a need-to-know basis. When determining the key digital metrics, we should do so with a clear understanding of our business goals (see Chapter 3 on strategy) and how we expect our users to act (see Chapter 4 on customer behaviour). Using the customer relationship stages model in Section 5.2 we can begin to align the key measures that may help us to objectively understand the stimulus and response dynamics at play. Table 5.4 explores the organisation's objectives and the key metrics attached to them at each stage of the relationship cycle. This should be read in conjunction with Chapter 2, which explains the metrics in more detail.

Table 5.4 Customer relationship stages: potential metrics

Stage	Business objective	Potential metrics
Approach	Awareness of the organisation/ brand lines/products	• Search engine optimisation: – Search engine referrals vs direct visits – Page impressions/unique visitors – Browser type – User country of origin – Cost per acquisition • Site optimisation: – Bounce rates – Site dwell time and number of pages viewed – Arrival and departure pages – Most/least popular pages – Registrations – New user accounts – App downloads • Advertising effectiveness: – Online display advertising response (e.g., click-through rates) – Direct mail response rate and timing – Channel contribution (affiliates, online, offline)
Establish	Enquiry and/or purchase	• Conversion/attrition rates: – Product search to selection – Selection to add to basket – Add to basket to checkout – Cancellations/returns • Cost per sale • Search combinations • User ratings and reviews
Secure	Repeat purchase	• Cost per transaction • Purchase frequency • Purchase volume
Expand	Purchase of a range of product types	• Product search and purchase combinations • Special offer/recommendation responsiveness • Lapsed and declining customers • Loyalty schemes • Lifetime user value
Advocate	Positive non-transactional communication with the organisation	• Social media likes, comments, shares • Rewards for referrals • Prosumer behaviours

---

RESEARCH INSIGHT 5.3 **Measuring What Matters**

Fulgoni, G. M. (2016). In the digital world, not everything that can be measured matters: how to distinguish 'valuable' from 'nice to know' among measures of consumer engagement. *Journal of Advertising Research*, March: 9–13.

   This paper considers the driving factors of digital communication and how these have led to rethinking the traditionally accepted advertising metrics of brand recall, likeability, and purchase intent. A key issue is the ease with which advertisers can supply pop-up content to viewers. The volume and untargeted nature of this content has led to the rise of pop-up blocker functions within browsers, which in turn have created tensions within the industry as advertising clients seek reassurances from agencies that their content is getting viewed across a range of platforms, and is not getting blocked. Since many online business models are built on the premise that users consume content for free in return for viewing adverts which fund the platform, the advent of ad-blockers is forcing a rethink of the usefulness of customer engagement metrics.

5.12 Characteristics of Good Metrics

Table 5.4 is not an exhaustive list, but it is designed to get you to think about what you can measure, and how you may measure it. You should not try to implement them all since it would require too much time and effort, potentially with sub-par results, as some measures may conflict with your organisation's goals. Good practice here is to start with the organisational or campaign strategy (see Chapter 3) then work through prioritising what is 'need-to-know' over what is 'want-to-know'. These measures can be benchmarked against industry norms and the organisation's specific and quantified objectives. Over time it will become clear which metrics are useful and which are not, enabling you to fine-tune your approach, and potentially even your strategy. When developing your list of specific metrics, it is helpful to ensure that they are:

- *easily measurable* to minimise additional cross-referencing and analysis that may cause confusion and delay;
- *efficient to collect* since data is constantly changing, thus requiring constant updating to provide a current picture;
- *interpretable* for the wide range of functions involved in running the business, and not just the data/computer scientists;
- *robust* in that they can present a consistent picture if challenged;

- *generally accepted* to ensure consistent communication inside and out-side the organisation; and
- *linked to desired business outcomes* to focus upon 'need-to-know' and not 'want-to-know'.

CHAPTER SUMMARY

Building upon Chapter 4, which examined the customer–organisation relation-ship from the customer's perspective, we have now seen it from the organisa-tion's point of view in a way that takes a practical and operational approach to the strategy elements covered in Chapter 3. We can define digital customer relationships and how they change over time, considering how to stimulate relationships that are failing, and how to grow relationships that are successful. We can do this with significant support at all stages of the relationship from the functionality afforded us by digital processes. This chapter also discussed the key issue of customer experience and how we can engage and measure customer interactions at different stages of their journey. It is important to realise here that the customer relationship should never be fully automated. While digital processes are a great support, offering consistency of service and feedback on interaction and satisfaction, they are currently unable to provide the levels of empathy, understanding, and creativity which are some of the cornerstones of fulfilling interpersonal relationships. Also, data is not wholly reliable since it lacks an understanding of nuance in customer communications. Let's be honest – none of us truly means everything we say or write.

Review Questions

- Are the stages of the customer relationship lifecycle so different from one another in practice? Provide examples to challenge these categorisations and delineations. Should there be more or fewer categories?
- Search for examples of 'good' and 'bad' web design. How did the prin-ciples discussed in this chapter shape your view, or was there something about it that you instinctively did or did not like? From this, describe your own personal 'likes' and 'dislikes' in web design. How do they differ from those of your friends?
- When was the last time you had a great online shopping experience? When was the last time you had a bad online shopping experience? How do they compare? What factors did they have in common?

- Which websites or apps have you stopped using in the last year? What were the reasons for this? Do you receive email, text, post, or social media messages from them to get you to return and have they made you reconsider?

END-OF-CHAPTER CASE: ONLINE USER EXPERIENCE (UX) GONE WRONG

With a vast range of low-cost digital techniques available to us, it is easy to be too enthusiastic and ambitious (or the opposite: lazy and uncreative) when creating a positively unique and memorable experience for visitors. To put visitors at the centre of the experience it is important to think about the stories that they want to hear, being respectful of the time and attention that they are giving to your online presence. A bad experience can be off-putting, with the least impact being that a potential customer might take some time to convince as to your levels of care and consideration for their custom. On the other hand, it might be so bad as to act as an instant deterrent, with your competitor benefiting from your less-than-ideal approach. Reputations for poor performance spread quickly and are hard to change. We have the power of social media to thank for this. This chapter has discussed many of the principles for good practice, but now it is time to consider the bad practices that continue to be seen despite the many great tools and tips provided for free online by experienced web designers. Here are some examples of not-so-great practice:

- Third-party advertisements that dominate the page and distract your attention away from what you were looking for. The worst offenders overlay the page, preventing you from reading anything else until you have closed it down. These can be intrusive and annoying. They also say to you that the designer might be more interested in generating ad revenue from your visit than they are in understanding and meeting your needs.
- As our attention spans shorten and the connectivity and processing power of our devices speed up, we are becoming less tolerant of slow loading times. In periods of high demand this may happen occasionally, but with relatively cheap and ubiquitous access to storage and processing power (e.g., via cloud computing) there is little excuse for this from a data processing point of view. It might be more to do with poorly designed web processes that try to integrate multiple fragmented platforms. It may also disguise a bad link where attempts are being made to download malware to your device. If your page does not load within four seconds – ideally less – then you are almost certainly losing traffic.

- The best websites and apps tend to be the simplest ones. On the surface of it they do little, but they do it very well by offering a small number of choices which are presented intuitively to the user. Offering too much input, whether words, images, menus, sounds, or effects (e.g., flashing or moving) risk sensory overload which disrupts the cognitive processes and leads to confusion and uncertainty.
- Poor spelling, punctuation, and grammar can be distracting, and shows a lack of care and consistency. Likewise, repetition and verbosity can be boring. Long, rambling sections can seem self-important and boring as they can be more about how the company feels about itself than how it wants to help customers to meet their needs. In an era when customer feedback is easy to come by it would be strange if there were no customer views available for products that the company provides.
- 'Template' website layouts are available from many good online web design companies. These are a good start for those without programming or design experience. However, they can seem a little bland and may not help your company to stand out against its competitors. Use of generic (aka stock) images, and the use of poor-quality low-resolution images look shoddy and unprofessional.
- The site does not have the same look and feel across multiple devices (e.g., TV, laptop, tablet, phone). There might be a conscious decision to offer different formats for different devices, simplicity for small devices being a prime reason. However, offering multiple sites/apps can get confusing for both your marketing team and the customer!
- Unorthodox layout of key information (e.g., search bar, menus, FAQs, contact information, home button).
- Unhelpful or incomplete search results which do not include similar or recommended items, or corresponding/complementary items that most commonly get bought in addition to the primary product search (e.g., a belt with a search for trousers, or a shirt and tie with a search for suits).

DISCUSSION QUESTIONS

For each of these examples, answer the following:

1. What is the risk of this design flaw?
2. What do you think the designer was trying to achieve?
3. How could it be fixed?
4. How would you measure the subsequent improvement in UX?

Develop Your Skills

What Is the Skill?

To fully understand the customer's experience, we must see the interaction from their perspective. Using storytelling techniques, marketing researchers use customer journey mapping (see the example in Figure 5.2) to tell the story of the customer's experience from initial contact, through the process of engagement, and into a long-term relationship. It may focus on a part of the story or give an overview of the entire experience. What it always does is identify key interactions that the customer has with the organisation. It talks about the user's feelings, motivations, and questions for each of these touchpoints. It often provides a sense of the customer's greater motivation. What do they wish to achieve, and what are their expectations of the organisation?

Why Is It Important?

Stories have defined our world. They have been with us since the dawn of communication, from cave walls to the tall tales recounted around fires. They have continued to evolve, with their purpose remaining the same: to entertain, to share common experiences, to teach and to pass on traditions.

(Inchauste, 2012)

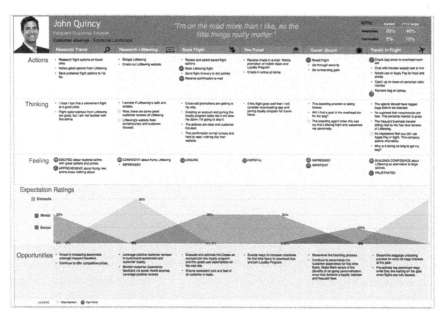

Figure 5.2 Nine sample customer journey maps, and what we can learn from them. Davey (2018). Copyright © 2018. Reprinted by permission of the author.

The key benefits of the customer journey mapping technique are:

- it helps designers understand the varying contexts of users;
- copy writers are helped to understand what questions users have and how they are feeling, so that they can develop the appropriate emotional stimulus;
- managers have an overview of the customer experience which can be benchmarked, resourced, and assessed;
- it considers multichannel, online, and offline touchpoints;
- it can identify gaps between channels and departments; and
- it puts the consumer at the centre of the organisation's thinking.

How to Develop It

Figure 5.2 gives an example of a typical customer journey map. You can also search online to see a range of examples and formats for this type of analysis.

How to Apply It

Develop your own customer journey map using an example of your choice based upon your personal experience as a customer. Use the following steps to tell the 'story' of your experience, identifying major and minor touch-points, and areas that create satisfaction or dissatisfaction.

1. **Define behavioural stages from the customer's perspective.** List your activity step by step, focusing upon what you feel you were trying to achieve at each step.
2. **Capture the customer's considerations.** What needed to happen to give you confidence to proceed to the next step?
3. **Detail every touchpoint.** How did the activity connect to, or interact with, the marketing activity of the organisation?
4. **Detail customer pain points.** To what degree did each of the interactions have the potential to cause you pain or pleasure? These could be scored or colour-coded.
5. **Chart changing customer emotions.** How did you feel about the experience at each stage? While some of this might be dictated by the quality of the service received, some other emotions may be a result of the scenario the customer finds themselves in and the goals they want to achieve.
6. **Consider what other detail can be added to the map.** The more comprehensive the map is, the more likely it is to accurately represent the customer's journey, and the higher the probability that you will be able to identify areas for improvement. What is the time-lapse expectation? Could a step have been avoided?

7. **Outline opportunities for improvements.** The process of building the map will emphasise to you what the pain points and opportunities for improvement are.

References

Chaffey, D., and Ellis-Chadwick, F. (2019). *Digital Marketing: Strategy, Implementation and Practice*, 7th ed. Harlow: Pearson.

Davey, N. (2018). Nine sample customer journey maps – and what we can learn from them [online]. Available from: www.mycustomer.com/experience/engagement/nine-sample-customer-journey-maps-and-what-we-can-learn-from-them [Accessed 10 July 2019].

Eigenraam, A. W., Eelen, J., van Lin, A., and Verlegh, P. W. J. (2018). A consumer-based taxonomy of digital customer engagement practices. *Journal of Interactive Marketing*, 44: 102–121.

Fulgoni, G. M. (2016). In the digital world, not everything that can be measured matters: how to distinguish 'valuable' from 'nice to know' among measures of consumer engagement. *Journal of Advertising Research*, March: 9–13.

Inchauste, F. (2012). Better user experience with storytelling. In Smashing Media (ed.) *User Experience Design*. Freiburg: Smashing Media.

Kumar, V., Petersen, J., and Leone, R. (2007). How valuable is word of mouth? *Harvard Business Review*, 85(10): 139–146.

McKinsey Global Institute. (2016). *The Age of Analytics: Competing in a Data-Driven World*. London: McKinsey & Company.

Peppers, D., and Rogers, M. (2002). *One to One B2B: Customer Relationship Management Strategies for the Real Economy*. Oxford: Capstone.

Rettie, R. (2001) An exploration of flow during Internet use. *Internet Research*, 11(2): 103–113.

Watkinson, M. (2013). *The Ten Principles Behind Great Customer Experiences*. London: Financial Times.

Zeithaml, V. A., Parasuraman, A., and Malhotra, A. (2002). Service quality delivery through web sites: a critical review of extant knowledge. *Academy of Marketing Science Journal*, 30(4): 362–375.

6 Digital Marketing Networks and Partnerships

Introduction

This chapter builds upon the internal view of marketing organisation in Chapter 5 to give an external perspective of how organisations sit within their wider marketing ecosystem to provide benefits to customers across a range of channels through a co-ordinated variety of activities. Digital technologies have forced a reconfiguring of traditional businesses who are vulnerable due to the high levels of resources committed to staff, accommodation, and facilities. Additionally, these established, incumbent businesses may feel that they do not need to change and that the market will eventually come around to their way of thinking, a misunderstanding of the wave of customer empowerment that runs throughout this book. So far in this book we have highlighted the risk of ignoring change, and the speed and certitude with which it is occurring to the benefit of agile, often newer, organisations, and to the detriment of more bureaucratic, often older, businesses. Let us explore how value networks have changed.

Learning Objectives

- Judge the importance of the integration of online and offline business activities.
- Consider how different physical and virtual business configurations add value to business activities.
- Discuss the changing organisational roles played by business partners.
- Summarise how new digital platforms transform the way in which organisations and markets interact.
- Appraise the threat of cybercrime and recommend cybersecurity countermeasures.

CASE INSIGHT: THE DEMANDS OF A MULTI-SCREEN WORLD

The ubiquity of online and offline channels, and the flexibility of a multitude of digital devices on which to access a rich wellspring of data, can make it hard for users to process data in a meaningful way to make informed purchase decisions. There is a corresponding challenge to organisations who seek to make the best use of their time and money to deliver the right marketing mix to the right people, in the right way, at the right time. It is no surprise that most of our media consumption is screen-based, be it smart-phone, tablet, PC, or TV. The nuance in their interrelationship is that devices and platforms (to include websites, apps, or third-party intermediaries) are considered by the user to be wholly interchangeable elements of the same relationship with the organisation. Users will flip and switch between devices to search, enquire, select, and pay for products. This may be a clear, spon-taneous, and rapid action in response to clearly defined needs, or a compel-ling promotional stimulus, or it may be slower and more considered, such as for a high-involvement purchase or the consideration of a complex range of alternatives. Either way, organisations need to design externally facing processes and partnerships to provide a rapid and cohesive user experience. As a diligent and motivated student of marketing I am sure that you spend evenings at home, and possibly even some lecture time, looking for alterna-tive media to improve your learning experience. This may come from the university's virtual learning environment, but is also likely to come from external news, journals, professional body, and social media sites. For example, your lecturer will describe a key theoretical concept, give examples of it in practice, and invite you to challenge or add to the discussion. You may be passively viewing the presentation notes on your laptop or tablet, you might also be annotating comments directly onto the presentation with a scribing function using a stylus and a screen, or you may be typing copious notes through your keyboard. You may choose not to make any notes at all and instead view the recording of the lecture at a later time, pausing and rewinding as your attention wanes or when you need to go over a concept again, or look elsewhere for more information through respected academic sources (e.g., an electronic copy of the recommended textbook or recom-mended articles) or social media/browser searches (e.g., TED Talks on YouTube, or SlideShare presentations on LinkedIn). Each of you will have your preferred manner for the timing, mode, and consumption level of learning materials, but how do *you* use the various platforms available to you, and how does this differ from a friend who is studying the same module?

Questions

- How, when, and how frequently do you access generic course materials provided by the university, such as the module guide, timetable, and past exam papers?
- For a given lecture, what materials did you access, on what devices, and for how long? You should consider this before, during, and after the event.
- How did you supplement this (e.g., by note-taking, participation in quizzes, accessing other material, emails to the lecturer, messaging other students)?
- In a lecture, have you ever used your digital devices for anything other than exploring the subject that is being discussed? Answer this honestly – we know that you sometimes get bored and need to reset your attention.

The answers to these questions will reveal the use of multiple devices, at multiple times, for multiple purposes, to enhance your learning. It will also help you to see the complex supporting web of knowledge that is developed for you both directly by the university and indirectly through partnerships with other organisations.

6.1 Market Channels

The relationship between end-users and original manufacturers can be complex. There are arguments for and against the use of intermediaries in the supply relationship, and it is every organisation's responsibility to assess what channel and intermediary options best suit their short-, medium-, and long-term goals. While intermediaries offer an increased scale and specialism for the activities of the organisation, they will also add cost (or erode margin) and potentially distort customer feedback. Intermediaries can be part of the organisation or separate organisations altogether with which the organisation has a mutually beneficial alliance. Fundamentally, the roles of the intermediaries are as follows:

- *Demand generation or selling to customers* to initiate the commercial relationship. Intermediaries will have a closer proximity to end-users and so can understand their motivations, behaviours, and competitive choices. Their insight can enable the tailoring and targeting of key messages to achieve greater effect.

- *Carrying of inventory and physical distribution* to enable local responsiveness and efficient supply chains for global and local customers. Customers prefer not to wait for extended periods for supply, and with globalised competition, hard-won customer loyalty could be at risk due to the organisation's failure to supply products within a reasonable period.
- *Aftersales service and the sale of complementary products* can be well served by local intermediaries who have their own specialist operations. It allows them to provide extra services to the customers so that they get more value from the manufacturer's products, potentially by selling complementary products.

6.2   Digitalisation of Intermediaries

Intermediaries come in many different forms and perform a range of roles within the supply chain between manufacturer and end-user.

- **Direct:** The direct linkage of the end-user to the product manufacturer is in theory the most effective and efficient relationship that can be had. The manufacturer and the end-user have a direct conversation which agrees product, price, and availability. At a small scale these relationships are relatively easy to manage. As the relationship increases in scale (i.e., size with many more customers) and scope (i.e., offering a wider product range across multiple countries) then relationship management becomes complex. For digital products such as music (e.g., iTunes, Spotify, BBC Sounds) and movies (e.g., Sky, Netflix, Amazon Prime, Disney+) this is not an issue as the marginal additional cost is almost zero and the product supply is virtually instantaneous. Digital technologies have enabled a growth in direct relationships through fast and accurate data-sharing through the Internet of Things (IoT), which is largely automated via machine learning/artificial intelligence.
- **Agents/distributors:** These intermediaries work on behalf of multiple manufacturers, providing them with market access and insight. However, many of their roles have become automated as their market knowledge (i.e., awareness of buyers and sellers) and contacts (e.g., professional service providers such as hauliers, shipping agents, import/export documentation, storage, and banking services) are no longer proprietary due to the Internet. They still have an important role to play in market-making – that is, understanding and interpreting market signals to identify opportunities and agree the deal. This nuanced and creative element of their role will be very difficult to automate.

- **Wholesalers:** The role of wholesalers is to receive bulk supplies from manufacturers or distributors, which are then held and broken down into smaller parcels of goods to be delivered to retailers or larger end-users (e.g., trade customers) as and when required. This has increasingly become a highly automated commodity service as wholesalers operate at vast scale, serving multiple manufacturers and industries. Their global presence benefits from highly integrated internal systems which also connect with upstream and downstream systems. Inventory handling and management systems allow for effective stock management and forecasting for peaks and troughs in demand. In a market such as perishable foodstuffs this fine-tuning of the supply chain, often using machine learning, is crucial to reduce product waste and improve customer satisfaction. Major online retailers such as Amazon have blurred the lines between wholesale and retail since their vast warehouses – and virtual third-party suppliers operating through the web portal – receive and hold large quantities of goods which are then distributed in small quantities as with a retail channel. This allows Amazon to reduce its operational costs and to gain significant market presence, which helps to secure significant discounts from manufacturers.
- **Retailers:** With the improved efficiency of upstream systems the role of retail is no longer principally about carrying a wide range of stock to satisfy the immediate needs of the customer. Retailers provide massive visibility of manufacturers' products, and convenience due to their proximity to target customers. They also carry some stock, but crucially they build customer relationships that lead to loyalty and long-term value. They also play an important post-purchase role in providing customer service for repurchase, complementary products, returns, and complaints. The role for digital here is to capture, access and analyse real-time sales and stock data which will lead to decisions regarding supply of further products, pricing, and sales promotions. It will also help the manufacturer or wholesaler to decide where to channel scarce stocks to get the best return. Retailers that operate loyalty schemes will also be able to attribute customer purchases to their segmentation profiles, which will help to inform further marketing campaigns and will enable the targeting of tailored offerings via email, messaging, and app notifications that are timely, appropriate, and attractive, further developing valuable long-term customer relationships.

The range of choices of channel and potential intermediaries create opportunities for manufacturers to achieve a global reach that can be monitored through complex supply chain programmes. The evolution of these strategies will be highly dynamic and data-driven, given the ongoing changes of consumer behaviours and local competitive conditions across multiple inter-linked markets, as the organisation seeks to be agile and efficient in the way it deploys resources to manage threats and capitalise upon opportunities. While the intensity of distribution is a strategic decision, the subsequent mix of channels can be difficult to control for the manufacturer whose desire might be to maximise market potential, but which can at the same time cause overlap and conflict in the marketing approach, leading to waste, delay, and confusion among end-users. This phenomenon is *channel conflict*, and it occurs when one intermediary perceives another intermediary to be acting in a way that unfairly disadvantages them. As an example of this, in the end-of-chapter case we will consider the potential channel conflict issues related to buying this book.

6.3   Informal Intermediaries

There are other less-formal intermediaries that play a role in connecting end-users with suppliers; they do this by exerting influence, which is either overt, covert, or somewhere in between. It is important to consider this influence in line with the discussion on consumer behaviour in relation to reference groups and opinion leaders in Chapter 4. These actors act as re-intermediaries, offering their help, views, and insight to assist us with making better decisions. Table 6.1 gives an overview of the parties, their roles, and their relative loyalty/independence.

Table 6.1 Range of informal intermediaries

	Imitators	Infomediaries	Social media	Affiliates
Acting on behalf of …	The buyer	Principally the buyer	Principally the buyer	The seller
Activities	Offering unauthorised copies of premium products	Offering price and product comparisons between competing offerings	New product reviews	Offer cross-selling recommendations for complementary products. May also come with an introductory promotional offer
Popular industries	Luxury goods such as handbags, jewellery, and watches	Financial services such as credit cards, personal loans, insurance	Cosmetics and fashion	Tourism and entertainment

Table 6.1 (*cont.*)

	Imitators	Infomediaries	Social media	Affiliates
Their interests	Selling large amounts of premium-priced products on the back of a global brand without the need for extensive marketing investment.	A popular site with lots of functionality will draw many users. The network effects of this audience make it valuable to sponsors who will pay for advertising and referrals.	To be relevant to their followers by offering insight, guidance, and advice.	To generate brand loyalty and income from referral fees.
Value to the buyer	Low cost and easy availability with the look and feel of the genuine article. Association with luxury brands may improve self-concept and lead to increased social status.	Transparency and choice. Site search functionality allows the user to tailor the query to their needs, subsequently adjusting it based on cost or product need.	Independent viewpoint from people that they admire who act within communities which users aspire to join and play a valued role.	Recommendation of complementary offerings which may lead to cost savings or increased satisfaction. Convenient connections avoid the need for extended searching.
Value to the seller	A negative impact could be lost sales and brand damage. A positive impact could be increased brand awareness and aspiration.	Reduces the need for customer enquiry and customer service support. Analytics allows instant tailoring of the product and assessment of its marketing effectiveness.	Trusted social media personalities offer source credibility to target audiences where direct involvement from the supplier (e.g., advertisements) might be less credible or compelling.	Minimises general promotional costs. Targeted activity is highly effective at the cost of a small share of the sales margin.

6.4   How Channels Add Value to the Marketing Relationship

Ordered channels of supply create a clear process for how the organisation and its customers reach each other. If you wanted to interact with a friend, you have the choice of physically visiting them, talking with them, or simply sending them a message; this also provides a range of complex options. If visiting, should you walk, cycle, drive, take the train, or fly? If talking, would you call by phone, Skype, or a messaging service, or possibly just send a video. Alternatively, you could send a letter, email, text message, or social media post. The key determinants here of what channel to use will depend upon:

- **Proximity:** This can relate to physical and relational distance. For example, if your friend lives in another country it may be more sensible to fly rather than walk. If they are not a close friend but only someone with whom you have a passing acquaintance, then you might try to reach them through a mutual contact with whom you are closer.
- **Complexity:** If we have lots to talk about, you may schedule a longer visit. If it is a brief update or a query, then maybe a text message or email will do the job.
- **Availability:** If you or your friend are too busy to meet up then you might agree to interact by talking on the phone or via text message. This way each side can interact in the way that is most convenient for them.
- **Frequency:** If you are in frequent contact regarding the issues then you will have a strong idea of each other's needs and preferences. This makes it easier arrive at the required result since less time will be needed to question the needs and explore different approaches.
- **Interactivity:** If the interaction is quite routine, where both sides are clear on the purpose and the nature of the conversation, things can move on quickly and smoothly, which would suggest a more functional approach such as text messaging, with copious use of emojis. If you have no specific outcome in mind and just want to share ideas and gain feedback, then maybe a phone call or face-to-face visit is appropriate.
- **Duration:** You might want to commit a greater amount of time to your interaction because you have complex issues to discuss, you enjoy the experience of spending time with that friend, or simply that by visiting them you also get the opportunity to visit other friends or places while you are in the area. So, visiting might be the preferred option over a phone call, email, or text message.
- **Urgency:** The need to ask or answer an urgent question might make physically meeting too slow or time-consuming. A call or text message could quickly resolve this.

If you can relate to these complexities of managing relationships with friends, family, and colleagues in your everyday life, just try to imagine the challenge faced in every hour of every day by global companies offering multiple product ranges. This is where digital technologies transform the way in which marketing relationships are maintained.

6.5 The Complementary Role of Online and Offline Channels

Given the global market access available from an 'always on' Internet, the external configuration of the organisation's activities to maximise the potential of customer relationships while minimising a debilitating drain on scarce resources is a constant and complex balancing act. The benefits accruing to an organisation because of the successful alignment of its online effort were termed by Evans and Wurster (1999) as the Three Dimensions of Navigational Advantage:

- **Reach:** This is the potential audience of the website as determined by its connection and accessibility. Reach can be increased by moving from a single site to representation with many different intermediaries. Reach has come to mean 'eyeballs' on the Web and is the most visible difference between virtual and physical businesses. Allen and Fjermestad (2001) suggest that niche suppliers can readily reach a much wider market due to search engine marketing, giving them a global presence from a local operational base.
- **Richness:** This is the depth or detail of information which is both collected about the customer and provided to the customer. Richness holds enormous potential for building close customer relationships. Traditional businesses have always had to make a trade-off between richness and reach. Doing both – getting highly detailed, customised information from a massive audience – was prohibitively expensive.
- **Affiliation:** This refers to whose interest the selling organisation represents – consumers or suppliers. It suggests that customers will favour retailers who provide them with the richest information on comparing competitive products. This customer-centric approach, through providing information, choice, and support, can affirm the relationship to be based on serving the customer's current and emerging needs over the long term rather than focusing upon the moving of product with short-term sales strategies.

The complexity of managing these relationships in a way that integrates online and offline activity can be illustrated by focusing upon the core of the customer decision-making process (Blackwell et al., 2001). In Table 6.2 we consider the role of online and offline channels through the example of the purchase of a car.

As it evolves, digital retailing is quickly morphing into 'omnichannel' retailing. This term reflects that retailers can interact with end-users through countless channels such as websites, apps, physical stores, automated kiosks,

Table 6.2 Online and offline channel activity for each stage of the customer decision-making process

Offline	Purchase stage	Online
Generic company display and broadcast advertising, sponsorship, and press releases to establish a clear brand identity. Mailshots or sales calls with trade-in/special offers to stimulate enquiry.	Need recognition	Generic company social media PR (owned), advertising (paid), and commentary (earned) to establish a clear brand identity. Emailshots or SMS with trade-in/special offers to stimulate enquiry.
Showrooms with specialist sales advisers. Product range leaflets. New vehicle reviews in specialist press.	Search for information	Rich array of photos and videos of the products. Interactive tailoring of product specification (e.g., vehicle type, colour, finish, wheels, windows, seats, control, livery) to see the 'ideal' purchase rather than be limited by the stock in the dealership. Independent user reviews and product ratings.
Test drive. Price lists showing a clear breakdown of basic price and optional extras, estimated service costs, and frequency. Limited-time special offers and promotions.	Prepurchase consideration	Check on product availability for new and used cars. Book a test drive. Instant trade-in and purchase quotation based on the required specification.
Payment by cash or cheque. Finance contracts delivered and signed.	Purchase	Payment by credit/debit card or bank transfer. Finance contracts delivered, signed, and enacted online.
Collection/delivery agreed in person or via telephone. Letters or phone calls to update on service requirements and issues.	Consumption	Collection/delivery scheduled via the website or app. Delivery updates via app, messaging service, or email.
The relationship is now largely handled by the service department, which takes a problem-based approach based on dealing with emerging vehicle defects and repairs.	Post-purchase evaluation	Real-time fault detection through vehicle sensors connected to the dealership to proactively arrange repair and provide a courtesy car. Service reminders and requests for customer feedback via app, messaging service, or email.
Trade-in events and offers promoted by display, print, and broadcast advertisements. Letters and phone calls to existing customers of older vehicles.	Divestment	Instant valuation comparisons if sold independently vs a direct trade-in against a new purchase.

direct mail, call centres, social media, mobile devices, gaming consoles, TV, and networked appliances. Unless conventional suppliers can integrate these disparate channels into a single seamless omnichannel customer experience they are unlikely to thrive with the weight of changing customer attitudes, constant technological innovation, and economics against them. This requires the careful monitoring and management of these channels through a variety of digital sales and product-based systems, and should lead to a co-ordinated approach which balances customer satisfaction with market growth and profit generation using analytics that assess the environment and organisation performance.

RESEARCH INSIGHT 6.1 Planning Omnichannel Programmes

Berman, B., and Thelen, S. (2018). Planning and implementing an effective omnichannel marketing program. *International Journal of Retail & Distribution Management*, 46(7): 598–614.

This paper explains the difference between multichannel and omnichannel marketing in the context of the retail channel. Its systematic approach identifies four stages of transition which enables the organisation to assess its position and prepare to move ahead with more complex offerings. Barriers to implementation are also identified along with potential approaches for overcoming them.

6.6 The Flexing Relationship: Disintermediation and Reintermediation

We have already explored the emergence of digital products, dynamic pricing, and analytics that have had an impact on our customer behaviour. However, in many ways this transformation can be interpreted as an augmentation of existing activity rather than its radical reframing. For example, when we stream film, TV, and music the process of consumption is not radically different from when we buy CDs or DVDs. However, it is the Internet's effect upon the role of intermediaries that has redefined how customers are served. The highly efficient nature of digital communications and supply chains has allowed for the greater use of timely and accurate intelligence regarding which products are required to be in which place and at what time to be best placed for when we anticipate that the customer will need them. This approach also allows for 'lean' supply chains as data is shared between the organisations that comprise the supply chain. The emergence of Internet-based retailing has led to customers making routine purchases online due to the convenience of being able to browse 24/7 for products, checking for availability, making payment, and then having the goods delivered directly to them. As software systems became more sophisticated, communication speed and capacity improved, and new devices such as tablets and smartphones arrived, and online competition exploded. Seeking new ways to create convenient and compelling customer interactions that kept customers loyal led to the development of web applications, known as apps. Instead of accessing supplier websites via a search engine or address bar, apps create a separate tailored 'walled garden' experience for the customer which, through convergence with mobile hardware and communications technologies (e.g., Wi-Fi and Bluetooth), enabled a mobile capability to fit in with users' needs for flexibility and convenience in their everyday lives. If we connect this further with the geolocational potential of your networked devices, a locational advantage is created which replaces the traditional high street buying behaviours with more exploratory shopping experiences. The ensuing movement of offline purchases to take place online, along with ongoing increases in store rental, storage, and transportation costs, has forced many retailers to close. The retailers that survive have done so by reconfiguring their approach to being less like a warehouse where customers view a wide range of stock, buy it, and take it home, thus enabling much lower rental, storage, stock, and staff costs. Instead, stores are behaving as showrooms for selected items in the product range, providing a rich shopping experience that aims to engage customers through sensory interactions which reinforce the organisation's brand identity, thus creating not just an economic but an emotional connection. These slimmed down retail customer experiences are designed to capture the full potential of the 'bricks and clicks' interaction between online and offline channels in the expectation that the customer will then go to the retailer's app to browse, select, and pay for their chosen goods. Unfortunately, this is not always guaranteed as many customers still engage in 'showrooming' behaviour, which is when a product is evaluated in a physical store and subsequently bought from a competing online store using a mobile device. Mobile marketing practices allow retailers to send special offers, reminders, and event invitations to potential customers who may be nearby at a given point in time, with the aim of stimulating a visit to the store to engage with the brand, perhaps by making an impulse purchase. This level of care and attention from the seller can appeal as a timely reminder to the customer to buy, with the added incentive of convenience, due to proximity, and cost saving, which may be in the form of a discount voucher sent with the reminder.

DIGITAL INSIGHT 6.1 The Future of Shopping: Omnichannel Retailing

Imagine that you are about to go away with your friends for an adventure holiday that will include climbing, biking, and skiing. Until recently you may have started shopping for clothes and equipment at your local shopping centre. This time, however, you decide to login to your user account at an outdoor sports store where you last year bought a walking jacket and replaced your ancient skiing boots. The website has a virtual assistant called Sherpa who makes some clothing recommendations, and because the styles vary and you are not completely sure of the look you are aiming for, Sherpa renders images of you in the clothes based on the physical characteristics and avatar of you that it has on record. You reject some of the suggestions and check out the reviews and prices of the others. In doing so you find better details for a couple of items at other online retailers, but decide to order the other items with Sherpa then drive to the store to try on the items that you like the look of, to make sure of their fit and comfort.

As you arrive at the store the sales assistant greets you by name (the app has registered your location) and shows you to the changing room, where your items are ready to try on. They have also set aside some additional clothing and equipment items that they think might complement your choices, based on your past online purchases. You like the walking trousers, but after scanning the price label with your smartphone you see that you can get them cheaper at another store. The sales assistant agrees to match the price but you are not so sure, so you try them on and stream a short video on a social media messenger to your partner and a couple of friends, but none of them respond positively to your suggestion, so you decide to stick with your original choice, collect your items, and move to the checkout. On the way you find a discount voucher on the store app, which saves you an additional 10 per cent, and you pay through ApplePay.

6.7 The Role of Supply Chain Partners in the Marketing Ecosystem

Configuring an agile and flexible organisational network carries both benefits and costs. Traditional organisational structures which are relatively fixed and largely proprietary (i.e., the organisation owns a controlling stake or has considerable influence upon how they operate) provide reliability of quality and lead time along with predictability of cost and capacity. However, should the market explode, vanish, or change, then the producer is left with significant operational and personnel costs that may not be easy to dispose of without incurring significant additional losses. On the other hand, a fully flexible virtual organisation offers versatility, creativity, and is cheap to run in the short term since the full costs of overheads will not be factored into the price as they will be shared across a range of other customers. The challenge is to plan for change that is both effective and efficient.

Porter (2004) described the organisation as a collection of activities that come together in the form of the *value chain* to serve its chosen market. Each activity has a distinct and valuable role to play to contribute to the overall effort to achieve sustainable competitive advantage and can be supported by digital technologies in the following ways:

- **Firm infrastructure** deals with planning, finance, quality control, and information management and uses a sophisticated range of data capture, reporting, and analysis tools to inform decisions regarding where to deploy scarce resources. Progress reporting of performance against target will also highlight corrective actions that need to be undertaken, measuring their subsequent success.
- **Human resource management** deals with recruiting, training, developing, and rewarding employees. Digital technologies can enhance the recruitment process, with social media increasingly being used to identify candidates and pre-vet applicants as part of the shortlisting process. Online training is being used increasingly as a low-cost flexible activity that enables employees to learn on the job while also making a productive contribution. For more quantitatively driven organisations, employees' productivity can be measured and rewarded appropriately.
- **Technological development** includes research and development, product design, process development, and raw material improvement. Scientists and engineers are greatly assisted by data management, visualisation, and simulation tools. Using computer aided design (CAD) and computer aided manufacturing (CAM) software coupled with computer numerically controlled (CNC) and 3D printing equipment can create rapid prototyping of new products for testing ahead of being fully productionised.
- **Procurement**: locating, contracting, receiving, and paying global suppliers has never been easier. Search engine marketing, communities of practice, common software protocols, and electronic payment make it easy to buy from anyone at any time. Additionally, one of the major risks of buying from a new supplier, that of trust and reliability, can begin to be addressed by online searches of social media commentary, press reports, and statutory agency reporting to ascertain their reputation.

- **Inbound logistics** ensure the raw materials are received, stored, and distributed in as safe and efficient a manner as possible. Since a great deal of an organisation's cash can be tied up in unproductive materials, stock control systems allow this to be reported, flagged, and addressed. Materials will carry unique codes, which allows their origins to be identified for quality control purposes. Location tagging also allows for materials to be easily found and moved to where they are required for the production process.
- **Operations** brings together multiple raw materials to produce the finished product. Traceability is again important to ensure quality control. Once products are ready to be shipped, alerts that include packing lists can be sent to notify the logistics operation. Perishable finished goods that are ready for transport but may need to be stored for a while can be sent to the appropriate place and be monitored.
- **Outbound logistics** aim to balance timely despatch (to free-up storage space and working capital) with a minimum of activity in order to reduce fuel waste and pollution. Consignments will be carefully planned and scheduled, with progress reports for customers regarding delivery of their goods.
- **Marketing and sales** activity enables the organisation to understand and deliver on customer expectations in a manner superior to that of the competition. Within the *primary activities* this is essentially a promotional and channel management activity.
- **Service** includes pre-sales and aftersales activity that addresses customer queries, solves problems such as errors or faulty products, and will help the customer to get better value from their purchase, perhaps with the purchase of complementary physical or virtual products.
- **Margin** relates to the profit generated from higher income (i.e., price and place) or lower costs (i.e., product, process, partnerships). Data analytics will track organisational performance, allowing for the necessary financial adjustments to be made.

Since the organisation sits within a wider context of the marketing ecosystem that integrates to create extended value for a wide range of potential customers, we should consider the roles and relationships between parties. With an appreciation of the wider **value network**, the organisation has important decisions to make regarding its configuration. As discussed earlier, there are arguments to be made for and against wider control of the channels that lead to customers. With greater income and customer involvement come greater cost and risk of losing one's focus upon what the customer values that the organisation truly is, or aspires to be, better at than the competition. The options available to the organisation are essential dimensional choices:

- **Vertical integration**, by expanding their scope of control of 'upstream' activities (i.e., closer to the source), or by including more 'downstream' activities (i.e., closer to the customer). The organisation can choose to shift or expand its business model based on where it thinks the greatest value is to be had.
- **Horizontal integration** by closer connections with suppliers of competing or non-competing products to the same customer base. This can lead to a greater share of sales or can unlock further product development potential by the close alignment and creation of complementary and replacement product ranges.

6.8 Establishing Valuable Partnerships

Traditionally organisations have achieved integration benefits through a process of mergers and acquisitions which are highly expensive, of questionable long-term value, and can take a long time to facilitate. These are all risky propositions given their relatively rigid structure and static operational approach in a dynamic and radically changing marketplace. It is here that digital technologies enable a way of working which is both flexible and agile to respond to the important marketplace threats and opportunities in a timely and effective manner to achieve some or all the following aims:

- **Protect product quality**: ensures the desired quality of inputs and final product.
- **Improve scheduling**: easier planning, coordination, and scheduling of adjacent processes.
- **Reduce competitive pressures**: gaining control over the source of inputs and distribution outlets creates entry barriers and reduces the threat from existing competitors.
- **Invest in specialised assets**: gaining control over specialised assets avoids potential problems of 'holdup' and bilateral monopoly.

The Internet, and the technology and software platforms that it hosts, are ideal tools to identify, plan, and execute collaborative projects. Beyond the sharing of data it can also be used to evaluate past projects, assess risk (specifically the financial viability of partners where investment in a longer-term engagement is required), agree electronic contracts, and co-ordinate the efforts of diverse and dispersed global teams. This highly agile strategic response utilises cloud-based processes and a significant amount of automation to allow the organisation to quickly respond to market pressures without the time and expense of building new supply chains.

Open collaboration is defined by Levine and Prietula (2014) as 'any system of innovation or production that relies on goal-oriented yet loosely co-ordinated participants who interact to create a product (or service) of economic value, which they make available to contributors and noncontributors alike'. As a process of peer production and mass collaboration it has many features in common with crowdsourcing. Contributors will operate across a wide community, contributing ideas and completing tasks towards the goal. Peer-review will create feedback and discussion on the priorities and approaches to collaboration. Riehle et al. (2009) define open collaboration as based on the three principles of egalitarianism, meritocracy, and self-organisation, which place equal value upon all contributions since there is an absence of hierarchy and overriding approval systems other than changes which are widely adopted (representing acceptance by the community). Openness extends from the creation to the use of the product, which is made available to non-contributors and members outside the community.

Closed collaboration will see a small number of players work closely on projects, which may include product development, market entry, or serving a global customer. Projects will be short-term, oriented towards a specific goal, and will involve only selected parts of the organisation. Whatever new profits or assets are developed by the collaboration are owned jointly and exclusively within the group and not made freely available to non-members. Where a collaboration is co-ordinated to dominate a market at the expense of customer choice or to unfairly restrict competition it is referred to as collusion. In some jurisdictions this is seen as being anti-competitive and is illegal, often to be addressed via regulation or legislation.

Co-operative competition (aka coopetition) occurs when organisations who would otherwise be natural competitors choose to collaborate within a narrow scope of activity for relatively short periods of time to achieve a joint goal (e.g., cost savings in new product development), while at the same time competing fiercely on other levels and in other markets (Dagnino and Padula, 2002). One example of this is the arrangement between PSA Peugeot Citroën and Toyota to share components for a new city car, simultaneously sold as the Peugeot 107, the Toyota Aygo, and the Citroën C1, where the companies saved money on shared costs while remaining fiercely competitive in other areas. Such an arrangement can cause practical difficulties regarding control, ownership, and exploitation of the resultant intellectual property, equity and risk, complementary needs, and trust.

DIGITAL INSIGHT 6.2 Partnerships That Worked ... and Some That Didn't

GoPro and Red Bull are both companies that have established themselves as lifestyle brands, specifically a lifestyle that's action-packed, adventurous, fearless, and usually pretty extreme. GoPro sponsors extreme sports fans and provides equipment to capture races, stunts, and events on film from the participant's perspective. Red Bull uses its experience and reputation to run and sponsor these events.

BMW and Louis Vuitton are both in the business of travel. They are traditional brands that value luxury and are well known for their high-quality craftsmanship. BMW created the i8 sports car model, which was available from $135,700, while Louis Vuitton designed an exclusive four-piece set of suitcases and bags that fit perfectly into the car's rear parcel shelf, for 'just' $20,000.

Shell and LEGO partnered for over 50 years. LEGO got to use the logo for its sports cars and service station sets, while Shell built brand awareness in families from a young age. Greenpeace began to protest that it was not appropriate for children to play with toys that displayed the name of a petroleum company that had a history of questionable environmental practices and was pursuing aggressive oil drilling in the Arctic.

U2 and Apple partnered on the launch of the iPhone 6 and Apple Watch, with U2 providing an entire new U2 album for free for all iTunes users, but the automatic download into libraries upset Apple's legions of iTunes users. The move was considered intrusive by individual users who valued the personal space of a carefully curated music collection. The move backfired on both partners.

6.9   Crowdsourcing

Crowdsourcing is not an invention of the Internet. It has been used for centuries as a sourcing model that allows an end-user to obtain goods and services from within and across communities as opposed to from individual parties, such as an organisation or an individual (commonly referred to as 'outsourcing'). Defined by Brabham (2013) as an 'online, distributed problem-solving and production model', it provides significant improvements in project costs, speed, quality, flexibility, scalability, and diversity over traditional static models of controlled collaboration. Brabham puts forth a problem-based typology of crowdsourcing approaches:

- Knowledge discovery and management are used for information management problems where an organisation mobilises a crowd to find and assemble information. It is ideal for creating collective resources.
- Distributed human intelligence tasking is used for information management problems where an organisation has a set of information in hand and mobilises a crowd to process or analyse the information. It is ideal for processing large data sets that computers cannot easily do.
- Broadcast search is used for ideation problems where an organisation mobilises a crowd to come up with a solution to a problem that has an objective, provably right answer. It is ideal for scientific problem solving.
- Peer-vetted creative production is used for ideation problems, where an organisation mobilises a crowd to come up with a solution to a problem which has an answer that is subjective or dependent on public support. It is ideal for design, aesthetic, or policy problems.

The process involves the broadcasting of a problem to the community, or general public, with an open call for contributions to help solve the problem. Contributors then submit proposals to solve the problem. It is not always expected that contributors will be paid as it is anticipated that they will gain intellectual satisfaction and community recognition from helping to solve the problem. In some cases, such as microtasking, contributors will be paid small sums to perform tedious activities. Crowdsourcing may produce solutions from amateurs or volunteers working in their spare time or from experts or small businesses. Examples of Internet-based crowdsourcing activities include the following:

- Ideas and innovations competitions such as those regularly organised by LEGO, where fans from around the world compete to win recognition from their peers and prizes such as gift sets and trips.
- Crowdfunding for commercial or charitable projects through multiple small donations by a multitude of people who each contribute to pre-purchase products, buy experiences, or simply donate. Kickstarter is an example of this.
- Macro-tasking work can be done independently, takes a fixed amount of time, and requires special skills. Tasks may include graphic design, software development, translation services, location and return of lost items, pets, or persons. Amazon's Mechanical Turk is a portal for outsourcing processes and jobs to a distributed workforce who can perform these tasks virtually.

- Microtasking work allows users to do small tasks for which computers lack aptitude for low amounts of money, such as writing survey feedback or programming a database. TaskRabbit is a portal that matches freelance labour with local demand, allowing consumers to find immediate help with everyday tasks, including cleaning, moving, delivery, and repair person work.
- Content-rating services such as Reddit aggregate web content through its rating and discussion website. Users submit content to the site such as links, text posts, and images, which are then voted up or down by other members.
- Crowd-shipping is a peer-to-peer shipping service where travellers heading in the direction of the buyer are willing to bring the package as part of their luggage for a reward; for example, a truck driver whose route lies along the buyer's location and who is willing to take extra items in their truck.

RESEARCH INSIGHT 6.2 Crowdsourced Journalism

Dailey, D., and Starbird, K. (2014). Journalists as crowdsourcerers: responding to crisis by reporting with a crowd. *Computer Supported Cooperative Work*, 23(4–6): 445–481.

The Internet and social media are disrupting traditional models of news production and distribution, forcing an evolution of the role of the journalist. This case is set in the context of the reporting of Hurricane Irene in 2011, and examines how journalists transformed their practice to serve in a new capacity as leaders of an online volunteer community which included citizen journalists, online volunteers, and collaborating journalistic institutions to provide real-time event coverage. In an environment of variable communications support this ad hoc effort bridged gaps in ICT infrastructure to unite its audience. The role of the 'human powered mesh network' is also explored.

6.10   Cybercrime and Cybersecurity

The Internet is built upon the principal of openness, access, and sharing to achieve common goals through trust-based relationships. As in the physical world there are actors at play (see the discussion of consumer misbehaviour in Chapter 4) who may disrupt the activities of others with innocent, mischievous, or malicious intent. Think about your data as you would think about your money, your car, or your home. We wouldn't leave our cash or credit cards lying around in public places; we'd put them somewhere out of view, where we could monitor them, in our pocket or a bag perhaps. If we have significant sums of money, maybe they are best kept in a safe at home, a safety deposit box, or a bank vault. A digital equivalent might be our login details, passwords, and data. These will be stored securely in password-protected areas on your PC, on websites, and in the cloud. Would you leave your car unattended or unobserved for an extended time on a public road with the driver's door open and the engine running? Probably not. You might park it under cover in a secure area such as a lockable garage with CCTV cameras and security patrols. You would certainly lock the car and place any valuables out of sight so as not to tempt intrusion from an opportunistic passer-by. In this scenario the security guard on your device would be security software and the device might be behind locked doors in a server room, or again in the cloud. At home, do you leave the doors and windows open at all hours, allowing strangers freely to visit and explore the house, taking or damaging items as they go? You'd probably close and lock the doors even when you are home. When you away at night you might leave the lights on to make potential intruders think that you are home. You may even get a dog, install a motion-sensitive intruder alarm, or install internal cameras that you can access and control remotely. However, all these pro-tections will prove ineffective to the most organised and determined criminal elements. No security system is completely effective and may at best deter efforts. So, when planning for potential scenarios you should consider how to prevent them by use of deterrents, reasonably protect your assets, and plan for recovering from the effects of the breach to ensure continuity in your business.

RESEARCH INSIGHT 6.3 **Human Error and Cybersecurity**

Hadlington, L. (2017). Human factors in cybersecurity; examining the link between Internet addiction, impulsivity, attitudes towards cyber-security, and risky cybersecurity behaviours. *Heliyon*, 3(7): e00346.

This paper studies the relationship between risky cybersecurity behav-iours, attitudes towards cybersecurity in a business environment, Internet addiction, and impulsivity. The results of the study demonstrated that the factors of Internet addiction and impulsivity were significant predictors of risky cybersecurity behaviours. These individual differences indicate good cybersecurity practices, highlighting the need to focus directly on more effective training and awareness mechanisms.

6.11   Common Cybersecurity Threats

System intrusion does not simply mean accessing and downloading private data. There are a range of ways in which malicious actors (internal and external to the organisation, human-based or automated) can have a damaging and lasting impact upon the software, hardware, and networks which are integral to the organisation's systems that operate to support the business and its customers on an ongoing basis:

- **Ensuring the integrity and validity of input, work-in-progress, and output data.** Data poisoning occurs when users amend or delete data inappropriately. This can be difficult to detect so the organisation may adopt protocols that require any such actions to be validated by another, more senior, employee with a clear audit trail of all changes.
- **Data access and its theft.** If data is stored it can be viewed or extracted. Do you need to store all data? For example, data relating to payment cards should never be stored. Under the GDPR (see Chapter 2) we should also be clear about what personal data we need to keep about employees and customers, and whether it is stored in an appropriately secure manner away from access keycodes and other sensitive data.
- **Malicious file execution** occurs when files that are uploaded from external sources (e.g., email or external drives) are not what they seem. Such malware includes viruses which destroy data, worms which spread from computer to computer on their own, ransomware which makes all of your files unreadable, holding your data hostage until you pay the hacker the ransom, spyware which steals your data (e.g., login information) and may be used to spy on you by using your webcam or microphone without your knowledge, and Trojan horses that deliver other types of malware by hiding them in files or programs that look legitimate. Email firewalls, the blocking of certain file types, 'detect and destroy' security software, and user training to help identify potentially dangerous sources or material all help to offer some form of protection from malware.
- **User authentication and session management** control access to the system and the levels of access allowed. They also track user activity while inside the system to prevent access to prohibited sites and material (i.e., those which are inappropriate to the user's role or represent a potential security risk). Systems can operate an automatic logout procedure after a prolonged period of inactivity, which assumes that the user is no longer present at their device and so running the risk that an unauthorised user could access the system. There may also be a requirement for a level of complexity in the login password to include upper

case, lower case, numbers, symbols, or to be of a minimum length. Additional authentication data may also be required, such as a personal identification number (PIN), keyword combination, or one-time access code sent to a separate device that is controlled by the user.

- **System manipulation** occurs when network IoT devices can be turned off, overwritten, or misdirected. Consider networked medical devices, power generation and distribution, air and rail traffic control, security systems, military hardware, and financial systems. It is a key theme in many crime dramas on TV in which criminal elements have sought to manipulate automated systems to effect blackmail, thefts, and other crimes. How would your life be affected right now if the power went off, your devices no longer communicated with each other, or any other parts of the Internet, or your electronic financial identity was wiped clean?

- **System configuration** should avoid over-dependency upon one system, server array, or back-up control. Sensitive data should be distributed in multiple copies rather than clustered in a single version. The cloud and outsourced server arrays offer a temporary solution, but this should not be the only back-up in case of emergency.

- **Phishing** is where users are misled into believing that a communication originates from a legitimate organisation. This could be a cover for malware or data theft. User education can help to reduce the risk.

- **Denial of service** attacks overwhelm the web server with messages, file downloads, and requests for connection that lead to a deterioration or collapse of the service. This can lead to hold ups of legitimate internal and external electronic communications due to a reduction in processing capacity.

6.12   Potential Cybersecurity Measures

Servers, websites, and user accounts are under attack 24/7 on a global basis from individual hackers, hacking organisations and collectives, and automated programs. Any security expert will tell you that there is no guaranteed protection from a determined assailant, but what you can do is to understand, plan, and execute reasonable measures to protect your business and the people it supports.

- Get help from cybersecurity experts. You may not be able to afford a team of dedicated in-house specialists, but you should be able to run security software programs that monitor and report activity to a responsible person in the organisation who will be able to assess the threat and co-ordinate the organisation's response. The services of consultants can be used to help with the design and periodic testing of the system architecture and its protocols (including who has what access to the system).

- Have a security process which users sign up to individually. This policy will include rules on downloads, uploads, personal use, prohibited material, and keeping the device secure when travelling and offsite (including how to avoid connecting to unsecure public networks).
- Train and test users frequently to keep them updated on risks and prevention measures that they might not naturally be aware of. Individual security elements include password complexity, multiple login factor levels, and biometrics. Data and systems misuse are increasingly becoming disciplinary issues within businesses, which means that systems can also be at risk from disgruntled current and former employees – supervisors and managers need to be trained in how to spot and address these behaviours. This will also need support from the IT department to identify and flag suspicious internal activity.
- Run frequent system diagnostics and tests. Networked devices that do not allow the automatic download of software security patches are highly vulnerable.
- Plan for a security breach to organise and practise the response. This will require the prioritisation of threats based on the potential damage to the business. Get appropriate business insurance in case you need significant extra resources at short notice to tackle the problem, or if by the nature of your business you become legally responsible for consequential losses incurred by your customers, investors, employees, or the general public.

These measures will not guarantee protection, but education can prevent a significant proportion of unintentional errors, oversight can act as a deterrent, and contingency planning makes sure that the organisation is prepared should the worst happen.

DIGITAL INSIGHT 6.3 Some of the Biggest Cybercrimes ... so Far

Yahoo (2013–14): Three billion user accounts were compromised by, it was presumed, a 'state-sponsored actor', revealing real names, email addresses, passwords, dates of birth, and telephone numbers of users.

Home Depot (2014): The details of 50 million credit cards were stolen when hackers used a vendor's name and password to get onto the

DIGITAL INSIGHT 6.3 (cont.)

company's computer network, then installed malware on its point-of-sale systems, which meant that customers swiping their credit cards were handing over their data to the criminals.

Twitter/PayPal/Netflix (2016): In the first instance of the IoT being used in a cybercrime, a distributed denial of service (DDOS) attack on one of the companies that host the Internet's Domain Name System, a directory of internet addresses, taking down many of the Internet's most popular sites.

UK National Health Service (2017): Hackers gained systems access and installed the ransomware software 'WannaCry', which was delivered via email in the form of an attachment. Once a user clicked on the attachment, the virus was spread through their computer, locking files and demanding payment for their release. The attack caused chaos in the UK's medical systems, and at its height infected computers in 150 countries.

CHAPTER SUMMARY

We now have a comprehensive oversight about how digital technologies have changed the 'space' in which organisations interact with their customers. These channels have grown significantly in the scale and scope of business operations to audience sizes that were previously unknown to any organisation with fewer resources than governments or global enterprises. The marginal costs for this exposure are low and getting lower due to the rise of alternative physical and virtual channels, and the many different types of ways that users and organisations can interact and co-operate to achieve their goals without ever physically meeting one another or with physical cash changing hands. Partnerships are at arm's length, are frictionless, create convenience, and can be an instant and rewarding experience. However, these network effects can also represent a significant threat as our organisations are exposed to threats we are unfamiliar with, from actors that we don't know.

Review Questions

1. How would an organisation decide on the best mix and configuration of channels that enhances the customer experience but minimises

organisational complexity? Illustrate your example through a business or product with which you are familiar.

2. What test would you use to decide whether the business performs an activity in-house or with the use of external partners? How would you decide which type of external relationship to have?

3. There is inevitably a constraint placed on the effective and efficient running of a business by any security measures it employs. Explain both the costs and benefits of the protection measures described in Section 6.12.

END-OF-CHAPTER CASE: IDENTIFYING AND RESOLVING CHANNEL CONFLICTS

When developing the marketing channel strategy for this book, the publisher had to consider a range of challenges and opportunities. As this is a first edition of a topic which is growing in its global relevance in higher education, we are eager for the readership to be global. To achieve this, we have considered where it might start selling (i.e., our target market) and where in the world sales will grow over time, potentially with subsequent editions. From a product point of view, an international publication might require translation and the provision of examples and cases that are more familiar to local audiences. Let's look at the distribution side first. The book will be offered in physical 'hard copy' form that you could buy from retailers such as your university's campus bookshop, larger generalist booksellers in a nearby town, online via hyperscale book retailers such as Amazon, or directly from the publisher's website. All of these might offer you slightly different prices which would represent a *horizontal channel conflict* – that is, between retailers. When selling a book, the publisher designates a recommended retail price (RRP). Behind this the publisher (i.e., the manufacturer) and the book seller (i.e., the retailer) will negotiate a level of discount that is based on potential projected sales and their relative market strength. For example, large-scale national and international wholesalers represent significant sales potential for the publisher, and they might offer a bigger discount accordingly. Smaller-scale retailers run the risk of low levels of sales, with the potential for slow-moving or unsold stock, which represents waste in the supply chain. Physical retailers will come under price pressure from online retailers, who may benefit from lower-cost operating models or superior market strength that enables them to negotiate a bigger discount on the RRP. There is also a significant threat from resellers, who may offer a platform for students who bought copies of the book that they no longer need and are now seeking to clear from their bookshelves and recoup some of their investment by reselling their copy. The challenge for buyers here is whether to buy a cheaper, older edition or pay full price for the up-to-date edition.

If you are accessing this book via your university library, as a soft or hard copy, you are essentially utilising a wholesale channel where supply is bought in bulk from the publisher (i.e., the manufacturer) and made available to a trade customer base (i.e., the academic community of researchers, teachers, and students) for a fixed fee. This is an example of *vertical channel conflict* – that is, between wholesaler and retailer. For the publisher there is a trade-off to be made that these copies might be used in lieu of full-cost copies that could be sold via the university bookshop or by another specialist online/offline book retailer. Usually, the determining factor here is the preferences of end-users. Those that will dip into the book in exceptional circumstances, for revision or research purposes, potentially using it alongside other resources to support their work, may prefer to periodically access hard copies in the library. Those that will use the book as a key aid throughout their time studying the subject and who may anticipate using the book in their future academic and professional activities may prefer their own hard copy, which makes it easier to cross-reference multiple sections, annotating ideas as they go along.

Finally, if you only access textbooks via the university e-library, this creates a *multichannel conflict* – that is, online vs offline. Many organisations have different price offerings for online and offline sales. Given that their online activities are geared more towards serving remote customers with specific requirements, and their offline activities are focused upon the needs of local customers seeking to browse and explore, it is common for buyers to visit shops to physically engage with the product before buying it online, perhaps from another retailer, at a discount. This phenomenon is known as 'showrooming'. It is easy to understand how and why this conflict occurs between companies but can be embarrassing when it happens within an organisation and has led to complaints from offline customers who feel exploited due to higher prices. This conflict is forcing organisations to rethink the role of their retailing activities from being less about stocking and selling products, and more about providing a high-quality customer experience that later leads to online sales, which are cheaper and easier to serve.

DISCUSSION QUESTIONS

Considering the issues covered in this chapter, we will now think about the supply chain and distribution issues that might arise should this new book become a roaring success.

- The first edition sells well in the UK market due to the connections and reputation of the author and the publisher. It very quickly overtakes its competitors for popularity and demand increases rapidly. With the new academic year only a few months away, how would you use market insights (see Chapter 2) to ensure there was enough stock in the right place at the right time?
- As the subject matter undergoes constant change there is a need for a fully updated second edition within a couple of years. However, with many heavily discounted used first edition copies in circulation there is a chance that buyers will opt to buy the older, cheaper version over the newer, updated version. Using the knowledge from Chapter 3, how would you provide a better value proposition for buyers to prefer the new edition?
- As global demand grows there is a need for specialist regional editions with a focus on local examples and case studies. Also, with the expense of printing and shipping textbooks across the world, it might be more sensible to consider local manufacture and distribution. How can the publisher do this through partnerships rather than through expensive and slow organic growth?

Develop Your Skills

What Is the Skill?

Risk management is the systematic identification, evaluation, and planning of a range of incidents that pose a threat to the organisation. It can only deal with known threats that the organisation might have previously experienced or that may have been experienced by other organisations. It cannot guarantee protection, but it can help to avoid the excessive effects of failure and go some way to protecting users and ensuring business continuity.

Why Is It Important?

Cyberthreats to individuals, organisations, and networks are ubiquitous and relentless. All of us at some point in our lives could be victims to online fraud, phishing attacks, data corruption or theft, ransomware, or DDOS attacks. Identifying and mitigating these threats is good business practice to ensure that resources are channelled towards developing a strong and loyal customer relationship, and not fire-fighting malware and hacker attacks.

How to Develop It

Step 1: Identify a hazard in your business and put it into a specific context. For example:

- an email is opened and the attachment which carried a virus was opened and downloaded;
- when travelling a user accessed an unsecured public Wi-Fi network, allowing their laptop to be accessed and the data cloned, leading to ransomware demands;
- your website and online systems have collapsed under a DDOS attack.

Step 2: Identify the people who are at risk from the hazard.

Step 3: What is the specific potential risk? In other words, how will the person be impacted by the hazard?

Step 4: Evaluate the likelihood of the event occurring (from 1 for low to 5 for high) and the potential severity of the impact (from 1 for low to 5 for high). Multiplying these numbers will give the risk rating. This helps to prioritise the risks. To increase visibility and focus upon the riskiest hazards they can be colour-coded as follows:

Risk rating: 1–8   Acceptable

Risk rating: 9–15   Improvable

Risk rating: 16–25 Unacceptable

Step 5: Describe measures to either prevent the event or to provide contingencies if it happens.

Step 6: Consider the residual risk after the controls have been considered using the same measures as described in Step 4.

Step 7: Share your assessment across the organisation to gain awareness and support for the resources and processes required to protect the business and its publics.

How to Apply It

Table 6.3 shows a worked example of the issues and methods described above.

Table 6.3 Worked risk analysis

Hazard	Persons at risk	Potential risk	Risk before controls	Controls to reduce risk	Residual risk after control
An email is opened and the attachment which carried a virus was opened and downloaded.	Sales and finance personnel	Loss of confidential data regarding orders and payments	Likelihood: 3 Severity: 4 Rating: 12	Staff training to recognise threats Virus software to embargo suspicious emails and attachments	Likelihood: 1 Severity: 3 Rating: 3
When travelling a user accessed an unsecured public Wi-Fi network, allowing their laptop to be accessed and the data cloned, leading to ransomware demands.	The individual user Data security personnel	Harassment and ransomware demands that cause anxiety	Likelihood: 4 Severity: 2 Rating: 8	Staff training to recognise and avoid unsecure networks Software alerts when unsecure wired and wireless networks are detected Change passwords and security protocols for data that may have been exposed	Likelihood: 2 Severity: 2 Rating: 4
Your website and online systems have collapsed under a DDOS attack.	Customers and end-users	Loss of supply could cause a critical failure in the customer's manufacturing process	Likelihood: 4 Severity: 5 Rating: 20	Back-up servers and parallel systems Buffer supply, such as emergency generators Hazard management protocols within the customer's organisation	Likelihood: 4 Severity: 3 Rating: 12

References

Allen, E., and Fjermestad, J. (2001). E-commerce marketing strategies: an integrated framework and case analysis. *Logistics Information Management*, **14**(1–2): 14–23.

Berman, B., and Thelen, S. (2018). Planning and implementing an effective omni-channel marketing program. *International Journal of Retail & Distribution Management*, **46**(7): 598–614.

Blackwell, R. D., Miniard, P. W., and Engel, J. F. (2001). *Consumer Behaviour*, 9th ed. Mason, OH: Southwestern.

Brabham, D. C. (2013). *Crowdsourcing*. Cambridge, MA: MIT Press.

Dagnino, G. B., and Padula, G. (2002). Coopetition strategy: towards a new kind of interfirm dynamics for value creation. EURAM 2nd Annual Conference, Stockholm School of Entrepreneurship, Sweden. Available from: http://ecsocman.hse.ru/data/977/644/1219/coopetition.pdf [Accessed 31 July 2019].

Dailey, D., and Starbird, K. (2014). Journalists as crowdsourcerers: responding to crisis by reporting with a crowd. *Computer Supported Cooperative Work*, **23**(4–6): 445–481.

Evans, P., and Wurster, T. (1999). Getting real about virtual commerce. *Harvard Business Review*, **77**(6): 84–94.

Hadlington, L. (2017). Human factors in cybersecurity: examining the link between Internet addiction, impulsivity, attitudes towards cybersecurity, and risky cyber-security behaviours. *Heliyon*, **3**(7): e00346.

Levine, S. S., and Prietula, M. J. (2014). Open collaboration for innovation: principles and performance. *Organization Science*, **25**(5): 1287–1571.

Porter, M. E. (2004). *Competitive Advantage: Creating and Sustaining Superior Performance*. New York: Free Press.

Riehle, D., Ellenberger, J., Menahem, T., et al. (2009). Open collaboration within corporations using software forges. *IEEE Software*, **26**(2): 52–58. Available from: https://ieeexplore.ieee.org/document/4786953 [Accessed 31 July 2019].

7 Promotion in a Complex Online Environment

Introduction

This chapter aims to dispel two common misunderstandings of marketing. The first is that 'marketing' is just advertising or sales. Hopefully, now that you have reached Chapter 7 via product, price, people (in the form of customers), process, physical experience, place, and partnerships, we may have convinced you that marketing is a complex, sophisticated, and dynamic discipline that adds significant value to organisations and the customers that they serve. The second misunderstanding is that simply by having a website or a social media account, your message is ubiquitous and compelling. Yes, your message will be ubiquitous since the Internet is a global entity. However, whether it even reaches the intended target audience and gains their attention can be a lottery given the plethora of media platforms used by many organisations to send out frequent marketing messages. So, while digital technologies offer simple and relatively cheap communications platforms, they can be hugely wasteful of time, effort, and money that the organisation could put to better use. This chapter will help you to focus upon a few disciplines to gain real value from your communications activity rather than being falsely content that once the 'send', 'post', or 'share' icon has been clicked, everything will be OK because our message is now 'out there'.

Learning Objectives

- Judge what constitutes an effective message.
- Recommend permission-based relationships.
- Appraise digital media channels.
- Evaluate interactive and integrated marketing communications.
- Consider the key characteristics of digital branding.
- Summarise how effective campaign design can limit costs and maximise impact.

CASE INSIGHT: CRISIS? WHAT CRISIS?

There is a rich history of mistakes, miscommunication, and mischief in corporate promotions where good intentions and seemingly sound marketing principles have spiralled into public relations (PR) disasters:

- In 2012 Mountain Dew's 'Dub the Dew' campaign, which aimed to crowdsource ideas from loyal customers, created an online poll for naming their new green apple-infused soft drink. The top-ranking among these names were 'Hitler Did Nothing Wrong', 'Gushing Granny', and 'Frapple'. Mountain Dew's subsequent statement claimed that 'Dub the Dew' was a local market promotional campaign created by one of their customers, not Mountain Dew, and closed it down.
- After the 2017 Boston Marathon Adidas sent an email to participants congratulating them for surviving. Considering there was a bombing at the race in 2013 that led to three deaths and hundreds of injuries, people took to social media about the thoughtless subject line, and the company quickly apologised.
- Also in 2017, United Airlines, faced with an overbooked flight, demanded that an elderly doctor leave one of its planes. When he refused, United's security personnel intervened, violently dragging the man from the plane in full view of everyone's camera phones. United's CEO, Oscar Munoz, made the situation worse by saying he apologised 'for having to re-accommodate these customers'.
- In 2018, Lockheed Martin, the world's largest weapons maker, tweeted 'Do you have an amazing photo of one of our products? Tag us in your pic and we may feature it during our upcoming #WorldPhotoDay celebration on Aug. 19!' Pictures were submitted showing the impact of its weapons, including an image of bloody UNICEF backpacks belonging to children killed in Yemen with a bomb made by the company. Lockheed Martin later deleted the tweet.

Questions

- Were the companies' public responses adequate for the offence that they caused?
- What internal processes would have helped the organisations avoid such errors?
- In your own experience, is there 'no such thing as bad publicity'?

7.1   The Message and its Purpose

Fill (2013) defines marketing communications as 'a management process through which an organisation attempts to engage with its various audiences'. By understanding an audience's communications environment, organisations seek to develop and present messages for their target customer groups. These messages need to command the intended receiver's attention and to be so compelling as to ensure a timely and positive response. This requires a clear and consistent approach to the 'call to action' (i.e., the response that the stimulus of the message is trying to elicit) that aligns with the organisation's goals for the relationship, which we explored in Chapter 5. The messages may seek to do the following:

- **Approach** customers with whom the organisation has no previous, or a lapsed, relationship with a view to renewing awareness of the organisation and its products and registering a point of contact to pursue the action.
  Call to action: 'Get in touch!'
  Digital stimulus or response may include: website visit, app download, social media post 'like', store locator, offer of a free sample.
- **Establish** a relationship based on a satisfying customer experience.
  Call to action: 'Make a purchase!'
  Digital stimulus or response may include: create a user account on the website/app (rather than checking out as a guest), sign up to a mailing list, follow a social media account, 'buy it now' button, coupon downloads, limited time special offers.
  Secure product loyalty by the repurchase of the same or similar products.
  Call to action: 'Buy again!'
  Digital stimulus or response may include: leave a product review, set up a repeat order.
- **Expand** the relationship to the purchase of unrelated products which further demonstrates the enhanced level of trust between the organisation and its customers.
  Call to action: 'Buy something else!'
  Digital stimulus or response may include: accept a recommended purchase ('other customers who bought this product also bought …'), buy a recommended product package (e.g., a collection of books by a single author or a box set of movies), a complementary product purchase (e.g., a belt with a pair of trousers).
- **Advocate** to their friends on the organisation's behalf through electronic word-of-mouth (eWOM), and, potentially, social media.

Call to action: 'Tell others about us!'

Digital stimulus or response may include: share purchases, product/company recommendations, and specific product feedback on social media, either as a general post or tagged with specific contacts in mind.

However, it would be easy to get carried away with the personalisation and targeting potential of digital communications. Try as we might to craft attention-grabbing and compelling messages for customers who we believe will benefit from our products, we must have a clear understanding of the processes by which organisations and customers communicate with each other on a message-by-message basis.

7.2   The Communication Environment

While every message will have a specific intent, it will also exist within a complex and noisy environment that creates the potential for mis-targeting, misinterpretation, distortion, and loss. The Shannon and Weaver (1962) model of communication is a classic interpretation of the process and its complications, which we can use to identify potential failure points, and opportunities, in the digital communications process:

* **Message encoding and decoding:** Keyword analytics will help us to understand enduringly popular, or merely just currently trending, terms that our target customer profile group or segment will recognise. Translation devices, although not entirely reliable in accurately representing the intended sentiment, can help copywriters to develop effective material. Campaign testing, particularly for new markets with languages and cultures different from our own, should be used to check the idea and its execution.
* **Transmission and feedback** may not always happen via the same media channel. For example, the success of pop-up adds may be measured via click-through rates. In contrast, the success of social media posts may be principally measured via likes, comments, and shares, rather than whether they result in a purchase in the short term.
* **Noise** interferes with effective communication in the following ways:
  - volume, variety, and frequency of competing online messages;
  - volume, variety, and frequency of competing offline messages;
  - poor wired or wireless connectivity resulting in inaccessibility, slow download, or poor image resolution;

- environmental noise will interfere with audio unless subtitles are provided;
- broken links included in messages;
- too many images which do not download or dominate devices, requiring extensive scrolling to find the core of the message; and
- alerts and notifications interrupting the user's attention.

DIGITAL INSIGHT 7.1 Do I Have Your Attention?

Any parent, partner, friend, or workplace supervisor will lament that attention spans are shortening. Is it all the fault of social media or is it a natural phase in the evolutionary process as our cognitive processes try to adapt to complex lives and communications? How much attention is enough? Psychologists identified the phenomenon of heuristics (also called 'mental shortcuts' or 'rules of thumb') which are efficient mental processes that help humans solve problems and learn new concepts. These processes make problems less complex by ignoring some of the information that's coming into the brain, either consciously or unconsciously. So, are our narrowing attention spans less about receiving, processing, and deciding based on data inputs and more about social etiquette as most of our relationships and interactions become encoded through screens and emojis, allowing for simpler, less nuanced communication?

7.3 The Tailoring Potential of Digital Media

Godin's (2007) work champions a 'Permission Marketing' approach which has the customer's wants, needs, and preferences in mind. The key principles of this approach are that the communication must be anticipated (i.e., not interruption marketing), relevant (i.e., not spam), personal (i.e., tailored to the recipient's preferences, requiring opt-in but giving the opportunity to opt-out at any stage), and timely (based on past decision behaviours and an understanding of when need is likely to arise). Godin distils this philosophy into the key 'right-touching' guidelines and test questions that we should ask ourselves when designing and evaluating a communications transmission schedule (Table 7.1).

Table 7.1 The tailoring potential of digital media

Godin's 'right-touching' guidelines	How digital technologies can support
'A multichannel communications strategy	Digitisation allows for the careful planning and release of multiple interconnected campaigns within an overall plan.
customised for individual prospects and customers forming segments	Customer analytics via steady-state algorithms augmented by machine learning gives insight into patterns of behaviour of individuals and their contacts.
across a defined customer lifecycle	Not all customers have the same needs or behave in the same way. Customer relationship management (CRM) protocols help to market to individuals rather than homogeneous groups.
which delivers the right message	Key word analytics and message testing help us to get the wording right.
featuring the right value proposition (product, service, or experience)	Connecting the CRM insight with the priorities of the business to sell the product it is manufacturing and storing to create value (most often in the form of profit) for investors. At this point marketing is not simply a 'selling' process but an integral operation of an effective and efficient organisation.
with the right tone	Using words and images to stimulate the required call to action depending upon where customers are in their decision-making process.
at the right time or context	Matching the likelihood of a customer responding to a call to action with the needs and capabilities of the business (i.e., if we get the order do we have the stock and logistics to deliver it in the required timescale?)
with the right frequency and interval	There is a careful balance to be created between not over-communicating (which might lead to boredom, or even hostility from customers due to the perceived nuisance) and not under-communicating (meaning that potential customers forget about you). Databases and analytics are core to getting this right.
using the right media/communications channels	Business analytics will track the effectiveness of campaigns and tactical approaches, helping the digital marketer to understand which 'levers to pull' to get the desired result from a situation.
to achieve the right balance of value between both parties.'	A combined business analytics effort to see if we have satisfied and loyal customers at the scale and scope that are required for the sustained success of the business.

7.4   Characteristics of Digital Media

The function of digital communication is nothing new. For many years we have used advertising, publicity, and personal selling to build relationships with segments and individual customers which range from the 'broad and shallow' approach of mass display advertising and TV and radio broadcasts aimed at building and maintaining customer awareness, to 'narrow and deep' relationships through personal selling and aftersales customer service operations which aim to maintain loyalty which can also be expanded into the purchase of other products. Based on the work of Peppers et al. (1999), McDonald and Wilson (1999), and Chaffey and Ellis-Chadwick (2016) we can identify the key ways in which communications technology has changed how suppliers and customers interact:

- **Ubiquity:** due to multiple software (e.g., website, app, social media) and hardware (e.g., smartphone, tablet, TV, laptop, desktop) platforms. This is amplified by the wide reach and 'always on' nature of the Internet.
- **Insight:** with significantly improved market transparency for the customer, vast sources of market and customer data available to the supplier, and access to widely available analytics tools to create meaning from this data, suppliers are in an unprecedented position to understand and influence consumer behaviour.
- **Leadership:** interactions are as likely to be initiated by customers as they are suppliers, which makes customers less passive in the process and more likely to contribute, but not necessarily in the ways that the supplier hoped or expected.
- **Complexity:** communications could be one-to-many (e.g., broadcast via a website or app), one-to-some (e.g., targeted activity through database profiling), one-to-one (e.g., individualised social media chat), and many-to-many (e.g., group conversations within online communities). This also includes the growing role of intermediaries, infomediaries, and affiliates, as discussed in Chapter 6.

For an overview of the complex choice of media platforms and how they relate in terms of level of leadership of the supplier–customer interaction, see Figure 7.1. Some of these elements have been explored in previous chapters.

Advertising is a broadly targeted mass communication approach which is designed to build company, brand, or product awareness through maximising exposure. It is highly impersonal but can communicate large amounts of information to a wide audience of users and non-users. Attention, recollection, and conversion rates are low due to low customer involvement and the significant

One-way ←――――――――――――――――――――――――――――――――→ Two-way

Advertising	Publicity	Affiliations	Sales promotion	Direct marketing	Personal selling	Customer service
Company websites	Blogs	Event-specific interactive displays	Product reviews	Apps	Recommendations	Downloadable/ saveable content
Pop-up ads	Online communities		Rebates and price discounts	Email	Augmented reality	
Banner ads	Polls	Comparison sites		Newsletter	Virtual reality	Loyalty programmes
News sites	Webinars		Samples, coupons, and	Messaging	Multimedia experiences	
Online publications	Live broadcasts	Third-party sellers	gifts	Location-based		One-click purchases
		Resellers	Competitions		Analytics	Easy return and replace procedure
On-demand TV/radio		Group discounts	Auctions		User preferences	
					Intelligent search	
					Virtual assistant/ chatbots	FAQs

Figure 7.1 The digital promotional mix.

number of competing messages. **Publicity** relies less on the selling of a specific product than on the sharing of stories associated with it, such as novelty and high levels of customer benefit, or associations with other popular brands – for example, by sponsoring the arts, sports teams, or community organisations. The purpose here is to access large segments and to create positive associations with the brand in the minds of the potential customer. **Affiliations** were explored in Chapter 6 and benefit from a reciprocal co-marketing approach to accessing markets in an efficient manner. **Sales promotion** activities are often linked to a specific product or range for a specific timescale (e.g., at product launch or product retirement). Their aim is to generate sales, but due to the targeted communications effort and offering of discounts, these might be at break-even or loss. **Direct marketing** is a dated term which still suffers from the poor image of junk mail and spam emails. It is, if properly done using a 'right-touching' approach, a highly effective promotional activity since it relies on insight gained by the seller on the past behaviours and preferences of the recipient. **Personal selling** is greatly aided by a selection of CRM and sales management tools, many of which can be automated, allowing the greater use of virtual sales agents (or chatbots) to improve that organisation's availability and responsiveness in dealing with customer enquiries. **Customer service** is not traditionally considered to be part of the traditional promotional mix. However, with more of a shift away from physical retail outlets to online purchases there is an increased propensity to return items that are no longer wanted (i.e., they may have been an impulse purchase) or are not what the buyer expected in terms of their feel, touch, or look (e.g., clothes, accessories, furniture). This is a crucial process to establish customer loyalty and build high levels of post-purchase satisfaction that can lead to customers sharing their good experiences as recommendations within their online communities.

7.5   Categorising Digital Media

We will now focus on some of the key media platforms that are available for the organisation to deploy. You may have noticed that the promotional efforts of a seller can be driven and facilitated across a range of marketing disciplines. For example, the bundling of complementary products with associated special offers if done well can build the relationship; if done poorly it can lead to the seller being regarded as a nuisance and the buyer being more distanced in their relationship (see Chapter 3). The theme, tone, and timing of our communications, if greatly out of step with the customer's attitudes and behaviour, can affect their preferences and their propensity to buy (see Chapter 4). The context in which the customer buys – online or offline – can greatly affect their perceived experience (see Chapter 5). The channels used by an organisation can affect the accuracy and consistency of their message to different audiences (see Chapter 6). While this broad mix gives us comprehensive representation across multiple channels, such exposure comes at the risk of a potential loss of control of the message and its transmission. It is possible to differentiate within the digital promotional mix between media that is owned, paid, shared, and earned (Table 7.2).

Table 7.2 Comparing levels of digital media ownership and control				
	Owned	Paid	Shared	Earned
Definition	Hosting, structure, and content is under the exclusive control of the organisation	Message exposure in a specific place and time is rented by the organisation	Content which is designed to be viral	Public feedback on satisfying (or unsatisfying) customer experiences
Examples	Website, app, email, messenger	Advertising, affiliations, games, samples, coupons	Blogs, social media	Reviews, recommendations, links
Purpose	Global presentation of a consistent generic message	Promote a specific product or range in a limited timescale	Generate positive community engagement and feedback	Maximise positive and manage poor customer experiences before they damage community attitudes
Effectiveness	Low	Medium	Medium	High
Efficiency	High	Low	High	High

It is important when considering these different channels to be aware of their different purposes and relevance to the customer. While social media channels might be 'free', they should be carefully nurtured to ensure the continuity of brand values and messages from the 'owned' and 'paid' media efforts. Social media also acts as a message amplifier, which enables you to reach more potential customers via a more credible source (i.e., recommendations by fellow users). When positive messages are being shared, this is good news. When negative news and opinions are being shared, it is important to act promptly and clearly, since ignoring or counterattacking is likely to lead to escalated levels of customer dissatisfaction, and the discouragement of potential customers.

RESEARCH INSIGHT 7.1 Online vs Offline Word-of-Mouth Effects

Drozdenko, R., and Coelho, D. (2016). Sentiment of online reviews are consistent with conventional word of mouth effects. *International Journal of Business, Marketing, and Decision Sciences*, 9(1): 55–69.

With the increased migration of promotional spending from offline to online channels, it is time to evaluate the attendant word-of-mouth (WOM) behaviour change in relation to this switch to digital media. While the generic online behaviour of consumers is well documented, there is little insight into how the posting of favourable and unfavourable reviews differ by product category. Overall, it was discovered that consumers were more likely to write a favourable review and there were significant interactions of gender with product type and sentiment type. From a psychological perspective, traits such as self-acceptance, positive attitude, and peer conformity were related to posting reviews.

7.6   Website and Search Engines

As discussed in Chapter 1, individual websites are hosted on the servers of the World Wide Web, which communicate via the software protocols of the Internet. If a user knows the website they want to visit, then they will input the uniform resource locator (URL) into the browser's address bar and will be directed to the desired site and page. If you are a frequent visitor, then the cookies on your device will inform your browser of the desired page by auto-completing the search after the input of only a partial URL. However, if you do not know the specific seller, brand, or page that carries the information you need then you will type the keywords into your browser's search bar. Your browser will then return a link to every site that is relevant to the keywords used in your search, a list of results that may stretch to many thousands of options. To be picked up by the search engine, the supplier needs to embed certain keywords, either as actual content or as page or image descriptions known as meta-tags, which the search engine will recognise as being pertinent to the keyword search. This process is known as **search engine optimisation.**

Given the significant range of available choices, the search engine will need to decide in which order they will be presented to the viewer. Initially they are ordered organically based on the presence of all or some of the keywords, but browser search history cookies and location data from the user will help the search engine to further refine and prioritise the results organically (i.e., with no external interference). However, search engine companies quickly recognised the potential to offer a preferential service to sellers and generate significant incomes by 'selling' keywords based on demand to the highest bidder, which would allow the advertiser's search return to appear above that of a competitor who perhaps did not bid for the same keywords or opted for only organic unboosted returns for their webpages. The target here is to appear on the first page of the search engine results, which is normally in the top 10 returns. This process is known as **search engine marketing.**

Following on from the completed search, should the user then click on the organisation's promoted link, this will trigger a payment of the agreed sum, a process known as **pay per click.** There are several additional factors within the organisation's control which will affect how well such campaigns succeed in their goals:

- **Budget size and distribution:** when designing a campaign, the search engine will ask the advertiser to set a maximum budget, a period over which the campaign runs, and where the spending should be concentrated to benefit from potential peak interest. For example, if you are a local restaurant that has a lunchtime special menu, then perhaps you would tailor your campaign to run from 11.00 a.m., when customers may be considering where to eat. While it is a straightforward task to predict customers' daily routines, it begins to get more complex when considering their weekly, monthly, and annual routines. If you represented a supermarket, when might you promote your special offers that might fit in with the weekly grocery shop? Friday afternoon, maybe, on the assumption that shoppers will pop in on the way home from work. Likewise, if you were a recruitment company, when would you advertise your jobs? Sunday afternoon or Monday morning may be popular, when many employees are facing a long week at work because they feel it is time for a change and to try another role. When it comes to bigger treats like clothes or a trip to the theatre, you might aim for when users may have more disposable income, say in the last few days of the month soon after their salary has been paid. Annual purchase patterns can also be planned for. Traditionally in the UK, the Christmas and New Year festive period has been popular, when the weather is cold, wet, and dark, to promote next year's summer holidays and gym membership (when we all promise to get fitter and healthier next year).

- **Quality of the design and content:** while the budget will influence placement of the search result, it is its creative qualities that will add to the customer experience, encouraging users to visit the link. The associated metric here is click-through rate (CTR). The website's designers need to ensure minimum service outages and that there is enough server capacity to handle all the likely requests that the campaign could generate. The creative team will ensure the appropriate content, keywords, meta-tags, images, and accessible layouts are used. They will also determine the landing page to which the visitor will be routed to quickly deal with their query, since the homepage might not be the relevant response to every query. The webmasters will ensure that all live pages within the website are up-to-date, and that all links to additional content or links to other pages are working. Search engines will assess your site for these elements, allocating a *quality score*, which will augment your budgeted campaign to improve visibility to whoever is doing the search.

7.7   Online Display Advertising

Any communication medium that commands access to a sizeable and loyal audience will have the potential to attract significant revenues from a range of advertisers who wish to access that audience, whether they are based on events such as sports and music, destinations such as cities or other popular tourist destinations, print such as high-selling newspapers or magazines, or on commercial TV, where slots next to shows with high viewing figures sell for significant amounts. Internet advertising mimics many of the behaviours of the offline world, particularly in relation to the placement of static advertisements within websites. However, where the Internet has a significant advantage is in dynamic advertising, which tailors the user experience based on their recent purchase history and search behaviours. While it can be a little disconcerting when you are searching for a product in your web browser or in an online store for that product to then appear in your social media news feed, it is an example of your user history cookies being utilised across multiple sites and platforms. While advertising helps the organisation to generate instant sales, change attitudes, reinforce attitudes, and raise awareness, it also allows for a repetition of the message to a wide audience. However, there is competing research on the effectiveness of online advertising. Winer and Ilfeld (2002) found that online advertising leads to more website traffic, but may not increase brand awareness, whereas Drèze and Hussherr (2003) found display advertisements increase brand awareness and subsequent recall. Display advertising that is interactive, in that it is hyperlinked to rich content such as a product page, videos, enquiry pages, or social media sharing, comes in a range of formats.

Banner advertisements that are embedded within a webpage are available in a range of display formats to fit with the budget and placement preferences of the advertiser. As with any advertising effort, there is no guarantee of success. Chatterjee et al. (2003) found the customers' responses to banner advertisements depend on the frequency, cumulative exposure, and elapsed time since the last click. As the same banner advertisement is repeatedly shown to the customer, they are less likely to click on it. Customers who revisit after a longer timeframe are more likely to click on banner advertisements than those with a shorter revisit interval. That is, customers who are new to a display advertisement, or less frequently exposed to it, are more likely to click. Manchanda et al. (2006) showed that a greater number of exposures to a banner advertisement accelerates a purchase.

It is important to consider the relevance of the advertising content to the audience of the hosting websites. The tailoring potential offered by website and app data analytics has given rise to the practice of **native advertising**, which matches the advertisements with the form and style of the platform upon which it appears, with the use of the term 'native' referring to the coherence of the content with the other media that appear on the platform. This approach aims for consistency of language and tone of voice between the owned content of the website, designed by their own developers, and the advertising portion. The power within native advertising is to inhibit consumers' recognition by blending the advertisement into the native content of the platform, making many consumers unaware they are looking at an advertisement to begin with. To comply with trading regulations, and to avoid unfairly misleading the consumer, there is often a requirement for the publisher to state clearly that the content is sponsored and is not part of the editorial output.

Other non-embedded forms of advertising are also available on the Internet, over which there is a variable relationship between website owners, advertisers, and consumers. **Pop-up advertisements** are a cheap and effective medium for advertisers, a highly effective way to monetise free content for website owners, or an interruption and nuisance to customers. Pop-ups occur separately to the desired content, drawing the viewer's attention away for another purpose, in a manner dissimilar to that of native advertising.

With the prevailing model on the Internet that users will generally not pay for basic content (i.e., the freemium model), website owners need to find a way to generate income to sustain the venture until it can charge users a fee for membership, which opens up premium content free of advertising. Most users prefer the free access to content on the acceptance that they may engage with the advertising content, but have a choice to ignore it if it's not relevant or of interest to them. The main forms of this interruption advertising include *interstitial banners*, which are shown between pages on a website; *floating advertisements*, which open in a smaller window and appear in a layer over the content; *wallpaper advertisements*, which change the background of a webpage; and introductory content on free video sites, such as YouTube, that gives the viewer up to five seconds of additional content until they can skip the advertisement to watch the desired content. The risk with using pop-up advertising is that it is unexpected, thereby creating a sometimes-unwelcome interruption to the user experience. This may give rise to irritation with the brand, which is counterproductive to the aims of any promotional campaign. However, in response to consumer complaints about this practice, web browsers offer an ad-blocking function within their user preferences which may force websites to charge for content to bridge potentially lost income from the reluctance of advertisers to pay for pop-up campaigns that can be skipped by the user.

DIGITAL INSIGHT 7.2 Eye Tracking for User Experience Design

We make 3–5 eye movements per second, and these movements are crucial in helping us deal with the vast amounts of information we encounter in our everyday lives. Through the development of eye tracking technology it has become possible to measure these movements, and to understand how we attend to and process the visual information we encounter. The seminal works of Bergstrom and Schall (2014) and Holmqvist et al. (2015) explore the many applications of eye tracking to better understand how users view and interact with technology. Eye tracking research is utilised in the design and development of websites, games, mobile devices, large screen displays, and video game consoles. Eye tracking helps us to understand viewers' behaviours in relation to where they are looking, how long they are looking, what parts they miss out, and how they are navigating the length of the page. Tracking and heat map reports capture the intensity (Figure 7.2) and the direction (Figure 7.3) of the viewer's attention, often leading to improved design.

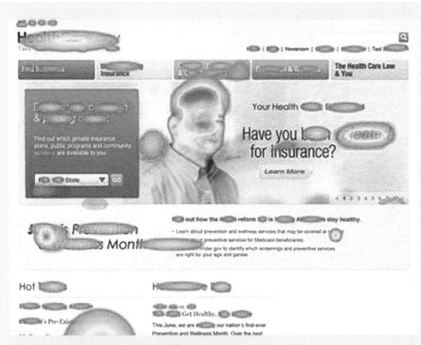

Figure 7.2 Heat map example (Usability.gov, 2019).

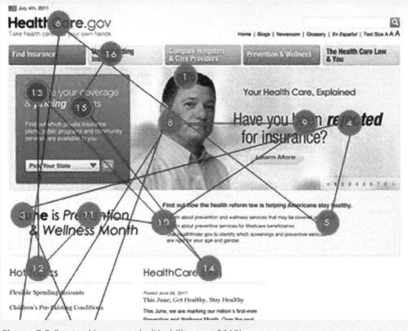

Figure 7.3 Eye tracking example (Usability.gov, 2019).

7.8   Social Media

This section connects to Chapter 4, which discussed the role of online communities and how users behave within them in terms of group power and influence through eWOM, sometimes also known as 'word of mouse'. Social media is a complex field, with new platforms arriving frequently. While it is easy to prefer a few of our preferred platforms, such as Facebook, LinkedIn, Twitter, YouTube, Instagram, Snapchat, and WeChat, to be effective communicators we need to have a clear understanding of the form and function of this important part of the promotional mix. The key distinction to be drawn is between content-driven platforms whose key purpose is the creation and dissemination of user-generated content (i.e., a **'push'** or **'input'** model of communication), as considered by Cavazza (2021), and user-driven platforms whose key purpose is to channel and harvest this content to serve the specific purposes of the consumer (i.e., a **'pull'** or **'output'** model of communication), as considered by Tuten and Solomon (2017).

Cavazza (2021) offers an illustration of the push or input social media functions (Figure 7.4), which provide the foundations of communication activity by creating and placing content in a way that audiences can interact with to a greater or lesser degree:

- **Publishing** of content in the form of commentary (e.g., blogs and posts), written documents (e.g., PDF files), images (e.g., photos, illustrations, and

Figure 7.4 Social media landscape (Cavazza, 2021). Used by permission of Frederic Cavazza.

animation), audio (e.g., podcasts, music), and film (e.g., livestreams and vodcasts). This material is rich and varied in both its range of content and its quality of presentation.

- **Sharing** involves the connection of users with common interests. These may be quite passive in nature (e.g., the sharing of information about an entertainment event or a special offer purchase) and can be largely driven by the entertainment value of the content.
- **Networking** involves the connection of users with common objectives. This takes place within online communities that are formal (e.g., LinkedIn, where the objective is principally career and business development) or informal (e.g., a group of parents sharing educational ideas to aid child and family development).
- **Messaging** of short communications has gradually shifted from PC-based email and mobile phone-based text services to messaging apps such as WhatsApp, Facebook Messenger, WeChat, and Snapchat. This has occurred as messaging becomes less of a casual activity and instead is preferred over telephone calls due its ease, speed, and the utility offered by apps to engage in and moderate many concurrent conversations.
- **Discussing** differs from messaging in its focus upon a core theme or specific content. Discussion forums are particularly popular for user reviews, ranking, and feedback. They also serve to galvanise opinion on political, community, or environmental issues. These platforms allow more focused engagement than discussion, but a less action-based approach to addressing these issues than there would be via collaboration.
- **Collaborating** is a formal arrangement towards the achievement of a key output or goal. Such arrangements can be based on an equal relationship and so are co-operative in nature (e.g., the sharing of information to achieve a common approach) or they may involve crowdsourcing activity such as microtasking or macrotasking.

The work of Tuten and Solomon (2017) focuses on the purpose and function of social media content and platforms in the eyes of the customer. This utility-based approach determines the key purposes, or zones, of social media activity:

- **Social community:** The purpose is to recruit, connect with, and share relevant material and information to a group of individuals with a common purpose. Objectives may be creative, community, or professional in nature. Examples of platforms include Twitter, Facebook, and LinkedIn.

- **Social commerce:** Goods and services are traded on a peer-to-peer basis (e.g., eBay), through independent infomediaries (e.g., TripAdvisor, Yelp), and through affiliates (e.g., Groupon). Contributors share their opinions and recommendations of suppliers that offer value for money to customers.
- **Social publishing:** Contributors can post content or information about a certain topic that is referenced using keywords and/or hashtags, which enables users with a specific interest to source relevant input from the broader community. Examples include BlogSpot, Tumblr, Flickr, SlideShare, and YouTube.
- **Social entertainment:** These activities comprise the social media channels that are used for play, enjoyment, and entertainment. This includes games, art, and videos. Platforms include MySpace, Instagram, and Come2play.

Social media is a substantial subject, with the frequent arrival, consolidation, and obsolescence of competing platforms. The larger media companies, seeing the popularity and versatility of this medium, will continue trying to launch or acquire 'killer apps' which dominate the market for the long term. But what we have seen is the evolution of both the technologies and the audiences that they serve. For example, when Facebook launched it was highly popular with younger audiences. However, as these users began to be joined online by their parents, it became a less 'cool' place to hang out with their peers and instead they migrated to other platforms such as Snapchat.

As professional marketers your success will be determined by the range of tools that you have, and how skilfully you deploy them to address a specific opportunity or threat. Social media is often poorly defined and poorly deployed, leading to good, bad, or indifferent results. However, the brand-building potential and community-based nature of these multiple and complex platforms make them seem like the 'silver bullet' for every marketing situation. To ensure fitness for purpose when considering social media, it is important to remember that, on one hand, it is possible to reach a large audience at a relatively low cost; on the other hand, it can be difficult to control targeting and the brand risks damage since unsolicited messages may be received. So, when discussing social media, let's make sure that we understand the purpose, platforms, and processes to get the best possible value for both our organisation and our users.

DIGITAL INSIGHT 7.3 **How to Manage a Social Media Crisis: A Practical Guide for Brands**

On social media things can move blindingly fast, leading to a publicity crisis that seems to come out of nowhere. How can we prepare in advance, either to minimise the effect of the error, or to avoid it altogether? Here are some tips developed by the popular social media aggregation service Hootsuite (2019):

1. Create a social media policy that covers copyright with regard to the use of third-party content, privacy regarding the status of public versus private conversation, confidentiality of sensitive information and clarification of what can be shared, and brand voice to be clear of the level of formality on behalf of the organisation in social media interactions.
2. Use social listening to identify potential issues before they turn into a crisis. Social listening programs can help you to monitor brand mentions, which can be a positive or negative outcome, but you should also be monitoring social sentiment.
3. Be clear what counts as a crisis, since that sudden spike in social media mentions could be a good thing – that's why you should get a more accurate picture via sentiment analysis. For negative comments to count as a crisis there also needs to be potential long-term damage to your brand.
4. Prepare a communication plan which automatically kicks in when a crisis is triggered. Responses should be swift, moderate, and clear, not an overreaction, or a lack of response which shows that you just don't care. The plan should make clear who is responsible, how updates will be communicated internally, and what are the pre-approved responses.
5. Engage, but don't argue, so keep it short and avoid getting pulled into a long public discussion of what went wrong. If the respondent persists, try to move it to more private communication such as phone or email.
6. Learn from the experience by debriefing the team and examining the detailed records of what happened, and whether it worked or not. Are new guidelines or responses required?

7.9 Databases

The sales function within an organisation, through a variety of CRM systems, will carry a significant amount of customer-specific data that can be used to initiate and maintain direct customer contact. Such a relationship can be personalised based on the user's communications preferences (i.e., post, phone call, text message, or email), tailored to meet their specific interests, and trackable in its effectiveness to achieve the desired 'call to action'. The ease with which databases can be built (based on existing in-house information or through the purchase of third-party databases) and the low cost and high scalability of email and text messaging platforms make this a popular approach used by many organisations, which can lead to excessive 'noise' in the communications process, with users receiving too many messages and too much information which at best are ignored or at worst succeed in building user hostility to nuisance organisations. Additionally, with the increased focus upon cybersecurity, antivirus software programs scan incoming emails to ascertain the risks of potentially malicious content from known and unknown users. Spam filters will be constantly updated by your security software providers, so make sure that you sign up for automatic updates which will include new security patches.

Emails can carry large amounts of information, attachments, and hyperlinks to other sites, enabling a comprehensive approach/response to the customer. Ansari and Mela (2003) showed that emails with customised design and content can increase website traffic. However, firms should not overuse email communication. Ansari et al. (2008) found the overuse of email targeting could have a negative impact. Thus, one of the key issues in email approaches, given the volume of other solicited and unsolicited messages that are competing for the customer's attention, is to get the customer's attention and convince them to open the message and read the content. This will depend largely on the relevance and timing of the message, but the sender can aid their purpose by clearly stating the theme and 'call to action' of the message as a priority. Email offers significant analytics potential which can provide feedback in real time on the delivery rate, opening rate, CTR, and unsubscribe requests from campaigns. Response rates can be very low from such campaigns, in some cases less than 5 per cent, which is an important consideration when determining the size of the target audience, the 'call to action', and how to evaluate the relative success of the campaign against creative or targeting criteria. This low response rate creates a dilemma when maintaining database lists. Should the fact that the recipients repeatedly fail to engage with messages mean that they are no longer potential customers, or their contact information is out of date? What percentage of unsubscribe requests is standard and at what number should we begin to reconsider our value proposition, creative strategy, or targeting approach?

Mobile text messaging can build relationships by sending permission-based information where consumers want to receive it. This can include product service reminders (e.g., for your car or your domestic gas appliances), confirmation of appointment (e.g., to see your physician or to attend a planned business meeting), travel information (e.g., flight or train tickets, or notifications of travel delays), or release alerts for entertainment events (e.g., new movies, albums, festivals, concerts, or theatre shows).

With the increased migration from PC-based systems such as email and browsers to app-based communications which offer a richer and easier customer experience, in turn allowing for greater customer insight using analytics, the use of traditional database marketing methods, while important, is in decline.

RESEARCH INSIGHT 7.2 Customer Databases: In Whom We Trust?

Martin, K. (2018). The penalty for privacy violations: How privacy violations impact trust online. *Journal of Business Research*, 82: 103–116.

Do online customers have an explicit expectation of information privacy or is permission to use their data implicit within their online interactions? With privacy legislation in some jurisdictions (see Chapter 2 and the discussion of GDPR) information misuse can be a significant risk both to the user and to the organisation. This study measures the relative importance of violating privacy expectations and the effect upon levels of consumers' trust in a website and finds that violations of these privacy expectations, specifically the secondary uses of information, diminish trust in the integrity and ability of the offending organisation. Violations of privacy may place firms in a downward trust spiral by decreasing trust in the firm.

7.10 Long-Term Campaigns: Branding

Branding seeks to establish a unique name and image for a product in consumers' minds, which they associate with a satisfying experience, preferably to be shared with others. It aims to establish a significant and differentiated presence in the market that attracts and retains loyal customers. Viewed holistically (i.e., online and offline branding activities) branding activities are driven by:

- **Domain:** key target markets, where the brand competes.
  Digital contribution: using market and customer analytics to understand the behaviours and potential of different groups of customers and

articulate this back to the organisation in a way that can lead to positive augmentations to the eight drivers of digital marketing.

- **Heritage:** the background and culture of the brand.
  Digital contribution: website pages that explain the origins of the organisation and the milestones in its development. Introductions to the key people explaining their history, roles, and interests. Telling the story of the brand through its people creates an authentic and compelling narrative.

- **Values:** the core characteristics (e.g., price, quality, performance).
  Digital contribution: this is reflected in the questions that we ask of customers and the questions that we ask of ourselves. What are the key messages that we push to customers? Is it any combination of 'we're cheap', 'we're good', 'we're fast', 'we're helpful'? Equally, how we benchmark our own performance internally is a telling reflection of our values. Whether we value sales growth, profitability, loyalty, or a sense of community and sharing will all have a big impact upon the organisation's values. Customer service and order fulfilment performance will serve to heighten or erode the brand's image.

- **Assets:** distinctive names, symbols, images.
  Digital contribution: artefacts such as logos, images, photos, illustrations, documents, videos, and podcasts create a rich online experience for customers. Interactive and immersive technologies such as personalisation, augmented reality, and artificial reality create a more powerful sensory experience.

- **Personality:** the character of the brand.
  Digital contribution: character is best understood by observing behaviour. There is no better way to do this both historically and in real time than through social media feeds (posts and responses), particularly in challenging times such as a product or process failure. Is the brand empathetic, responsive, and humble, or reticent, slow, and arrogant? Site design, flexibility, and interactivity play important roles in the perception of personality.

- **Reflection:** how the customer perceives themselves because of buying the brand.
  Digital contribution: customer satisfaction and dissatisfaction are highly visible, given the potential for direct response in terms of product comments and ratings, and messaging to the company. Indirect feedback via user-to-user and user-to-community comments is harder to monitor and control, but can be highly influential upon existing and potential customers.

Within a medium with such a high potential for measurement – even as we have discussed the questionable value of some of these measures in

Chapter 2 – as the Internet, it is sensible to consider how we might consolidate a wide range of communications activities to give an overall assessment of online brand performance. The work of Christodoulides et al. (2006) provides a series of measures where customer sentiment can be self-measured via a Likert scale (Likert, 1932) – that is, strongly agree, agree, neutral, disagree, strongly disagree – and analysed by the organisation.

1. Emotional Connection
    Q1:   I feel related to the type of people who are [X]'s customers.
    Q2:   I feel as though [X] actually cares about me.
    Q3:   I feel as though [X] really understands me.
2. Online Experience
    Q4:   [X]'s website provides easy-to-follow search paths.
    Q5:   I never feel lost when navigating through [X]'s website.
    Q6:   I was able to find the information I wanted without any delay.
3. Responsive Service Nature
    Q7:   [X] is willing and ready to respond to customer needs.
    Q8:   [X]'s website gives visitors the opportunity to 'talk back' to [X].
4. Trust
    Q9:   I trust [X] to keep my personal information safe.
    Q10: I feel safe in my transactions with [X].
5. Fulfilment
    Q11: I got what I ordered from [X]'s website.
    Q12: The product was delivered by the time promised by [X].

The ideal end-state for a branding campaign is to create advocates – that is, customers who have favourable perceptions of the brand who will talk favourably about a brand to their acquaintances to help generate awareness of the brand or influence purchase intentions (see Chapter 5). This is supported by compelling, interactive experiences which include rich media that reflects the brand and considers how the site will influence the sales cycle by encouraging product trialling.

RESEARCH INSIGHT 7.3 Digital Darwinism

Bughin, J. (2015). Brand success in an era of Digital Darwinism. *McKinsey Quarterly*. February.

This paper studies the relationship between the level of digitisation across the consumer's decision journey and the likelihood that a consumer will select a brand after considering and evaluating its qualities. The base data set for this study is significant in its coverage of a diverse selection of

> **RESEARCH INSIGHT 7.3 (cont.)**
>
> over 1,000 brands and their interaction with 20,000 consumer journeys. The research focuses upon the factors involved in a consumer's purchase choice (also known as brand conversion), finding that as consumers become more digitally empowered, brand messages lose their impact, and the likelihood of conversion, on average, decreases. Consequently, the brands most likely to convert digitally jaded consumers into purchasers offer the strongest array of digital experiences.

7.11   Medium-Term Campaigns: Public Relations

Kotler and Armstrong (2005) describe the process of PR as the 'development of good relations with the company's various publics, by obtaining favourable publicity, building a good corporate image and handling or heading off unfavourable rumours, stories and events'. In the context of user-generated content via unmediated social platforms, user dissatisfaction, misbehaviour, or mischief can quickly grow into significant PR challenges for the organisation. Likewise are the potential effects of 'good' stories spreading virally among the organisation's past, current, and potential customers and consumers. However, the influence of good or bad PR goes beyond the organisation's customer base to include news agencies, shareholders, financial institutions, employees, suppliers and distributors, government, and the local community. The key areas of online PR are:

- attracting visitors through competitor research, keyword analysis, search engine optimisation (SEO), pay per click (PPC), inbound link building, affiliations, content creation, blogs, and press releases;
- engagement and dialogue using insight from surveys and polls, audience research, initiating social media discussion by the production and seeding of content, and engagement with user-generated content;
- building campaign buzz using display advertising, teaser campaigns on social media, opinion leader endorsement, web editorial contacts, and press releases; and
- defence in the time of a crisis through sentiment monitoring of key news and social media feeds, keyword trending searches, proactive reporting, and selective responses on social media.

7.12   Short-Term Campaigns: Sales and Income Growth

The launch of a new product is a turbulent and uncertain period in an organisation's development. When planning our communications, we will have clear goals and timelines in mind to guide operational planning in relation to products (their range, volume, and quality), processes to ensure adequate preparations are made in the supply chain to deliver a reasonable amount of stock, and sufficient logistics capacity without over-investing and placing unnecessary pressure on the organisation's cashflow. However, it is worth considering what patterns of market response can affect new product launches. It is in this respect that the Gartner Hype Cycle (Gartner, 2019; Figure 7.5) can offer some insight into the peaks and troughs of market response and how we might tailor our communications activity in a way that drives effective and efficient sales growth in the light of this.

The 'hype' theme within this model relates to the bold promises made in relation to the launch of new technologies. The expectation and ensuing challenge for the market are how and when we can discern between the hype surrounding the promotion of the technology and its realistic potential. The Gartner Hype Cycle provides a graphical representation of the evolution, maturity, and adoption of technologies over time, which helps to tailor the

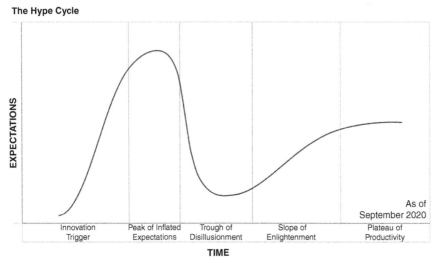

Figure 7.5 Gartner Hype Cycle (Gartner, 2019). Gartner® Hype Cycle™ From Gartner®, Understanding Gartner's Hype Cycles, Philip Dawson, Alexander Linden, Keith Guttridge, Katell Thielemann, Nick Jones, Jackie Fenn, 2 July 2021. Reprinted with permission.

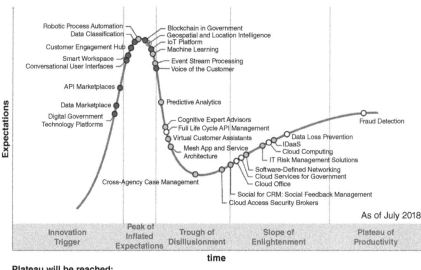

Figure 7.6 Top trends from the Gartner Hype Cycle for digital government technology (Gartner, 2018). Gartner® (2018). Top Trends from Gartner Hype Cycle™ for Digital Government Technology, 2018. Reprinted with permission.

organisation's collective marketing activities to meet its goals. Each hype cycle (see the example in Figure 7.6) gives a detailed illustration of the five key phases of a technology's lifecycle.

- **Innovation trigger:** a new technology – often in concept or prototype form – is ready to be marketed. Press releases attract media interest and generate publicity. It is early days as the technology has neither been manufactured nor used at scale.
- **Peak of inflated expectations:** the use of protypes and early production versions has led to some successes, but these are often outweighed by incidents of products not working to their envisaged potential, being incompatible with other devices, or not working at all.
- **Trough of disillusionment:** weaker organisations cannot recover from the early setbacks. Some may choose to abandon the new technology in the belief that the market has moved on. Some organisations continue to invest and develop the technology, building strong relationships with early adopters.
- **Slope of enlightenment:** more potential applications for the technology are identified and explored. Investment begins in next-generation versions, but the memories of earlier failures are still strong, leading to a more cautious approach.

- **Plateau of productivity:** mainstream manufacturing and sales take off. Specifications are standardised and technology diversity reduces as standardised technologies are adopted.

7.13   Planning and Budgeting

So how do we plan our communications to deliver different messages in a complex and noisy environment, through channels over which we have only partial control, that utilise a wide variety of different media, that need to integrate with our offline promotional activity, to deliver long-, medium-, and short-term goals? Not easily. We need to take an integrated marketing communications (IMC) approach, which is described by Fahy and Jobber (2015) as 'the system by which companies co-ordinate their marketing communications tools to deliver clear, consistent, credible and competitive message about the organization and its products' to deal with this complex and challenging problem. The key IMC issues to address and clarify before we begin the campaign planning process include:

- **Goal setting and tracking:** which specific goals should be set for online campaigns and how do we measure success? What response mechanisms will be most effective? See Chapter 3.
- **Campaign insight:** which data about customer and competitor behaviour is available to inform our decision? See Chapter 2.
- **Segmentation and targeting:** how can we target and reach our different audiences? See Chapter 4.
- **Offer and message development:** how do we specify our offer and key messages? See Chapter 3.

The final two planning elements will be covered in this section:

- **Budgeting and selecting the digital media mix:** how should we set the budget and invest in different forms of digital media?
- **Integration into overall media schedule or plan:** how should we plan the media schedule which incorporates different waves of online and offline communications?

7.14   Framework for Media Selection

Choosing the promotional mix needs to begin with a clear articulation of the objectives of the campaign and an agreement of the time (perhaps with staged milestones to allow for reflection and reconfiguration if necessary), people (creative/production/media buying expertise, along with follow-up sales and customer service capacity), materials (what is already available to be re-used and what needs to be created afresh), and money that are currently available to the campaign team. Once these are in place, the campaign team – using a consideration of market size and concentration, customer information needs, and product characteristics – will select the mix based on a selection of the following criteria (Coulter and Starkis, 2005):

- Quality:
  - attention-grabbing capability which targets focal rather than peripheral attention;
  - stimulating emotions to create positive feelings towards the product/brand/organisation;
  - information content and detail that can be accessed via scans, links, and click-throughs to ensure access to rich information without overloading the viewer;
  - credibility/prestige/image of the channel which reflects that of the product/brand/organisation; and
  - clutter reduction to avoid message distortion or loss due to noise in the communications process.

- Time:
  - short lead time to ensure responsiveness to campaign plans and effectiveness data, and control of the overall progress of the campaign to refocus objectives, media, message, and spending as required;
  - long exposure time, which allows repeated contact with the customer to build recognition and familiarity with the product/brand/organisation. This needs to avoid becoming a nuisance, boring, or irrelevant.

- Flexibility:
  - appeal to multiple senses for a richer experience but also caters for the differing communication preferences of the customer to appeal to them on their own terms;
  - personalisation based on user preferences (e.g., via a website or app login) or the capability for the user to tailor the content and presentation to their own preferences;
  - interactivity to increase engagement and feedback; and
  - right-touching to ensure a positive disposition to the sender and the message, which is a balance between too much and too little communication. This is largely a process of experimentation linked to the intelligent and selective use of data analytics.

- Coverage:
  - selectivity based on segmentation criteria and targeting choices;
  - pass-along audience which enables sharing to enable virality;

- frequency/repeat exposure which needs to be held in balance with the principles of right-touching; and
- average media reach to understand the potential scale of distribution and likely number of audience impressions.

7.15   The Integrated Promotional Plan: Media and Budget

To co-ordinate the integrated promotional mix around a specific branding, PR, or sales effort, the organisation will draw up timescaled plans which work to build awareness and interest prior to launch, maximise sales in the crucial early days, and build growing and sustained levels of income within the anticipated lifecycle of the product. Online activity should also support and integrate offline activities, and the level to which this is achieved depends upon the nature of the product and the market (to include customers and competitors).

When planning the expenditure for a campaign it is important that costs are transparent and controllable to ensure budget allocation that maximises the targeted returns within a given timeframe while achieving the delicate balance of avoiding an overspend which would risk the profitability of the project, or underinvesting, meaning that sales may fall short of their goal. For budget forecasting purposes we need to differentiate between fixed costs, which *do not* vary based on the volume and frequency of use (e.g., website content, apps, games) and variable costs that *do* vary based on the volume and frequency of use (e.g., PPC, banner advertisements). These costs will differ based on the stage of the process:

- **Development** costs will be incurred for idea and creative development to assist the visualisation, perception, and testing of a range of content and imagery to determine its suitability for the message and the audience. These costs are typically related to the services of illustrators, graphic designers, copywriters, and market researchers.
- **Production** costs will cover a range of artefacts such as website programming, app and game programming, social media content creation and moderation, films, podcasts/radio, augmented reality/virtual reality hardware and software.
- **Delivery** costs include SEO, PPC, banner advertising rates, sponsorship of prominent bloggers, database rental, and affiliate and intermediary promotions.

The fictional example in Table 7.3 considers the promotional effort in support of the release of a new movie in a popular superhero franchise. Please note that this example covers promotional costs only and makes no

Table 7.3 Some media options for a new movie release in a superhero franchise

		Fixed costs	Variable costs
Online	Movie website with information on other films/characters in the franchise, photos, character and creative information, cast interviews, teaser trailers, downloadable/shareable images	Concept generation, graphic design, coding and testing Content creation	–
	Apps/games		
	Competitions to win tickets/merchandise	Concept generation and graphic design	Advertising
	Pay per click	Copywriting and coding	Cost per click
	Banner ads	Copywriting and graphic design	Advertising rate card based on user impressions, size, placement, occurrence, and duration
	Social media pages with curated content and moderated feeds	Copywriting and content uploading	Moderation of user-generated content and commentary
	AR/VR experiences at retail and entertainment venues	Software concept, programming, and testing	Hardware purchase and maintenance Space rental
	Fan clubs with preferential ticket access or exclusive merchandise	Set up and recruit to online community	Based on group scale
	Movie review sites	Copywriting and content creation	–
	Movie bloggers/podcasters		
	Extracts for TV/radio		
	Interaction with virtual character chatbots	Concept, design, building, and testing	–
	Movie downloading / streaming	Negotiation of distributor/broadcaster deals	–

Table 7.3 (*cont.*)

		Fixed costs	Variable costs
Offline	Press releases to print media Magazine and poster advertising	Copywriting Concept, copywriting, graphic design	Distribution of press releases Advertising rate cards
	Point-of-sale displays	Concept and graphic design	Printing and distribution
	Sponsorship	–	Negotiations with partners
	Character licensing	Licensing agreement	Based on the complexity of the deal
	Merchandising of replica characters, costumes, equipment	Concept, design, and testing	Based on scale and variety
	Premiers and other events	Concept, graphic design, production	On an event-by-event basis to include exclusive venue use and display materials
	Cosplay conventions		
	Character/cast visits and interviews		
	DVD/Blu-ray discs	Artwork	Printing and distribution of point-of-sale materials

consideration for other costs incurred by the eight drivers of digital marketing, such as product development, manufacturing, distribution, sales incentives, etc.

In the Develop Your Skills section at the end of this chapter you will have the opportunity to programme this activity during the pre- and post-launch phases of the fictional campaign for the new movie.

CHAPTER SUMMARY

As with any professional communication, it is essential that both the sender and receiver of the message are clear as to its content and intent. Digital communications platforms make it possible to contact many more people than ever before with a relentless promotional campaign across multiple devices which can be tracked, reported, tweaked, and refined. However, the pressure on receivers is significant, given the volume of communications traffic to which they are exposed online. This can leave the receiver overwhelmed, confused, or just intransigent. None of these are states of feeling that marketers want to achieve in potential customers. We have explored the key vehicles for online promotion, their uses, and relative strengths and weaknesses within the process. In the final section on planning, we explored the factors that influence media selection and deployment over time, and how these might integrate with offline activities to create a single cohesive and coherent effort.

Review Questions

1. Consider two different purchases that you make on a regular basis. What 'noise' exists in the communications environment that prevents the full intended message from reaching you?
2. Keep a log of unsolicited digital communications that you receive over a week. These will include emails, social media adverts, mobile messaging, and pop-up advertisements. How closely do they meet the 'right-touching' criteria?
3. Find an organisation that is currently in the news for suspected wrongdoing. Visit their social media pages and undertake a keyword or hashtag search. How is the organisation responding to negative comments about it?

END-OF-CHAPTER CASE: WITH SUCH EXTENSIVE INSIGHT, WHAT COULD POSSIBLY GO WRONG?

Adidas' Boston Marathon Email

Adidas was one of the sponsors of the inspirational Boston Marathon. Customers who participated in the 2017 event received an email from them with the subject line 'Congrats, you survived the Boston Marathon!' In the context of any other fitness event this might seem harmless. In fact, many people use this kind of phrasing when they refer to completing an event – some might say they survived their first Peloton class. However, this campaign ignored the context of the 2013 event in which three people lost their lives and a further 260 were injured as the result of a double bombing at the finish line. Naturally, Adidas' unfortunate choice of words went viral on Twitter. Spokeswoman Maria Culp said: 'We are incredibly sorry. Clearly, there was no thought given to the insensitive email subject line we sent Tuesday. We deeply apologize for our mistake. The Boston Marathon is one of the most inspirational sporting events in the world. Every year we're reminded of the hope and resiliency of the running community at this event.'

Audi's Chinese Wedding Ad

It's always important to check out a car before you purchase it. Audi turned this idea on its head. Audi came up with an ad in which a couple is about to say 'I do' at the altar when the bride's mother-in-law-to-be interrupts and goes on to assess the bride for perfection. She inspects her soon-to-be-daughter-in-law by pulling her lip to check her teeth and tongue, and pulls on her ears before giving a nod of approval to her son. Audi used the tagline: 'An important decision must be made carefully.' The commercial misses the mark by objectifying women and reducing their value to that of a vehicle. It was far more offensive than it was humorous. Audi came under some well-deserved social media fire.

Bic's Facebook Ad Campaign

The pen company came under fire when they posted an image on their social media account encouraging women to 'look like a girl, act like a lady, think like a man and work like a boss'. The sexist post was heavily criticised by women, leading to the company issuing a public apology.

DiGiorno's Use of Domestic Violence Hashtag

Over the past few years, many new movements have taken centre stage, with many using social media platforms and principles to spread awareness and gain support. Movements have become unified via the use of hashtags such as #metoo, #whyIstayed, and #blacklivesmatter. However, DiGiorno – the reheat-at-home pizza brand – went too far by co-opting #whyIstayed, a movement for domestic violence survivors to speak out against the weak victim stereotype, explain warning signs of abuse, and discuss their personal experiences with how abusers trap their targets. The company realised their mistake and had to issue a public apology.

Burger King: Smartphone Campaign

In what was initially a great marketing idea, Burger King created a campaign to run on smart devices that activated the device to read a list of burger ingredients posted on Wikipedia, the crowdsourced online encyclopaedia. This was a clever innovation which aimed to engage with customers at a deep level who were showing interest in health issues and sustainable farming. However, it was not long before mischievous hackers altered the Wikipedia post to include ingredients like cyanide. Inevitably the campaign was cancelled and a new channel to enhance the buyer–seller relationship had to be abandoned.

Snapchat: Would You Rather?

Snapchat found themselves in unpopular territory when an advert for the game app 'Would you Rather?!' asked users whether they'd rather 'slap Rihanna' or 'punch Chris Brown', an unfortunate reference to the events of 2009 when Chris Brown was imprisoned for severely beating up then-girlfriend Rihanna. Rihanna responded on Instagram, a rival social media platform, criticising Snapchat, stating they had 'made a joke' out of domestic violence and let down 'all the women, children and men that have been victims of DV in the past and especially the ones who haven't made it out yet'. Rihanna's comments caused the share price value of Snapchat's parent company, Snap, to plummet by almost 4 per cent, wiping $800 million from its market value. A spokesperson for Snapchat made the statement: 'This advertisement is disgusting and should never have appeared on our service. We are so sorry we made the terrible mistake of allowing it through our review process. We are investigating how that happened so that we can make sure it never happens again.'

DISCUSSION QUESTIONS

- What could have been the reasons for these errors of judgement?
- How appropriate were the companies' public responses?
- If you had worked for the companies, agencies, or platforms involved, how could you have prevented this from happening?

Develop Your Skills

What Is the Skill?

Promotional campaign planning is the process of selecting and combining multiple communications channels to deliver a coherent and compelling message to a target audience that stimulates them to act in a desired way.

Why Is It Important?

We have many online promotional platforms available to us, but there is a risk of failing to engage the customer with too little communication or making them hostile to us due to excessive and inappropriate

Table 7.4 Promotional plan format										
Offline media										
Earned media										
Shared media										
Paid media										
Owned media										
Timing (month)	−3	−2	−1	LAUNCH	+1	+2	+3	+4	+5	+6

communication. This task challenges the planner to reach out to customers in the right way and at the right time (i.e., 'right-touching'). From the organisation's point of view its budgets are finite and there is the constant challenge to find more effective and efficient ways to establish high-value, long-term marketing relationships with customers.

How to Develop It

Using the fictional example in Table 7.3 which considers the promotional effort in support of the release of a new movie in a popular superhero franchise, you are to develop a 12-month plan, detailed by month, to build customer awareness, launch the sales effort, and extend the product-market potential of the movie. In your introduction you will clearly describe the target segment (see Chapter 4 for guidance on this) and how your communications will progress them through their decision-making process towards a purchase (also in Chapter 4). The plan should be presented in a framework such as that shown in Table 7.4.

How to Apply It

Produce your plan and present it to the group for them to challenge your assumptions and proposals, and to provide feedback.

References

Ansari, A., and Mela, C. F. (2003). E-customization. *Journal of Marketing Research*, 40(2): 131–145.

Ansari, A., Mela, C. F., and Neslin, S. A. (2008). Customer channel migration. *Journal of Marketing Research*, 45(1): 60–76.

Bergstrom, J. R., and Schall, A. (2014). *Eye Tracking in User Experience Design*. Burlington, MA: Morgan Kaufmann.

Bughin, J. (2015). Brand success in an era of Digital Darwinism. *McKinsey Quarterly.* February.

Cavazza, F. (2021). Social media landscape 2021 [online]. Available from: www .socialmediamodellen.nl/social-media-kanalen-platformen-websites-voorbeel den/social-media-landscape [Accessed 11 June 2022].

Chaffey, D., and Ellis-Chadwick, F. (2016). *Digital Marketing: Strategy, Implementation and Practice,* 6th ed. Harlow: Pearson.

Chatterjee, P., Hoffman, D. L., and Novak, T. P. (2003). Modeling the clickstream: implications for web-based advertising efforts. *Marketing Science,* 22(4): 520–541.

Christodoulides, G., de Chernatony, L., Furrer, O., and Abimbola, T. (2006) Conceptualising and measuring the equity of online brands. *Journal of Marketing Management,* 22(7/8): 799–825.

Coulter, K., and Starkis, J. (2005). Development of a media selection model using the analytic network process. *International Journal of Advertising,* 24(2): 193–215.

Drèze, X., and Hussherr, F. X. (2003). Internet advertising: is anybody watching? *Journal of Interactive Marketing,* 17(4): 8–23.

Drozdenko, R., and Coelho, D. (2016). Sentiment of online reviews are consistent with conventional word of mouth effects. *International Journal of Business, Marketing, and Decision Sciences,* 9(1): 55–69.

Fahy, J., and Jobber, D. (2015) *Foundations of Marketing,* 5th ed. London: McGraw-Hill.

Fill, C. (2013). *Marketing Communications: Brands, Experiences and Participation.* Harlow: Pearson.

Gartner (2018). Top trends from Gartner Hype Cycle for digital government technology, 2018 [online]. Available from: www.gartner.com/smarterwithgartner/top-trends-from-gartner-hype-cycle-for-digital-government-technology-2018 [Accessed 12 August 2019].

Gartner (2019). The Gartner Hype Cycle [online]. Available from: www.gartner.com/ en/research/methodologies/gartner-hype-cycle [Accessed 12 August 2019].

Godin, S. (2007). *Permission Marketing: Turning Strangers into Friends and Friends into Customers.* New York: Simon & Schuster

Holmqvist, K., Nystrom. M., Andersson, R., et al. (2015). *Eye Tracking: A Comprehensive Guide to Methods and Measures.* Oxford: Oxford University Press.

Hootsuite (2019). How to manage a social media crisis: a practical guide for brands [online]. Available from: https://blog.hootsuite.com/social-media-crisis-manage ment [Accessed 14 August 2019].

Kotler, P., and Armstrong, G. (2005). *Principles of Marketing.* Hoboken, NJ: Prentice Hall.

Likert, R. (1932). A technique for the measurement of attitudes. *Archives of Psychology,* 140: 1–55.

Manchanda, P., Dubé, J. P., Goh, K. Y., and Chintagunta, P. K. (2006). The effect of banner advertising on internet purchasing. *Journal of Marketing Research,* 43(1): 98–108.

Martin, K., (2018). The penalty for privacy violations: how privacy violations impact trust online. *Journal of Business Research,* 82: 103–116.

McDonald, M., and Wilson, H. (1999). *E-Marketing: Improving Marketing Effectiveness in a Digital World*. London: Financial Times/Prentice Hall.

Peppers, D., Rogers, M., and Dorf, B. (1999). Is your company ready for one-to-one marketing? *Harvard Business Review*, 77(1): 151–160.

Shannon, C., and Weaver, W. (1962). *The Mathematical Theory of Communication*. Chicago, IL: University of Illinois Press.

Tuten, T. L., and Solomon, M. R. (2017) *Social Media Marketing*, 3rd ed. London: SAGE.

Usability.gov (2019). Eye tracking [online]. Available from: www.usability.gov/how-to-and-tools/methods/eye-tracking.html [Accessed 14 August 2019].

Winer, R. S., and Ilfeld, J. S. (2002). Generating website traffic. *Journal of Advertising Research*, 42(5): 49–61.

8 Digitally Enabled Creativity and Innovation

Introduction

This chapter considers how organisations reinvent both themselves and the marketing relationship with their chosen customers. Creativity can occur at the microscale with improvements and breakthroughs from promotional taglines and product enhancements and through transformational changes which may create new product ranges and access new customer segments. Creativity is often considered to be a random or serendipitous event which occurs with no clear advanced planning, but this is misleading. Organisations and individuals can organise themselves, and create cultural mindsets, that open the door to creative opportunities which may fail – causing the organisation to question its priorities and approach – or succeed, thus creating value for the organisation and its customers. Many organisations realise the importance of the reinvention opportunities that creativity brings, but struggle to nurture sustained sources of worthy ideas that can be transformed into solid customer offerings at a speed and scale that achieves widespread commercial success. We will explore how ideas originate and are developed and moved through the organisation to maturity (see the product lifecycle in Chapter 3). We will also examine the organisational structure, leadership, and culture which creates and nurtures the creativity and innovation process.

Learning Objectives

- Classify different types of creativity within the organisational context.
- Distinguish between internal and external sources of ideas.
- Explain the open innovation phenomenon and how it relates to value co-creation.
- Summarise the role of creative strategy.

- Consider the organisational capabilities required to support innovation.
- Recommend a dynamic culture that champions speed, agility, and resilience.

CASE INSIGHT: WILL DATA CRAMP CREATIVITY'S STYLE?

Marketing, long seen as a highly creative right-brain qualitative activity, has often had an uneasy relationship with left-brain more quantitative practices of analytics, statistics, and detailed forecasting. However, with the rise of big data and analytics it has become increasingly possible to quantify insight throughout the lifecycle of the customer's experience. Marketers value their role as being inherently empathetic to customer needs and see this relationship as being largely emotional rather than a rational affair, and those that protect this outdated isolationist attitude are paying the price in terms of lost market opportunity, according to research undertaken by Gregg et al. (2018), which shows that companies that harness creativity and data in tandem across the marketing mix – from brand strategy and consumer insights, to customer experience, product, and pricing, to content, creative development, and media – grow their revenues at twice the average rate of S&P 500 companies: at least 10 per cent annually versus 5 per cent. Marketers that integrate data and creativity do so in the following ways:

1. They treat **creativity and data as equal partners**, with creative functions becoming more data-driven (e.g., customer experience research is growing its use of data analytics and can uncover customer intentions, triggers, and interests that reveal subtle pain points and unmet needs), and data-driven functions are growing more creative (e.g., customer insights researchers are collaborating with content producers and experience designers to actively test the effect of new marketing mixes).
2. They build **integrated teams** which are small, nimble, cross-functional, co-located, and relatively autonomous that execute targeted marketing projects, designing-out potential blockages such as a complex approvals process and enabling the frequent and rapid testing of new ideas, content, messages, and value propositions. In such cases the process of creating new campaigns or marketing initiatives often shrinks from months to weeks or even days.
3. They seek **'whole-brain' talent** from people who have both left- and right-brain skills, even though their primary function will utilise one more than the other. However, in a recruitment context it is often not

possible to develop or attract the best talent, but nevertheless these organisations are fully aware of skillsets and capabilities that they need to bring into the team.

Questions

- In what ways could this approach add to, or detract from, the different types of innovation (i.e., incremental, radical, transformational)?
- How does the organisation choose between 'safe' innovations which are strongly supported by the data, or 'risky' innovations which are driven by the marketer's understanding of the relationship between the organisation and its customers?

8.1   Can Creativity be Digitised and Automated?

Creativity is a process whereby something novel and useful is originated (Mumford, 2003). This new item might take an intangible form, such as a theory, or a physical object, such as an invention. Torrance (1966) explained the drivers of creativity as being 'a process of becoming sensitive to problems, deficiencies, gaps in knowledge, missing elements, disharmonies, and so on; identifying the difficulty; searching for solutions, making guesses, or formulating hypotheses about the deficiencies: testing and retesting these hypotheses and possibly modifying and retesting them; and finally communicating the results'. These definitions help us to understand what creativity is in its broadest sense and the problem-solving task that it performs. Schumpeter (1942), however, explains the economic role of creativity and its importance not only to satisfy our basic problem-solving instincts, but also to drive forward the development of the marketing effort, often in a disruptive fashion (see Chapter 1):

> The fundamental impulse that sets and keeps the capitalist engine in motion comes from the new consumers' goods, the new methods of production or transportation, the new markets, the new forces of industrial organization that capitalist enterprise creates.

Creativity in a digital environment gives unparalleled opportunities and threats to organisations and individuals. The scope for global collaboration in real time to develop and deploy new marketing mixes is breath-taking in its power and speed. On the other hand, it is easy for customers and supply chains to be overwhelmed by the pace and extent of change. But does creativity still have a role in the age of artificial intelligence and machine learning? Many authors believe that the unique and unprogrammable nature of human creativity, along with our abilities to collaborate and empathise with others, will, based on current and foreseen technologies, make it impossible for the process of creativity to be automated. This is not a guarantee but a short-term best guess. As machine learning develops it is a reasonable assumption to anticipate that growing connectivity, richer data, and greater insight and mapping of cognitive processes will eventually enable artificial intelligence to become truly creative, initially in its basic form and eventually in more sophisticated iterations.

8.2   The Role of Digital Technologies in Idea Creation

Due to the apparent 'accidental' nature of idea generation, creativity is often treated as unpredictable. However, neuroscientists (Boden, 2013) have revealed the processes that lead to creativity, distinguishing them by the sorts of cognitive processes that are involved in idea generation:

- **Serendipitous creativity** occurs when suddenly some ideas which prove to be very creative emerge in the mind during the process of thinking, which is stimulated by a pleasant event, usually rest and relaxation. These appear in the form of inspiration but are the result of complex psychological ruminations at a subconscious level. Digital communications, through the volume, range, and ubiquity of stimuli to which it exposes its audiences, creates untold numbers of opportunities to chance upon new ideas for products and their potential applications.
- **Normative creativity** requires the finding of new solutions for specific problems that have comprehensive requirements. New alternatives or new concepts are sought to address identified issues. The scope of the problem may be narrow, since it will need to sit within the constraints of a wider system, potentially requiring an incremental rather than radical level of change. Commonly understood problem-solving techniques such as brainstorming, mind mapping, attribute association, 5W/1H, and left–right brain techniques are utilised in this approach. Digital technologies provide access to a global selection of potential solutions for practical problems that are both existing and anticipated.
- **Combinational creativity** generates new ideas through a combination of old ideas. There are four generally accepted steps to generate combinational ideas: collect as many old ideas as possible, let them incubate in your brain, force a trigger event, and finally engage in a relaxing activity that will allow combinations and connections to occur and generate new

ideas. Data analytics and the integration of customer data across multiple online and app-based platforms help organisations to identify and anticipate patterns of consumer behaviour that might lead to non-traditional sales opportunities. For example, if you are a keen gardener then your purchase of books on the subject would also be linked to purchase of seeds, compost, tools, equipment, and clothing, thus allowing for great cross-selling and up-selling opportunities for suppliers.

- **Exploratory creativity:** while still guided by old ideas in your brain, this method seeks to extend beyond what you currently know. Experimentation without knowing what the outcome will be, and curiosity for the unexpected, will lead to ideas that would not normally arise through combinational creativity. Here, digital gaming and virtual reality technologies enable users to enter and investigate situations with which they may only have a passing familiarity. As they progress through the immersive experience, they will gain new knowledge and situational awareness which will stimulate the need for creative solutions to new, and potentially unfamiliar or unanticipated problems. Experience of such immersive worlds can lead to the development of new cognitive competencies as a result of unique problem-framing approaches and new techniques and approaches that are evaluated based on their relative success or failure within the game, such as collaborative problem solving with players/participants who are unfamiliar to us, who are largely anonymous, and may come from diverse cultures and environments.

- **Transformational creativity** occurs by adjusting the problem's frame of reference or changing 'the rules of the game' by identifying a barrier (real or perceived) that is preventing a clear solution and hypothesising what would be possible if that barrier did not exist. It empowers free-thinking beyond the limitations of individual barriers, which may be negotiable as part of addressing the wider problem. Again, digital game playing, and virtual reality experiences can help us to understand different situations through a simple of adjustment to the game's rules or settings. Simulation software enables assessments of the impact of the adjustment of certain variables, where their correlation with other factors is clearly understood. Such programmes are developed from the rigorous collection and updating of data in the context of a robust understanding of the cause-and-effect relationships between multiple variables.

The potential contribution of digital technologies to the process of organisational creativity is significant. Sophisticated data packages can model and predict potential outcomes at operational, financial, and market levels, giving an organisation an early indication of the feasibility of the potential project in a range of customer and market contexts. Data from previous efforts can be used to identify organisational strengths and weaknesses in its ability to identify and respond to emerging customer needs with a new marketing mix. Competitor benchmarking is also possible so that the organisation can model the ideal scope, scale, and timing of its creative effort to achieve maximum value without overloading the organisation and the market with too many initiatives which could devalue the hard-won existing marketing mix and risk initiative fatigue among its established customer base in its efforts to expand and attract new customers.

RESEARCH INSIGHT 8.1 Digital Creativity

Lee, M. R., and Chen, T. T. (2015). Digital creativity: research themes and framework. *Computers in Human Behavior*, 42: 12–19.

When searching with the terms 'digital' and 'creativity' there is precious little return in the academic literature. One paper that does stand out is this effort by Lee and Chen to map digital creativity research to date – defined as the creativity manifested in all forms that are driven by digital technologies. They confirm that due to its novelty and interdisciplinary nature, the scope, perspective, and main research themes of digital creativity study are unclear. The diverse nature of creativity as a domain is demonstrated by mentions in the disciplinary literature of design, ergonomics, music, media, drama, games, computing, and economics. The paper results in a framework which provides possible future research directions around the themes of design contexts, creative arts and learning, human–technology environments, and support and policy.

8.3   Creativity within the Organisational Systems Context

Organisational contexts can provide a strong canvas against which stakeholders can express their creativity. Here are some of the principal aspects of creativity along with explanations of their digital components:

- **Environments** both physical and virtual can create opportunities for skills, knowledge, problems, and collaborators to collide. Physical workplaces are frequently being redesigned away from separate spaces into common spaces, particularly when employees are less task-driven and may be relaxing – for example, coffee shops, restaurants, sports activities, leisure, and entertainment facilities. Collaboration here can be encouraged through ubiquitous Wi-Fi coverage. Virtual employees (i.e., principally stationed off-site and engaging via the Internet) and associate employees (such as project-based or casual employees) can be harder to engage. Here, employers make a trade-off between the 'presence' of their colleagues, who will typically have traditional work patterns in traditional work-places, and the opportunities offered by digital technologies such as cloud storage and document sharing and virtual meeting technologies, which allow for a wider, potentially global, network of collaborators with highly diverse cultural and educational backgrounds and expertise, each with their own separate personal and professional networks, who can build new solutions from a deeper well of source material.

- **Experiments** need to be encouraged and visible, and their results should be made transparent since success and failure create significant learning opportunities for both the participants and the wider organ-isation. An experimental culture should not encourage reckless risk taking, but this highly exploratory approach could also lead to either significant losses or even breakthrough discoveries. O'Reilly and Tushman (2004) wrote of innovation where organisations are dually challenged by the need to look backward, attending to the products and processes of the past, while also gazing forward, preparing for the innovations that will define the future. Experimentation is supported by the rich availability of data within the organisation and analytics programmes that can determine complex interactions between mul-tiple factors. Production, financial, and market data can be harvested in real time to understand which actions are having the desired effect and which are not.

- **Storytelling** is at the heart of how from a young age we are trained to interpret the world, its challenges, and its successes and failures. Many classic films aimed at younger viewers tend to follow the same dramatic arc:

ONCE UPON A TIME . . . there was a person . . . who was great at some things but not so good at others . . . who was loved but sometimes misunderstood . . . one day a baddie came along . . . who threatened the person and/or their loved ones . . . they realised they had to change, but how? . . . they considered lots of things then eventually decided on a solution . . . they fought the baddie . . . and lost . . . they had been betrayed by someone or had misunderstood the situation . . . they reflected, worked hard . . . and fought the baddie again . . . and won . . . and lived happily ever after . . . THE END

While the context, character, and plot devices have changed, the narrative thread of what constitutes a story remains the same. This narrative thread provides the core for simulations that take historical data to understand the step-by-step impact of decision-making, connected with the principles of game theory to understand the likely competitive response. Computer simulations utilise the data and parameters to help us design and launch better products. Data from the subsequent 'real' events also get fed into the process to improve decision-making via machine learning and artificial intelligence.

DIGITAL INSIGHT 8.1 Everything Is Awesome

LEGO, the manufacturer of plastic construction toys, based in Billund, Denmark, has been in business since 1932. In 1949 the company began producing an early version of the now-familiar interlocking plastic bricks. In an extension of the individual bricks, LEGO has released thousands of construction sets with a variety of themes, including space, robots, trains, castles, and other iconic buildings and feats of engineering. The company has also licensed-in themes from TV, movie, and video game franchises such as Batman, Harry Potter, and Star Wars. Beyond bricks and sets, LEGO also operates theme parks, a movie franchise, TV series, retail stores, and games. To feed this corporate machine and satisfy its diverse and growing fan base, LEGO needed to adapt the scope and scale of its innovation process, launching Future Lab using agile methodologies to build multi-disciplinary teams with a skeleton structure that draws on experienced staff only when and where their input is required. This was an essential response to a marketplace where 3D printing, virtual reality, the Internet, and technology shaped the attitudes of competitors, customers, and consumers alike.

Despite initial feedback from parents that it would not be a good idea to bring digital innovation into the practical, physical building block, LEGO realised that such innovation needed to happen. In 2011, the company created its first integration between LEGO bricks and a digital game, called *Life of George*. In order to see photos George had taken, users had to build the items George built and take a photo of their own creations with their phone. Another venture, LEGO Fusion, was released in 2014. It matched builders with virtual games, a bit like *Sim City*. The success of these games helped to prove that there's a balance between technology and creativity. Today, plenty of LEGO apps now blend technology and play.

Through LEGO Ideas the company has built an online platform that encourages user engagement to develop new product ideas. The benefit to the contributor is the satisfaction of engaging with their community of interest, possibly even winning recognition as a LEGO Master Builder. Participants can enter prize competitions, showcase their proposals for new LEGO Ideas sets, and vote for models that have been developed by fellow fans. In addition to receiving ideas that have been developed and reviewed by its customer base, LEGO also builds its strong sense of community and brand loyalty.

8.4   Platforms for Aggregating Ideas

The organisation can stimulate ideas from within its own structure via **research and development** departments that should normally be aware of new technologies that present new opportunities to meet customers' current and future needs, such as biotechnology and nanotechnology. This technology-focused perspective should be augmented with a focus on competitor actions and potential customers offered by the **marketing** department, who will continually monitor the external environment for ideas. At the operational level we will utilise **service** records to identify product needs and gaps in quality. Similarly, **sales** employees are the front-line contact with customers and will gain short-term insight into how well the organisation's current marketing mix is delivering value for the customer. Overseeing these internal and external operations and current and future perspectives will be **top management**, who will act to co-ordinate, consider, and synthesise this feedback to determine a coherent response by the organisation. These highly integrated data sets will be rigorously collected and interconnected by the organisation's enterprise-level management information system.

Externally, ideas can be sourced at an individual/organisational level by **lead users** (von Hippel, 1986) whose needs will typically be common to others in a marketplace but who are in a unique situation where they tend to be 'ahead of the curve' by facing them months or years before the bulk of that marketplace encounters them. In this sense, lead users currently experience needs that are still unknown to the public and will gain a significant comparative advantage if they obtain a solution to these needs ahead of the general competition. Since lead users innovate, they are one example or type of the creative consumer phenomenon – that is, those 'customers who adapt, modify, or transform a proprietary offering' (Berthon et al., 2007). Research into the needs of lead users can be undertaken through **voice of customer** techniques (see Chapter 2) and the insight that is generated can lead to the development of product and service ideas. However, the lead user presents one part of the story; it is then down to the data modelling presented by the organisation's insights into how the customer behaves and what this means for the supplier's marketing mix to extrapolate the complexities of any new requirements and their likely impacts, both inside and outside the organisation.

Value co-creation is a form of collaborative innovation with external individuals during a new product or service development process which is initiated and facilitated by a company (Piller and West, 2014). The concept has its roots in the user innovation phenomenon (von Hippel, 1998) and is beneficial to the organisation in that it benefits from the creation of a continuous feedback loop involving collaboration with all stakeholders within a value network throughout innovation processes (Kirah, 2009). Made possible by digital collaborations, value co-creation helps the organisation to break free of its creative confines, to create timely and relevant innovations that can be quickly researched (see Chapter 2), prototyped, evaluated, and deployed in a way that hopefully achieves mass adoption within the marketplace, and financial sustainability for the venture (see Chapter 3).

At a collective level, ideas can be sourced across **brand communities** (see Chapter 4) via innovation contests, which are online competitions for innovators who use their skills, experience, and creativity to provide a solution for a particular challenge set by an organiser (Bullinger et al., 2010; see also Haller et al., 2011; Adamczyk et al., 2012). The problem set can be explicit, carrying a description of the specific purpose and the solution limitations, or it can be general and more speculative, calling for broad solutions that may be inhibited by fewer limitations. Communities will typically operate online and can be stimulated by the simple desire to contribute to a community discussion of a shared challenge/objective, or they can be more explicitly motivated by competitive elements and the desire for success, recognition, and reward (e.g., naming rights for the new product, to be recognised as a co-inventor, receipt of an award with the associated publicity, or a financial reward such as a cash prize or discounts against future purchases). **Open innovation**, popularised by Chesbrough (2006), begins when organisations look outside their own doors for innovative ideas, and for ways of exploiting their own ideas which they may not currently have the strategic capabilities or commercial interest to pursue. This externally oriented co-creation philosophy emerges from a wide range of market environment drivers, many of which are technology-based. For example, the increasing scope and pace of technological change has led to significant adaptation of job roles in recent years as traditional skills may become redundant or replaced by automation, requiring workers to develop new, more flexible, skillsets. Also, with the changing role of the organisation, with a move away from large and rigid structures to smaller, more versatile teams of workers, people generally change their job more often than they used to and they carry their knowledge away with them. This knowledge represents a significant loss for the organisation, so it is sensible that they seek to reconnect to access this knowledge on an ad hoc basis in the future. Additionally, the international spread of industrialisation, made possible in large part by the development and global dissemination of affordable and high-quality information and communications technologies, has produced a huge proliferation of small firms who may act as collaborators, developing new ideas and technologies all around the world. This globally connected innovation activity may occur 'inside out', where organisations spin out ideas or early-stage product prototypes to other organisations who can develop them further as a result of their market-specific expertise, manufacturing, logistics, or investment. Alternatively, the organisation might choose to play host to the inventions of others that can thrive within its own unique organisational ecosystem.

8.5   How Does Innovation Add Value?

Innovation is the process of introducing something new. It differs from the process of creativity in that creativity *originates* ideas for something new (many of which will never see the light of day in a commercial sense), whereas innovation activates these ideas into tangible products which are widely utilised, thereby creating new value for customers (which represents a tiny proportion of the ideas created). The digital technology drivers were discussed in detail in Chapter 1, but it is worth refining this analysis to understand the role those digital technologies play in pushing forward innovative activity within the organisation itself. Sheth and Ram (1987) identify five key forces which create the impetus for an organisation's innovation effort:

- **Technological advances** through the connectivity of the World Wide Web, the common language of the Internet, sensor technologies which allow for the interaction of smart devices, computer processing power to make sense of the deluge of data fed from these devices and interactions, and the ability to deploy this new knowledge through automated responses and robotics via machine learning and the resultant artificial intelligence.

- **Intensified competition** from strong local competitors who can now project their activities onto a global stage. Digital has to some degree led to the 'death of distance' as a barrier to competition, given instantaneous global communication and highly integrated physical infrastructure of global supply chains, mainly due to logistical developments in containerisation and the globalisation of organisations via foreign subsidiaries and local partnerships.

- **Changing business environments** due to the expansion and projection of strong local and regional competitors onto a global stage, which was made possible by the increased market visibility and access of the World Wide Web and the adoption of common standards as exemplified in the coding of the Internet. This digital enabler has worked to support political and financial efforts to create an open and globalised economy. However, while local organisations can now expand to compete with global rivals, so foreign competitors can be more active against an organisation in its local market.

- **Strategic intent** has changed as organisations are required to think on a bigger scale and at a faster pace, and competition for global supply chains, customers, and workers intensifies. This significant increase in strategic opportunities and threats can cause confusion within the organisation as structures and decision-making processes struggle to keep up with the new rules of the game. Larger organisations have seen their market heft undermined by smaller, younger, and more agile challengers. This has led to a significant number of large corporate failures, with those who have survived having done so by slimming down, targeting their marketing mix, and working with a more flexible and devolved structure.

- **Changing customers and needs** as a result of the explosion of choice from a global supplier base, increased organisational responsiveness to customer needs (e.g., next-day delivery, 'no quibble' returns, digital payments, and tailor-made products). Additionally, the emergence of social media has altered the power balance between customers and suppliers, with organisations having the opportunity to create, identify, and exploit loyal fans to higher levels of personal and reference group loyalty.

8.6   Scope and Scale of Innovation across Marketing Functions

This dynamic environment leads to strategic dilemmas for how the organisation should deploy its resources to mitigate the threats or maximise the opportunities of digital technologies. For example, should the organisation invest heavily in research and development, and its wider marketing mix, to proactively push new technology, or wait to respond to changing market needs and await the 'market pull' effect as customer needs stabilise and become clearer, thus reducing the risk of the organisation investing significant funds in a wide range of products, many of which will fail? Another dilemma is where the organisation should focus its innovative efforts – in products that benefit customers, the processes that support and enable them, or a fundamental reimagining of how the business sees itself? Opposing the scope of change is degree of change:

- **Incremental:** a series of small improvements, such as upgrades or product line extensions that address the same existing markets, and which are focused on improving an existing product's development efficiency, productivity, and competitive differentiation. These are relatively easy to develop, but growth is only usually possible through taking market share. In Figure 8.1 changes to product base and range have been developed over time by extensive analysis of customer choices and combinations, both in terms of category sales within a given time period and also more explicitly when connected to the customer's Clubcard loyalty scheme, which connects actual purchases to the customer profile so as to further enhance the company's understanding of past and potential behaviour (i.e., purchase frequency, timing, and combinations). The Metro brand developed from an understanding of customers' needs for specific products, at a specific place and time (i.e., city-centre locations, operating principally in the daytime, to serve workers and visitors who will buy for same-day convenience consumption).
- **Radical:** new offerings with unique features that provide substantial benefits to customers. These are difficult to develop as they require deep customer insights. They generate growth through opening new, adjacent markets, and may take time to generate sales. In Figure 8.1 customer data and the tracking of external trends has helped Tesco to provide an integrated health-oriented element to its brand. Besides the provisions of fresh foods, the company also offers brand extensions which prioritise the provision of products that meet the needs of those with specific dietary needs (e.g., low-sugar, gluten-free, free of artificial additives

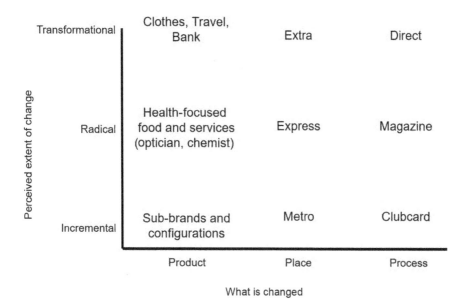

Figure 8.1 Dimensions of Innovation: Tesco example.

and preservatives) and ethical requirements (e.g., free-range, Fair Trade, vegetarian and vegan). Online, Tesco also provides dietary, wellbeing, and recipe advice through its *Tesco Magazine*. In addition to groceries, larger Tesco stores offer health support services such as optometry consultation and dispensing, and a dispensing pharmacy.

- **Transformational:** seeking to serve anticipated markets that do not yet exist; this may often require new business models to achieve the vision. Tesco and such stores have used their market power and presence, coupled with extensive customer insight, to further expand their domination of our shopping habits both offline – by the development of the Extra out-of-town superstore model – and online with its Direct service, which enables customers to buy online or via the app, with deliveries made at a time and place designated by the customer. Products are further developed to expand into unrelated markets of clothing retail, travel, and financial services.

8.7   Innovation as an Organisational Capability

Digitally enabled innovation creates significant impact across the organisation. Here are some examples in practice. These will be of varying relevance depending upon the type of organisation you are working in, its goals, and its customer base.

Cash: digital recording, reporting, and forecasting play a significant role in cost accounting and management accounting in many organisations. Since a shortage of cashflow is the single biggest limiting factor on an organisation's development, such techniques enable managers to stay informed of the current cash position of the business, with visibility of future issues (based on creditor- or debtor-related commitments) to understand whether the organisation can anticipate a surplus, which could be channelled into reserve funds or enable additional investment, or a shortfall, which would require cost-cutting, accessing reserves, or raising capital on external markets. Internal accounting systems can integrate with electronic banking and external fundraising to ensure the smooth and efficient running of the organisation, free from interruptions and the erosion of confidence that cashflow problems can cause.

Operations: operations management tools make it possible for the organisation to assess how well it is utilising its storage, manufacturing, and logistics capacity. Organisations may also set benchmark performance criteria to identify the optimum range for the process. Sensors in the production process can assess productivity rates and quality levels in a way that allows for real-time identification of issues, so that they can be rectified with the minimum delay to the process, and so that there is not a significant build-up of faulty goods at the end of the process. Environmental conditions in storage areas (e.g., temperature, moisture, air quality) can also be monitored to avoid spoilage. Radio frequency identity (RFID) tags and automated barcode scanners and printers are also widely used to aid product traceability – that is, the origins of the raw materials – in case of quality concerns. This process can also track the location of products both within the organisation and within the distribution and logistics network to provide customers with delivery updates and, where necessary, to trigger payment when the goods are received or used by the customer.

Costs: identifying waste and duplication within an organisation has become a matter of great financial, quality, and environmental concern. Digital technologies, from the data gathered through sensors that are embedded in connected devices, can interpret performance against agreed benchmarks and provide real-time feedback to identify areas for improvement. This might relate to energy consumption which is too high or too low, pollution and air quality levels, percentage of raw material waste, product quality failure rate for errors that cannot be recovered or re-tasked, operational outages or downtime, and production, storage, or transport capacity which is under-utilised, perhaps offering the potential for re-use elsewhere or for disposal. These efficiency measures can also help the organisation to plan maintenance programmes that minimise disruption of the production process and prolong the useful life of equipment (reducing financial and environmental costs).

Research and development facilities will consult and develop detailed schematic models to design and test new products, enhance existing products, or explore new applications of older products to extend their market life. Scientists and engineers will act in a design capacity, testing new concepts in simulated physical (e.g., a wind tunnel) or virtual (e.g., through computer aided design and computer aided manufacturing software) scenarios. Their effects, and the variables that control them, will be analysed and enhanced to build a better product and will also be translated into the requirements of the manufacturing process to ensure that products achieve the same high standards in use that they would in the controlled laboratory or workshop environment.

Intellectual property: the coding and rapid sharing of knowledge made possible by digital technologies have significantly increased the value and use of intellectual property such as patents, trademarks, design rights, and copyright. These are ideas physically expressed, often in written form rather than the physical form of a product, which are sold to others who will invest the time, expertise, funding, and operational resources for them to be translated into useful goods and services. This knowledge within the organisation, put into a form where it can be recorded, protected, and commercialised, further adds to the organisation's competencies because it embodies its regenerative powers to sustain and grow its operations. Digital rights management (DRM) tools or technological protection measures (TPM) are a set of access control technologies for restricting the use of proprietary hardware and copyrighted works. DRM technologies try to control the use, modification, and distribution of copyrighted works (such as software and multimedia content). These tools aim to prevent intellectual property from being copied freely – that is, without recognition or recompense to the owner. Where the rights owner is prepared to cede some ownership/reward to see the work develop, then DRM helps to maintain artistic control and perhaps gain some additional income from the project.

Reputation: in an era where opinions and claims can be shared virally in real time via social media, there is every chance that the organisation will fall foul of a disgruntled customer, poorly motivated employee, over-eager competitor, or some other mischievous player who through online anonymity could make scurrilous claims about the organisation, its employees, or its customers. The commentary and response could have significant negative impacts upon company reputation, brand strength, and customer loyalty. It is important for marketers to be aware of trending behaviour both on the level and type of online interactions with the organisation and within indirect activity through social media, where they may be discussed but not explicitly tagged. A range of analytics platforms exist to scan media platforms for mentions of the organisation and to perform a sentiment analysis which enables us to understand the positive or negative intent and to plan a suitable response.

Learning: the organisation's approach to learning, enabling it to create, collaborate, and convert opportunities, can be supported by virtual learning environments (VLEs), which are software packages available online, as apps, or as standalone systems that provide structured learning and tailored content to suit employees' needs. They can integrate with external providers (e.g., colleges and universities) with input provided in written, video, and audio forms. They provide rich and varied content, so can be relevant for many different learning styles. It is also possible for learners to submit their work for feedback and formal assessment. Managers can engage with employee learning, integrating it into their daily work and thus increasing the likelihood of retention and reflection. Organisations can also use this activity to assess employees for promotion or for performance-based rewards.

People: keeping track of the expertise, or know-how, of a workforce can be a devilishly tricky challenge. It is easy to miss, ignore, or misclassify our knowledge resources in this respect. Nevertheless, many organisations use the recruitment process to identify the key skills and experience that are required to perform well within a role. Promotion or transfer to another role will likewise require compliance with a skills and experience specification. As employees become embedded within an organisation, a periodic performance and development review (PDR) should update the organisation's database of expertise, although this rarely occurs in practice as the PDR process is often viewed as a private reflection between the reviewee and the reviewer in order to positively encourage the reviewee to identify and reflect upon their performance. For technical and scientific employees, retaining current and relevant skills is crucial to the potency of the organisation's innovation efforts. This can be tracked through performance in training and development programmes and through the PDR process as it seeks to understand the adaptability and versatility of employees.

Culture: employee goodwill and loyalty retain talent that acts as a beacon for other high-performing people both inside and outside the organisation. Digital platforms provide places for employees to engage with the organisation outside their normal job role, for example in social events or special projects teams, creating new connections and sharing ideas. Organisations can also create online suggestion schemes, which can be anonymised should contributors feel the need to contribute their idea but would prefer not to be directly associated with it for internal political reasons. Virtual 'sand pits' can be created for contributors to come together to work on new ideas for continuous improvement. Lastly, employee attitude surveys have been used for issues as varied as job satisfaction, diversity, pay and rewards, flexible working, and mental health. These encourage employees to contribute in a way that is potentially honest but attributable.

8.8 Digital Competencies

Although we may have good things (i.e., resources), it is the skill with which they are deployed (i.e., competencies) which determines the organisation's strategic capability. Likewise, skills without resources means that the idea or the organisation is significantly less likely to achieve its potential impact in the marketplace. Examples of competencies include the following:

- Expertise in integrating multiple technologies to create families of new products. Such technology literacy can be developed informally through working groups to share their reflections on best practice, short-term multidisciplinary problem-based teams who come together to tackle specific issues with a clearly defined end result, or as part of a more formalised learning programme which is supported and assessed via technologies such as VLEs, discussed above.
- Know-how in creating operating systems for cost-efficient supply chain management. When supported by sensor and communications technologies that provide data that can be interpreted to provide timely insight for decision-making, this capability can transform how the organisation perceives its strengths and weaknesses, enabling it to take clear and determined action. Seeing the potential connections between different hardware and software systems is a highly creative skill which, coupled with experiences of the successes and failures of other similar efforts, can identify and implement effective solutions.
- Speeding new/next-generation products to market requires skilful manipulation of multiple skillsets, including research, commercial, and operational employees. This often requires online collaboration tools that enable information to be shared between users. It will also benefit from software that allows designs and plans to be contributed to in a single

version which is updated by team members as required. Access to such documents will need to be secure, with all changes tracked and attributed (with those directly affected by the change receiving electronic notifications which may require their approval) so as to maintain the quality and integrity of the process, while also maintaining pace so as to maximise the commercial benefit by getting to market more quickly and effectively than a potential competitor offering. Such technologies assist collaborative relationships across and outside the organisation.

- Better aftersales service capability is available with organisations who host customer accounts through in-house software, or apps, or online, enabling the customer to query or return their purchase (for exchange or refund) as efficiently as possible. Customers are also encouraged to provide feedback in terms of quantitative scoring systems, indicated by granting a score based on the Likert scale of five stars to indicate 'highly satisfied' or one star to indicate 'high dissatisfied'. Alongside this, customers can provide qualitative commentary to indicate the reasons for their satisfaction or dissatisfaction. This feedback can be channelled to the appropriate department, such as manufacturing for quality-related issues or logistics for delivery-related issues, to drive further improvement. Good feedback from satisfied customers can also be shared online in the form of authentic product reviews, thus aiding customer choice and driving further sales.

- Skills in manufacturing a high-quality product can be supported by in-house systems of training and development, quality benchmarking, and monitoring through integrated sensors, barcodes, and RFID tags to enable traceability of all products to help identify the source of any errors and ensure that the necessary corrective action can be applied to all work-in-progress goods as required. Sometimes product failures occur or are discovered by the end-user, so such tracking capability may also help the efficient communication and handling of product recalls.

- Customer service orientation to fulfil orders accurately and swiftly is increasingly being enabled in warehouse environments by either operatives who prowl the aisles equipped with wireless devices connected to geolocational software which helps them to quickly locate and access the required goods, which they will scan via barcode or RFID tag to confirm as 'packed' until they complete collection of their pick list. This information will transfer to the despatch system to trigger collection and delivery. This may also trigger a despatch notice to the customer, confirming that their order has been despatched and indicating the likely delivery window.

DIGITAL INSIGHT 8.2 **Are Your Employees Fit for the Digital World?**

In collaboration with UK higher education providers, JISC (2018) has developed a Digital Capability Framework to guide providers and students in targeting skills and behaviours to get them workplace-ready in the digital environment. Their Digital Capability Framework (Figure 8.2) positions skill-sets in relation to each other and in a wider organisational context. This framework has most often been used by digital leaders and staff with overall responsibility for developing digital capability in their organisation, and it can be utilised to discuss and agree the digital capabilities required by the organisation, which could lead to a review of its recruitment, training, and promotion criteria.

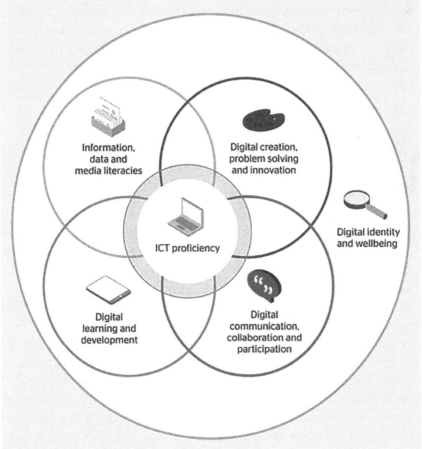

Figure 8.2 Digital Capability Framework (JISC, 2018).

> **RESEARCH INSIGHT 8.2 Complex and Dynamic Decision-Making**
>
> Nambisan, S., Lyytinen, K., Majchrzak, A., and Song, M. (2017). Digital innovation management: reinventing innovation management research in a digital world. *MIS Quarterly*, 41(1): 223–238.
>
> The explosion of digital technologies in recent years, coupled with the ever-increasing pace of change, has left no industry untouched by its disruptive influence. This fundamental disciplinary shift challenges the efficacy of existing theories on innovation management by calling into question fundamental assumptions about the boundaries for innovation and the relationship between innovation processes and outcomes. The authors propose a redefining of the foundations of research in innovation management in a digital context. **Dynamic problem–solution design pairing** recognises the fluid boundaries of the innovation space. **Socio-cognitive sensemaking** recognises the diverse range of parties engaged in the innovation process. **Technology affordances and constraints** recognises the varying distinctions, and occasional contradictions, of innovation processes and outcomes, and recognises how ownership and control of the innovation process can be distributed.

8.9   Innovation as an Organisational Behaviour

The organisational culture is a set of values, understandings, and ways of thinking that is shared by most members of a work organisation. It is recognised as a way of working which is typically made explicit when new employees join the organisation. Johnson et al. (2017) describe the respective components in the **cultural web** which we will use to explore how to build a culture for digital innovation.

Organisational structures are the formal structures and hierarchy which make clear departmental relationships and personal accountabilities. They will often take a top-down approach with the most senior manager, usually the chief executive or executive chairman, at the top, cascading down through divisions which, depending upon the scope and scale of the organisation, may be described by geographies (e.g., country or region), activities (e.g., operations, logistics, finance, marketing), or industries (e.g., automotive, retail, food). Each division may contain its own management team which runs the business unit in line with the requirements of company headquarters. Complex global organisations require a great deal of delegation of tasks and responsibilities, as such developing many layers of hierarchy between corporate leadership and customer service functions. In such 'tall' organisations this can lead to much duplication of activity (e.g., a marketing manager in each business unit) and slow decision-making since information will often have to be relayed 'up the chain' to gain the necessary approval. Due to the siloed nature of such organisations, and the accompanying financial and performance structures, decisions will often be made only in the self-interest of the business unit rather than to the overall benefit of the organisation. Digital technologies have helped to liberate organisational models from the extensive, wasteful, and bureaucratic nature of hierarchical organisations. The development of interactive software platforms has assisted inter-business communication and aided the internal visibility of company intelligence and operations. Central services that now need less business unit presence for strategic tasks include human resources, finance, and marketing. Those personnel that do remain within the business unit often perform customer-facing roles, supporting the business on a day-to-day basis. Team-based software platforms allow for flatter organisations which are easier to co-ordinate, collaborate with, and to combine their efforts to meet customer needs.

Robertson (2017) describes 'Holacracy' as a method of decentralised management and organisational governance, in which authority and decision-making are distributed throughout a holarchy of self-organising teams rather than being vested in a management hierarchy. However, team-based software platforms do not limit their scope to exclusively internal business functions. They can also encompass workers from other divisions, and workers who are not normally employed by the organisation except in a visiting or consulting capacity, whose expertise may be needed on a project basis for a standalone project. Such 'virtual teams' are supported by online or app-based platforms which enable team members to communicate, share information, plan together, and jointly create key documentation, all without ever having to meet. The flexibility of such software platforms allows for teams to be formed quickly around a specific challenge or opportunity. Their versatility of configuration can also make clear to each individual team member their specific responsibilities, hold them to account, and adjust and shape the team as its purpose changes over time. All of this is without the cost- and time-intensive requirements of office space, meeting rooms, and teams of administrators whose task it would be to marshal large volumes of paperwork. Instead, teams can be strongly focused on serving customer needs, which can be addressed through effective and diverse cross-functional teams. The speed and flexibility of this approach help the organisation to become more agile and versatile, enhancing its overall long-term resilience to change.

Power structures differ from organisation structures in that they deal with how informal power and influence are built and exercised throughout the organisation. They deal less with formal reporting lines and relate more to the people and the systems who have the power to get things done. They are related to the formal organisational structure, but are not easily recognisable from organisation charts. In contrast to organisational structures, power structures are a more human-based practice, much less formal in arrangement and seldom visible to the wider organisation. Power structures are built upon the perception and influence of individuals and small teams distributed throughout the organisation. Influencers leave their mark by judicious use of media, either as originators (i.e., opinion leaders), supporters (e.g., encouraging those who share their own core beliefs), and enablers (e.g., signposting support and guiding those they support through the politics and administration of the organisation). They may act in formal or informal mentoring roles. Influencers will often have a clear understanding of media channels (both internal and external) and will be highly visible in adding their endorsement to new initiatives. Powerful behaviours can be built through training, cross-functional rotation, and participation in communities of interest. All of this can be facilitated and tailored through digital tools such as team-based apps and VLEs. Communities of practice (CoPs) represent informal power structures that operate within and outside an organisation. A CoP is described as groups of practitioners who 'share a passion for something they know how to do and who interact regularly to learn how to do it better' (Wenger, 2000). CoPs can be facilitated from a blend of online or offline activities as required.

Symbols are physical artefacts that represent the organisation's culture. They can include advertising, logos, the style of the working environment, dress codes, and titles. Principally the domain of *promotion* within the marketing mix, these symbols should permeate throughout the organisation's online and offline communications and branding efforts. Since company logos and slogans are symbols, some companies update them regularly to ensure the typeface and style are modern. Displays of innovation successes and other artefacts in highly visible, high-traffic areas such as foyers and reception areas can present a powerful image of the organisation. In-store interactive display screens which regularly update the display can present a compelling and varied picture of what the organisation does, and increasingly whom it benefits. Social and environmental interest stories are becoming increasingly of interest to customers, so visuals of how the organisation is working to decrease the negative social and environmental impact of its work, either indirectly through its support of charitable organisations or formally by adapting its own supply chain, create a strong resonance.

Stories express how an organisation understands and explains itself. Every organisation has stories that capture the essence of key events and share a 'folklore'. Such stories are told to new recruits and visitors and act to reinforce behaviours. Stories tend to focus around key organisational values which it actively promotes, such as the taking of reasonable risks, perseverance, resilience, persistence, and positive and entertaining stories of mavericks. Effective stories and language will focus on learning rather than blame, and accept innovation success and failure. They will run as a thread throughout the organisation both as formal 'style guides' and histories of the organisation, but also in the terms that the organisation uses to describe its actions. However, stories are not just a matter for organisational historians and copywriters developing press releases around case studies of recent business successes. Stories (good and bad) develop within discussion threads on social media which may be led by the organisation posting on its own feed something which it hopes to share with its loyal audience (and which it hopes they in turn will share within their own online communities), or it may be posted by a stakeholder who may be pleased or displeased about something for which it sees the organisation as responsible. The organisation's considered response to this will establish new stories for its internal and external stakeholders.

Rituals and routines are the organisation's accepted norms and practices. They consider the ways employees learn to act towards each other and can enable the organisation to run smoothly. In addition to formal processes, organisations develop unwritten rules on how different departments interact during the innovation process. Routines can be difficult to change because they are often based on tacit knowledge and strongly support the overall paradigm of the organisation. Organisational rituals include regular meetings and traditions, and promotion criteria and appraisals. Businesses seeking to encourage innovation should work to promote new ideas for new products and new services and process improvements through internal and external communications and the formal/informal organisation. There may also be a process for internal venture management – making advice, support, and finance available for funding entrepreneurial ideas and opportunities – facilitated by online innovation disclosures which are quickly followed up and disseminated to pre-identified internal and external collaborators to verify and pursue the opportunity to its natural conclusion.

Control systems control how things are done, reported, and rewarded across the organisation. They act to integrate corporate objectives with measurement systems and reward and recognition systems. The most important control systems for innovation are those used to select ideas and implement them efficiently. For this work to support innovative activity, rather than unnecessarily impede it, the organisation must ensure that there are simple mechanisms for staff to propose ideas and obtain resources to investigate them. Most companies have introduced stage-gate processes, but leading organisations have moved to having a more flexible process for the whole of innovation. Well-defined and refined systems and processes should promote the freedom of entrepreneurial thinking within the scope of what the organisation considers to be its acceptable levels of risk versus potential reward. Metrics and goals should be cascaded to all levels of employees (internal and external) with rewards and recognition that link innovation to performance appraisals. Control systems should focus idea selection on growth (not costs) and support it with flexible but fast implementation processes.

RESEARCH INSIGHT 8.3 Digital Organisations

Davison, R. M., and Ou, C. X. J. (2017). Digital work in a digitally challenged organization. *Information & Management*, 54(1): 129–137.

This paper explores how digital technologies have transformed organisational forms and function,.creating significant benefits to employees and customers alike. To a large degree these organisations have benefited from employees with existing awareness and skills in digital technologies. However, not all digitally literate employees work in a digitally liberated environment. Instead, employees may experience significant barriers that hinder their digital engagement – for example, the organisation's governance approaches which may seek to curtail or reject technologies and persist with outdated patterns of work and control. This reticence by the leaders of the organisation can create tension with the irreconcilable demands of a digitally literate workforce. This study considers employee responses to such limiting factors and how they impact upon the organisation and the employees.

DIGITAL INSIGHT 8.3 Digital Culture Change: Evolution or Revolution?

The challenge of the increasing pace, scale, and scope of change thrust upon us as a result of technological advancements, and the threat of customers leaving us to move to our competitors to benefit from a more satisfying experience can elicit a multitude of responses from the organisation, from denial to outright panic. Do we ignore the changes in the belief that they are a mere fad and that customers will return to us in due course, or do we go all-out to invest in a radically different organisation to satisfy their current and emerging needs? From a capabilities point of view, it would minimise short-term disruption if a managed programme of transition, inclusive of all stakeholders, were to keep the essential culture of the organisation in place. However, it is not always possible to have this serene migration that keeps everyone happy. In the case of a significant step change in technological development which renders obsolete all that the organisation has become, then the only answer instead of a steady evolution is a rapid revolution. Significant change can be painful, principally due to uncertainty and feelings of dislocation in 'how things work here'. To manage radical change within the organisation we must first create a compelling case for change, challenging the taken-for-granted, supported by an extensive communications campaign which is transparent and accessible to all concerned. Operational processes and routines may also need a significant overhaul, involving data migration and integration, which despite our best planned scenarios will encounter teething troubles when rolled out at scale and when put into the hands of demanding users as opposed to sympathetic developers. To embed these changes, we must target quick wins that provide instant benefit to, and perhaps therefore minimise the resistance from, end-users.

CHAPTER SUMMARY

In this chapter we have explored the concept of creativity, how it occurs, and how to stimulate it inside the organisation and in concert with external partners. We follow the theme of external collaboration, in addition to the internal organisational effort, into innovation and idea generation, exploring the concept of open innovation. Further, we examined the different scopes and scales of innovation across the marketing mix. This led to a final discussion of how the organisation gears itself to be more innovative, both in terms of its 'hard' activity, which includes how its capabilities are configured to achieve short- and medium-term goals, but also in terms of achieving the organisation's long-term goals and mission through how it defines itself in cultural terms.

Review Questions

. . . .

1. Describe the different types of creativity and compare their roles in the innovation process.
2. What are the relative advantages and disadvantages of sourcing ideas from both inside and outside the organisation?
3. Using examples to illustrate your ideas, how do organisational resources and competencies support the organisation's ability to take new innovations to market?
4. Prioritise the aspects of an organisation's culture in terms of how you think they contribute to its ability to successfully innovate. Explain why you think that some factors are more important than others. Use examples to illustrate your ideas.

END-OF-CHAPTER CASE: PIXAR ANIMATION STUDIOS

Pixar Animation Studios has for the past four decades been synonymous with its pioneering use of digital technologies in movie production. Below is a summarised version of their history (Pixar, 2021). Acting as they do as leaders in the fields of creativity and innovation, we will later explore the role digital technologies played in the eras of development in its corporate history. This is also an excellent opportunity for you to binge-watch some of their movies under the guise of academic research! It certainly brought back some very happy memories of watching these films myself, and more recently with my kids. Enjoy.

1979 Lucasfilm begins the development and adoption of new computer technology for the film industry with film and sound editing systems, laser film printing, and computer graphics.

1982 The 'Genesis Effect' computer animated sequence for *Star Trek II: The Wrath of Khan* portrays the transformation of a barren planet into a vibrant ecological ecosystem.

1984 'The Adventures of André & Wally B.' features character animation, hand-painted textures, and motion blur.

1986 Steve Jobs, co-founder of Apple, buys the Computer Division from Lucasfilm and establishes Pixar as an independent company. Pixar and Disney begin their partnership to create animated films. 'Luxo Jr.' is the first 3D computer animated film to be nominated for an Oscar.

1988 Pixar's modelling environment system, Marionette, and its rendering software, RenderMan, are launched into the Pixar production system.

1989 Pixar begins making screen advertisements for commercial clients, developing their storytelling and collaborative skills.

1995 *Toy Story*, the world's first computer animated feature film, is released. It will go on to become the highest grossing film of the year, being critically recognised with multiple Academy Award nominations.

2002 'A Bug's Land', a Disney themepark spin-off from *A Bug's Life*, opens.

2006 The Walt Disney Company acquires Pixar Animation Studios.

2007 'Finding Nemo Submarine Voyage' opens in Tomorrowland at Disneyland Park in California.

2009 *Up* becomes the first animated feature film to open the Cannes Film Festival.

2012 Marionette is replaced by a new animation system, 'Presto'.

2013 'Toy Story of TERROR!' is transmitted on ABC.

2016 'The Toy Story Hotel' and 'Buzz Lightyear Planet Rescue' open at the new Shanghai Disney Resort.

2017 Pixar releases its RenderMan software for non-commercial use. Online educational program 'Pixar in a Box' is released in partnership with the Khan Academy.

DISCUSSION QUESTIONS

1. What have been the key themes of Pixar's creativity and innovation development over the timeline of its history? You may want to draw this.
2. What has been the impact of digital technologies upon the creative process (i.e., movie production)?
3. What was the impact of digital technologies upon the innovation process (i.e., the products and markets that it has developed)?

Develop Your Skills

. . . .

What Is the Skill?

Undertaking a digital innovation audit.

Why Is It Important?

To make good use in an organisational context of the knowledge discussed above, we need to have a process whereby we can objectively assess our digital innovation capabilities. This will help us to identify strengths that we can further enhance to create external market opportunities over rivals who are less well equipped. Similarly, we can identify weaknesses that need to be reconsidered in terms of their roles in creating value in the organisation. It may not be worth fixing every weakness in the organisation since that capability may have become weak because it is less valued or is considered to be less important. So, some prioritisation needs to take place before we invest heavily in something that we don't do that well because it isn't important. However, weaknesses in core capabilities need to be addressed quickly and effectively to avoid potentially crippling effects on the organisation's digital innovation effort.

How to Develop It

Goffin and Mitchell (2017) expand on the innovation pipeline of describing how ideas enter and progress through the organisation until a selected few go forward to market implementation. They augment this model to become the Pentathlon Framework (Figure 8.3) by also considering the roles of corporate strategy and the organisation configuration itself. We will use this as the basis for the digital innovation audit.

How to Apply It

Based upon this model, we can focus upon specific digital capabilities, rating ourselves against identified customer needs or the benchmark set by our closest competitors. With the use of the framework in Table 8.1 we assess three key digital innovation factors from each of the domains of the Pentathlon model.

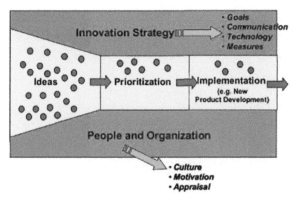

Figure 8.3 The Innovation Pentathlon Framework (Goffin and Mitchell, 2017). © Goffin, K. and Mitchell, R. (2017). *Innovation Management. Effective Strategy and Implementation* 3rd ed. Red Globe Press, used by permission of Bloomsbury Publishing, Plc.

Table 8.1 Digital innovation audit (adapted from Goffin and Mitchell, 2017)

	Aspect	Importance to the customer (1 = low to 5 = high)	Our performance (1 = low to 5 = high)	Closest competitor's performance (1 = low to 5 = high)
IDEAS	Use of digital technologies to collaborate with customers, suppliers, and other partner organisations			
	A single digital portal where all stakeholders can submit their ideas			
	Use of digital market research techniques to capture customer needs and preferences			
PRIORITISATION	Digital process to evaluate ideas based on scoring against clear criteria			
	Use of digital forecasting and simulation tools which consider potential risks and rewards			
	Online access to real-time measures of how efficiently we are using our resources			
IMPLEMENTATION	Visibility and status updates of projects in different stages of the innovation process			
	Digital tools that allow for stakeholder input and support as the product develops			
	Planning the prototyping, piloting, launch, and scale-up of new products into capacity utilisation of R&D, manufacturing, suppliers, and support functions			

Table 8.1 (*cont.*)

STRATEGY	Visibility of the innovation fund's current investments and their progress against objectives
	Use of digital media to communicate the organisation's innovation goals to all stakeholders
	Use of digital scanning techniques to identify key trends and market drivers in the operating environment
PEOPLE	Clear reward and recognition criteria for innovative and entrepreneurial behaviour
	Provision of online training for staff in innovation-related activities
	Use of digital platforms to observe, engage, and collaborate with the innovation team

References

Adamczyk, S., Bullinger, A. C., and Möslein, K. M. (2012). Innovation contests: a review, classification and outlook. *Creativity and Innovation Management*, 21(4): 355–360.

Berthon, P. R., McCarthy, I. P., Pitt, L., and Kates, S. (2007). When customers get clever: managerial approaches to dealing with creative consumers. *Business Horizons*, 50(1)

Boden, M. A. (2013). Creativity as a neuroscientific mystery. In O. Vartanian, A. S. Bristol, and J. C. Kaufman (eds.), *Neuroscience of Creativity*. Cambridge, MA: MIT Press.

Bullinger, A. C., Neyer, A., Rass, M., and Moeslein, K. M. (2010). Community-based innovation contests: where competition meets cooperation. *Creativity and Innovation Management*, 19(3): 290–303.

Chesbrough, H. W. (2006). *Open Innovation: The New Imperative for Creating and Profiting from Technology*. Cambridge, MA: Harvard Business Review Press.

Davison, R. M., and Ou, C. X. J. (2017). Digital work in a digitally challenged organization. *Information & Management*, 54(1): 129–137.

Goffin, K., and Mitchell, R. (2017). *Innovation Management. Effective Strategy and Implementation*, 3rd ed. Basingstoke: Palgrave.

Gregg, B., Heller, J., Perrey, J., and Tsai, J. (2018) The most perfect union: unlocking the next wave of growth by unifying creativity and analytics [online]. Available from: www.mckinsey.com/business-functions/marketing-and-sales/our-insights/the-most-perfect-union [Accessed 28 October 2019].

Haller, J. B. A., Bullinger, A. C., and Möslein, K. M. (2011). Innovation contests: an IT-based tool for innovation management. *Business & Information Systems Engineering*, 3(2).

JISC (2018). Building digital capability [online]. Available from: http://repository .jisc.ac.uk/6611/1/JFL0066F_DIGIGAP_MOD_IND_FRAME.PDF [Accessed 1 November 2019].

Johnson, G., Whittington, R., Scholes, K., Angwin, D., and Regnér, P. (2017) *Exploring Strategy: Text and Cases*, 11th ed. Harlow: Pearson.

Kirah, A. (2009). Co-creation: a new way of doing business in an age of uncertainty. *Technology Innovation Management Review*, November: 73–90.

Lee, M. R., and Chen, T. T. (2015). Digital creativity: research themes and framework. *Computers in Human Behavior*, 42: 12–19.

Mumford, M. D. (2003). Where have we been, where are we going? Taking stock in creativity research. *Creativity Research Journal*, 15(2–3): 107–120.

Nambisan, S., Lyytinen, K., Majchrzak, A., and Song, M. (2017). Digital innovation management: reinventing innovation management research in a digital world. *MIS Quarterly*, 41(1): 223–238.

O'Reilly, C. A., and Tushman, M. L. (2004). The ambidextrous organization. *Harvard Business Review*, 82(4): 74–81.

Piller, F. T., and West, J. (2014). Firms, users, and innovation: an interactive model of coupled open innovation. In H. W. Chesbrough, W. Vanhaverbeke, and J. West (eds.), *New Frontiers in Open Innovation*. Oxford: Oxford University Press.

Pixar (2021). Our story [online]. Available from: www.pixar.com/our-story-pixar [Accessed 31 July 2021].

Robertson, B. J. (2017). *Holacracy: The Revolutionary Management System that Abolishes Hierarchy.* London: Penguin.

Schumpeter, J. A. (1942). *Capitalism, Socialism, and Democracy.* New York: Harper & Brothers.

Sheth, J. N., and Ram, S. (1987). *Bringing Innovation to Market: How to Break Corporate and Customer Barriers.* New York: Wiley.

Torrance, E. P. (1966). *Torrance Tests of Creative Thinking: Norms Technical Manual Research Edition – Verbal Tests, Forms A and B – Figural Tests, Forms A and B.* Princeton, NJ: Personnel Pres. Inc.

von Hippel, E. (1986). Lead users: a source of novel product concepts. *Management Science*, 32(7): 773–907.

von Hippel, E. (1998). Economics of product development by users: the impact of 'sticky' local information. *Management Science*, 44(5): 629–644.

Wenger, E. (2000). *Communities of Practice: Learning, Meaning, and Identity.* Cambridge: Cambridge University Press.

9 Emerging Challenges and Opportunities

Introduction

This chapter considers some key digital trends and how they are affecting the ways in which we live, work, and play. The core focus is upon technological trends, but this discussion would be incomplete if it did not recognise other trends – political, economic, and social – that both feed into and are affected by digital change. The chapter largely takes a macro-level view of the immediate future and lays the foundation for a micro-level view in Chapter 10, where the implications for digital marketing practice will be explored. Since the future is by nature uncertain, we offer no firm models or theories to interpret 'reality'. Instead, this is a place for consideration of past developments, their trajectories and pace of development, and how they might combine to present consumers, commercial organisations, and regulators with challenges to be managed and opportunities to be explored.

Learning Objectives

- Evaluate current and emerging technology trends.
- Consider the impacts upon how markets behave.
- Appraise the threats and opportunities for buyers and sellers.
- Prioritise potential organisational marketing responses.

CASE INSIGHT: COVID-19

In December 2019, Wuhan, the capital of China's Hubei province, saw the first reports, of Coronavirus Disease 2019 (COVID-19), an infectious respiratory disease, which within a matter of weeks resulted in the declaration of a global pandemic by the World Health Organization. To control the rate of infection that threatened to overwhelm medical services and cause significantly higher death rates, governments across the world instituted social distancing measures, including the closing of non-essential businesses and population lockdowns, to slow the spread of the virus. All but essential workplaces, shops, and community venues closed. Businesses were seldom given more than a few days' notice that they were required to close. Where possible, employees were instructed to work from home as offices, factories, shops, and schools closed. Entertainment venues such as restaurants and cinemas were closed until further notice. Sports events, concerts, and theatre performances were cancelled. The COVID-19 pandemic caused significant loss of life and mental health issues. With the duration and extent of the lockdown uncertain, many businesses had no choice but to significantly curtail their workforce or close permanently, causing a significant rise in unemployment. Yet many organisations and self-employed workers managed to stay in business. Digital technologies played a significant role in:

- government crisis management processes (tracking the progress of the disease, communicating with the population, predicting potential future health and economic effects, deploying healthcare and financial resources);
- businesses expanding the use of existing online platforms to be the principal or sole route to supplying customers with meals (e.g., Just Eat, Uber Eats), groceries (e.g., Ocado, Asda), clothing (e.g., Next, ASOS), entertainment (e.g., YouTube, Disney+, Netflix);
- social contact via platforms such as Facebook, Messenger, and WhatsApp, which continue to thrive, but it was more the more personal live chat platforms such as Zoom, FaceTime, and Skype that provided sustained human interaction.

Questions

Reflecting upon your own experience:

- In what way did your work and social behaviour become more digital in this period?
- How did this change affect you emotionally, and the relationships you had with others?
- Were these changes temporary or permanent?
- What would you have done differently?

The sections that follow aim to distil the key technologies and applications that we have explored in the preceding chapters, to gain an overview of the themes for future development of digital technologies and how they will impact upon the ways that we live, learn, work, and buy. These discussions are not meant in any sense to be predictive, and do not give forecasts. Instead, we will revisit the technologies, discuss who will be impacted by their application, and identify potential opportunities and threats for some of those concerned. This section could help to form the basis of an assessment of the organisation's strategic fit, or SWOT analysis (see Chapter 3), informing the planning of the organisation's strategy to exploit and develop its resources and skills.

9.1   Data

Our ability to capture, transfer, and analyse data at scale is unparalleled. The World Wide Web provides the network, the Internet provides the common language, sensors provide the input points, algorithms provide us with an interpretation of what the data means, and automation enables a suitable response to the data based on defined parameters and objectives. Sales organisations are acutely aware of the potential to identify and respond to customers' existing and emerging needs. Data patterns from our browsing and purchase history can predict products that have a high likelihood of being of interest to customers and this visibility occurs across multiple platforms. For example, if you have an interest in cycling you might share cycling related content from YouTube on your Facebook, Instagram, or Twitter accounts. People that you are connected to, who may like and further share your content, will form a reference or user group within analytics packages. Perhaps you might choose to further act on your cycling interest by searching for and purchasing equipment and spares from eBay, Amazon, or specialist sites. Your integrated data profile is now flagging up opportunities for advertisers to make you aware of holidays, clothing, accessories, training supplements, maps, and books that may help you to get even more pleasure from your interest. This cross-platform integration can be a little unnerving at first. For example, when searching through sites that we consider to be independent of our social media activity, to then have the same product, or close relatives, to appear in our feed of notifications can make us question the privacy of our actions, which is a theme we will explore further in Section 9.6. However, buyers and sellers see it as an efficient marketing process to serve global product demand from a fragmented and widely distributed base of potential suppliers. The data and processing technologies have given rise to a range of machine intelligences that help us, both as buyers and sellers, in many ways:

- **Assisted intelligence** gives an incremental improvement to what people and organisations are already doing. Examples include predictive spelling in short message service (SMS) applications or a Global Positioning Satellite (GPS) navigation program that offers route advice to travellers, based on their preferred time and mode of travel. Chatbot technologies offer significant savings for service-based industries. Whether they use voice or character recognition, they are designed to interpret enquiries in order to give the desired response. Another example would be self-checkout facilities in grocery stores.

- **Augmented intelligence** offers a radical improvement on the user experience which enables people and organisations to do things they could not otherwise do. For example, the combination of programs that organise cars in ridesharing apps (e.g., Uber and Didi) or home-sharing apps (e.g., Airbnb) enables customers to connect with suppliers that could not otherwise exist.

- **Autonomous intelligence** transforms the supplier and buyer experience, using deep learning – otherwise known as machine learning – technologies which allow machines that act on their own. Here, sensor technologies are coupled with sophisticated algorithms and robotic process automation to give automatic responses through the Internet of Things (IoT). Simple examples include your refrigerator recognising that the stock of your favourite ice cream is running low and maybe placing an order with the grocery store for a delivery. More sophisticated examples include self-driving vehicles.

DIGITAL INSIGHT 9.1 Should Data Replace Intuition in Marketing Decisions?

While there is often tension between them, data and intuition are not necessarily mutually exclusive when it comes to making marketing decisions. Reid Hoffman (Hoffman and Yeh, 2018), founder of LinkedIn, describes one of the key transition points in enterprise development as moving 'from pirate to navy', indicating the changing level of responsibility as organisations move from creative and seemingly chaotic decision-making in small, tight-knit teams to larger and more accountable decision-making as the organisation grows, with more people, formalised processes, and budget lines. With early decisions free from the history of the organisation (which can be a significant limiting factor on the culture of decision-making and accountability), intuition has free rein and can create spectacular results, both good and bad. The work by O'Reilly and Tushman (2004) on ambidextrous innovation, which we explored in Chapter 8, also makes clear the need for risky and creative thinking (i.e., innovation) that helps the organisation to refresh, reset, and succeed. So, while we invest time and effort trying to get algorithms to think like us, they too will be guided by the biases in how we think, and our attachment to past behaviours. This occurs not necessarily because they are the right ones, but because they are the ones we are most familiar and comfortable with.

9.1.1 Opportunities

Industries such as food production (e.g., crop and livestock farmers and food processors) and utility suppliers (e.g., water, gas, and electricity), where timing is a crucial factor, will see benefits from more effective processes, which may lead to reductions in raw material consumption, production waste, and the spoilage of materials that cannot be stored in a good state for an extended period. Manufacturing organisations such as automobile and computer hardware makers will see more efficient and timely purchasing, reductions in inventories, and less waste in the manufacturing process as more popular products are improved and less popular products are retired or significantly revised. Service-driven organisations in healthcare, retail, travel, and tourism and entertainment sectors will build, maintain, and extend relationships using relationship management processes (e.g., order tracking, related recommendations, and social media content) to enhance the customer experience. Improved data management allows for better use of the organisation's people and cash, allowing for timely responses to customer needs.

9.1.2 Threats

The growing wealth of data available to us can carry many challenges. Which data to focus upon and which data to ignore? This will be driven by the reliability and robustness of the sources, but also by the perceived usefulness to the organisation. How do we differentiate between 'need to know' and 'want to know'? Analysing different data sources can take up much of our time, in many cases offering conflicting views, potentially leading the seller and the buyer to a state of 'analysis paralysis' where it is easier not to make a decision, given that there is no clear course of action that recommends itself to us. Data distortions and biases are common since we need to interpret the data so that it becomes meaningful to us. If we misunderstand or ignore events in our markets (such as a drop in sales or the emergence of a potential competitor) we may wrongly explain them away as fads rather than deeper trends for the future that need to be addressed sooner rather than later if we are to maintain or improve our market position. There are many ongoing ethical debates relating to what customer data can be captured, used, and shared by an organisation. The sale of customer data to other organisations, and the use of facial and voice recognition software continue to raise privacy issues among customers and legislators.

9.1.3 Conclusion

Data proliferation could be a blessing to make our lives simpler, easier, and more convenient. As consumers it takes away the need to think too much about what we want, since there are technologies to predict what we want to buy, when we want to buy it, and how we want it supplied, even taking away the need to make multiple transactions through the use of automated payments. On the other hand, there is also potential for data to enslave us to repeat the past, making us lazy in the development of our diverse and unrelated human activities. There is also much scope for confusion as the supply of data increases. It is important to remember that the information we receive from a system is only as useful as the data that feeds it and the decision-making parameters that guide it.

RESEARCH INSIGHT 9.1 How Might the Internet of Things Develop?

Ng, I., and Wakenshaw, S. (2017). The Internet-of-Things: review and research directions. *International Journal of Research in Marketing*, 34(1): 3–21.

This paper presents a review of the IoT research from a wide range of perspectives on its form and use. By reviewing the recent trends in both the practical applications and scholarly research of IoT applications it proposes a set of priorities for future research that extends beyond data science into design and innovation, organisational studies, and economics. The authors identify the following practice-based themes, which will frame, and be framed by, future IoT applications and configurations:

- Consumer experiences with physical products will be highly visible.
- Physical products are evolving into dynamically reconfigurable service platforms.
- Information is ubiquitous and difficult to control.
- Consumers' personal data allows for personalisation but also presents risks.
- Shifting boundaries due to information flows will transform markets and exchanges.

9.2   Humans

Technology revolutions have always changed the role of humans in society. They impact upon where we live, how we earn money, how we spend money, and how we relate to one another. **The first Industrial Revolution, mechanisation** (late eighteenth to early nineteenth century), was driven by the arrival of new materials, such as iron and steel, the scaled-up use of energy sources such as coal and steam, and new machines such as the spinning jenny and the power loom that enabled greater productivity for a lower input of human energy. This caused a significant dislocation of where people lived and worked. Dispersed, often rural, communities who would normally work in the same places as they lived gave way to a greater concentration of workers in towns and cities, working in factories where the scale potential of the new technologies could be fully exploited. Employment and living conditions were often poor but opportunities for education, economic security, and the development of specialist high-value skills could be much higher through the collective endeavours of large integrated communities. The need for traditional farming and crafting skills declined and the need for numeracy, literacy, and engineering skills rose with the introduction of technologies. **The second Industrial Revolution, mass production** (late nineteenth to mid-twentieth century), was driven by the generation and transmission of electricity, which in conjunction with assembly lines enabled mass production, and the internal combustion engine, and thus the automobile, leading to mass transportation. The expansion of steel production (which gradually replaced iron) enabled a growth in construction, industrial machinery, railways, and ships. The introduction of public electricity to light homes and factories replaced candles and gas lamps. Reduced reliance on daylight and increased use of machinery created more productive economies. Increasing mechanisation led to a deskilling of traditional craft-based roles and an increase in assembly-line operations. Professions began to emerge due to divisions of labour, as did awareness of the rights of the individual. Employee exploitation due to the excesses of some employers led to the politicisation of the workforce and the emergence of the trade union movement. Organisation and business management skills became necessary for the factory system to thrive. Employee rights were secured, health, education, and social security provisions were enacted. Due to production economies of scale and the growing wealth of the workforce, manufactured goods became affordable to the wider population. These include cookers, televisions, refrigerators, cars, and telephones. Leisure and mass entertainment became major industries. **The third Industrial Revolution, automation** (late twentieth to early twenty-first century), was all about computers. From the 1950s onwards, computers and digital systems enabled new ways of processing and sharing information. Transistors, microprocessors, robotics, and automation – not to mention the Internet and mass communications – would eventually allow for globalisation. A gamut of new technologies, including artificial intelligence, big data, drones, robots, the IoT, and 3D printing, holds out the promise of substantial economic advances. There is a broad range of opinions on the likely impact of these technologies. Optimists see strong prospects for a surge in productivity growth, rising living standards, and buoyant investment returns. Technologies could also have a substantially positive ecological impact on the grounds that they could use fewer resources in the production, purchase, use, and recycling of manufactured products. Think of how ride-hailing services such as Uber and Didi could reduce consumer debt, traffic congestion, pollution, and the storage space required when you buy a car. With the increased adoption of big data there will surely be a significant demand for the skills of cyber security professionals. The pessimists fear mass job insecurity (taking the above example and considering this from the perspective of the car manufacturer or taxi driver), widening inequality, and even the obsolescence of human beings who would be superseded as they may not be equipped to compete with their artificial counterparts. However, it is still early days to know the full impact for many of these developments, both from a technological and a social adoption viewpoint. The **fourth Industrial Revolution, robotisation** (from the early twenty-first century), centres around artificially intelligent cyber–physical systems – that is, the merging of the capabilities of humans and machines, leading to autonomous decision-making. Hyperconnectivity, cloud, and blockchain will create the intelligent factory, with little need for human operational intervention. Autonomous vehicles are just one example of the large integrated systems in action. Instead of technology being a thing we use, and which changes us, it will now be embedded into our lives – and our bodies – to affect great change. This revolution has the potential to bring us smart cities that reduce poverty and enhance standards of living, sustainable energy sources, environmental protection, more inclusive government process, social cohesiveness and collaboration, and to make us healthier. However, the shifts in power brought about by such human–technology systems could also bring about issues of inequality (who gets the benefits of what tech) and security (everything will be connected), as well as challenges to the very nature of identity (privacy) and community (global versus local). Business value chains will need to adapt – since the chain is only as strong as its weakest link – with versatility and resilience becoming key organisational competencies. The attitudes and roles of consumers will also change, since the monotony of frequent routine decisions will be taken away and choice will multiply. Experience, novelty, and creativity will become key criteria in customer satisfaction. To this extent the automation of buyer–seller engagements may lead to us feeling socially isolated to the extent that we seek out more opportunities for face-to-face human interaction and begin to leave our smartphones behind.

DIGITAL INSIGHT 9.2 Are Cyborgs Already Here?

Science fiction is rich with images of cyborgs, futuristic representations of an organism with both organic and mechanical parts with enhanced abilities due to the integration of technology that relies on some sort of feedback. In science fiction, the most recognisable portrayal of a cyborg is a human being with visibly mechanical parts, such as the superhero Cyborg from DC Comics, the Borg from Star Trek, or Darth Vader from Star Wars. Medical applications include cochlear implants and magnetic implants that assist hearing, brain implants that have been used to treat non-congenital blindness, and pacemakers that help to regulate the rhythms of the heart. However, more radical examples exist, such as the artist Neil Harbisson, who is the first person with an antenna implanted in his skull which sends information through his skull via audible vibrations, enabling him to take phone calls and listen to music. He is also the first person to be legally recognised as a cyborg. Does science fiction offer a reasonable prediction of how far human–machine integration might take us? Futurist Raymond Kurzweil (2005) writes about artificial intelligence and the future of humanity in relation to the Singularity (i.e., the point at which machine intelligence and humans would merge) when he predicts that machine intelligence will be infinitely more powerful than all human intelligence combined.

9.2.1 Opportunities

A range of technologies discussed in Section 9.1 increases our use and reliance upon technology through artificial reality and virtual reality, creating greater levels of human–digital integration. This has helped to relieve us of the mundane tasks of getting quotes for travel or accommodation insurance, visiting or calling multiple rental agencies to find suitable accommodation, and even placing orders for grocery supplies. While technology can relieve us of mundane tasks, it also opens new human capabilities (e.g., 3D printing of artificial implants or optical character recognition connected to voice synthesis that can read text to the visually impaired). Wearable technology can connect to biometric systems that monitor our health vital signs to warn us of the need to take any preventive action, such as medication or a check-up visit to a physician. Technology has the potential to make us more productive through the efficient deployment of our efforts and the elimination of waste.

9.2.2 Threats

Genetic engineering, enhanced humans, and autonomous systems have a rich history in the science fiction movie genre when it comes to dystopian futures. A few personal favourites include the rogue replicants in *Blade Runner*, the post-apocalyptic future of humans enslaved by machines as a source of energy in *The Matrix*, and of course the time-travelling cyborg assassin seeking to protect Skynet in *The Terminator*. When it comes to autonomous systems, the decision parameters are decided upon and controlled by the programs. There are ethical governance concerns as to how these systems are controlled, and the accountability of the controllers. The increasing speed, scope, and scale can cause anxiety as people's 'normal' lives face significant disruption.

9.2.3 Conclusion

While waves of technological change are inevitable, causing some lifestyles to retreat and others to advance, we should try to navigate these changes with empathy across the difficult transition stages, to ensure that the benefits, both social and economic, are maximised for all of humankind.

RESEARCH INSIGHT 9.2 Global Strategic Trends

Ministry of Defence (2018). *Global Strategic Trends: The Future Starts Today*, 6th ed. London: Ministry of Defence UK.

This extensive strategic review and foresighting programme identifies long-term threats and opportunities at a global level. Its analysis identifies key trends which are further developed in this chapter, but importantly sets them within a wider environmental context which demonstrates the breadth and depth of the effect of digital technologies. It does not attempt to predict the future but describes those phenomena that could have a significant impact on the future and combines these differing perspectives to produce a multifaceted picture of possible outcomes. The key thematic areas are:

- environment and resources;
- human development;
- economy, industry, and innovation;
- governance and law; and
- conflict and security.

9.3 Ownership

The development of the Internet has led to many fundamental questions about what property is, who owns it, how it can be protected, and how it can be shared. The publishing sector has experienced considerable disruption, which has forced a radical rethink of its business model. When it comes to digitised products the music industry has benefited greatly from an increase in product distribution and use both as a result of the software which enables songs to be downloaded and the hardware which enables songs to be retained and recalled at will. However, unsecure processes allowed for goods to be paid for once and then shared at will, with no additional income for the writers, performers, or producers. While this was illegal as it constituted a breach of copyright, it took the industry some time to develop the technologies and processes to create a more secure system. The piracy that ensued in the short term jeopardised the publishers, but also record producers, writers, and performers, since their main income stream (i.e., publishing royalties) was significantly reduced. This led to a rethink of the model. Whereas artists would tour to promote their back catalogue, with the tours operating as a price skimming or loss leader strategy on the assumption that overall money would be earned back by record sales, now the model has flipped. Artists now publish music that can be streamed or downloaded, but the true premium experience is attending the concert in person. The music industry is not the only one put in jeopardy by the digital phenomenon. Printed newspapers and magazines are no longer our main source of news; instead we are opting for social media or online sources such as bbc.co.uk. The sales of movie DVDs or Blu-ray discs has shrunk as more viewers choose on-demand streaming services such as Sky, Netflix, or Disney+. Book publishers have seen a resurgence of demand for printed copies, but there is still a strong demand for e-books (e.g., the Amazon Kindle) and audiobooks (e.g., Audible).

Even where the product is physical, the global reach of the World Wide Web and the empowerment of consumers to buy products from anywhere in the world has questioned the relevance of traditional retail supply chains and the role of retailing itself. Traditional retailers have existed to provide choice (i.e., alternative products and brands) and accessibility (i.e., in-store stock) for buyers. Since the Internet represents the ultimate 'shop window' for suppliers across the world, and high rents and the need for increased cash liquidity make it unattractive for retailers to devote space to speculatively storing stock, more retailers are changing their models. More often, retailers are designing their in-store experience to engage customers and expose them to the brand through richer store displays, supportive and interactive staff, and product sampling. They have no need to compete with internet competitors to provide choice and availability since they are focusing more upon the *first moment of truth* (Lecinski, 2011), which is when the customer gains hands-on experience with the product at the point of purchase, a significant stage in the decision-making and purchasing process.

Digital technologies have been a significant driver in our changing attitudes to purchasing, and owning products has led to the phenomenon of New Consumerism (Euromonitor, 2016; Figure 9.1). As consumers reassess their priorities and increasingly ask themselves what they truly value, a host of major consumer trends have emerged.

- **The sharing economy** has been around for hundreds of years and involves people sharing under-utilised assets so as to maximise their value. Such assets might include your professional skills (e.g., freelancing), your money (e.g., crowdsourcing), or your assets (e.g., your car via Uber or your home via Airbnb), and even your clothes (e.g., hurrcollective.com). Sharing is short-term, peer-to-peer access to goods and services which as a market phenomenon has seen significant growth in recent years, given the relative ease with which users and owners can find each other since the advent of the Internet, its use of big data, and the growth of community-based online platforms. This new approach to sharing rather than acquiring resources has faced significant challenges

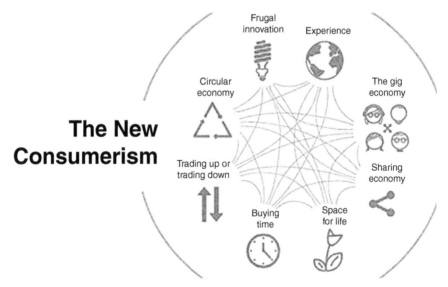

Figure 9.1 New Consumerism (Euromonitor, 2016). 'What Is the New Consumerism?', YouTube, uploaded by Euromonitor International, 12 May 2016, www.youtube.com/watch?v=0hVssoPcPg. © Euromonitor International Ltd.

in the form of regulatory uncertainty, questions about product liability, tax implications, and concerns about abuses.

- **The circular economy** is an alternative to a traditional linear consumption approach of make–use–dispose, which aims to keep goods in productive use for as long as possible (i.e., by repairing and re-using) and ultimately by recycling the raw materials (e.g., plastics, metals, and paper) into further applications. For example, platforms such as eBay.com are helpful to parents who no longer need expensive baby equipment such as prams, toys, and clothes as they can be resold to new parents on limited budgets. If you decide to upgrade your smartphone to the latest version you can sell your old model to musicmagpie.co.uk, who will refurbish and resell the model, helping the technology to become more accessible to less wealthy users and to avoid pollution from landfill.
- **Experience** is playing an increasingly important role in the marketing process. By relating to customers as individuals who will develop positive feelings towards our brand, we are building mutually beneficial and evolving long-term relationships. The Internet has rendered customer choice infinite, and since consumer decision-making research makes clear that our choices are both rational and emotional to different degrees in different contexts, it is customer experience in the purchasing process which often tips the balance in favour of a particular seller. However, there is another aspect of our behaviour where experience plays a crucial part. This is not only in *how* we buy (i.e., the customer experience journey), but more importantly in *what* we buy. There is evidence across a range of sectors, especially consumer electronics such as tablets and smartphones, that after many years of spectacular growth, demand is consistently slowing. This may be due to market saturation, it may be down to the expense of some items, but it could also be consumers prioritising doing, seeing, and feeling over having more 'stuff'. The trend is more than this, though, with many consumers seeking to 'do something different', searching for unique, often personalised experiences. Examples include learning a creative skill such as pottery, travelling to new parts of the world, meeting new people, or participating in a thrilling shared experience such as an escape room or a zombie apocalypse roleplay. Social media tracking and analytics are highly effective in targeting promotional campaigns at individuals and groups with such an orientation.
- **Buying time** is increasingly an option for today's consumers, for whom time has become a crucial commodity as a direct result of growing complexity in our lifestyles. Consumers in recent years have witnessed a 'choice explosion' in which the range of choices in various markets has grown exponentially. For example, when in a retail store take a moment

to consider how many different types of a specific product are on offer. Our ability to handle information has grown, but not at the same pace, causing anxiety. Despite unprecedented affluence, consumers seem little happier. Their expectations are continually increasing, bringing with them greater complexity. The growth of individualism is manifesting itself in a more internally focused definition of identity, with multiple identities simultaneously negotiated, often resulting in genuine, or perceived, 'anxiety'. So, in order to gain more time we are not just talking about convenience, but increasingly about outsourcing tasks. To this degree artificial intelligence, through algorithms embedded in devices such as digital personal assistants, along with automated repeat purchases, can take from us many of the monotonous routine decisions and purchasing activities to free-up time for more fulfilling pursuits.

- **Trading places** occurs where consumers consciously make the choice to reduce their expectations in some aspects of their spending to invest further in others. *Trading up* involves increasing the number of features (and their associated benefits) of a product, improving its quality, or backing it with a superior level of service to justify a higher price. This purchase decision represents a positive choice of goods and services that offers greater technical, functional, and emotional benefits. Alternatively, *trading down* involves reducing the number of features (and their associated benefits) or the quality of a product to suit the selling price demanded by its customers. Here, customers spend less in a few categories in order to spend more in others as a value calculation to maximise the benefits that are most important to them. For example, next time you do your grocery shopping, take a moment to consider the choices you make in store and for which categories you will consciously pay a higher price for goods that matter to you (in my case chocolate, coffee, and pizza all fall in this category!) or seek out lower prices for products that simply are not as important to you (which for me includes soft drinks, fruit, and toilet roll). Digital technologies such as price comparison websites have enabled consumers to become smarter shoppers who are not ashamed to look for bargains.
- **Frugal innovation** aims to eliminate non-essential and often costly features from a product or service. Drivers for this behaviour include socio-cultural attitudes towards sustainable consumption (i.e., the reduction in waste and unnecessary purchases) and away from contemporary consumer culture that has been dominated by ideas around abundance and excess. Technological innovations succeed when they create tangible benefits for consumers, such as longer-term cost savings from products which are designed to help them to consume less. In this case, consider

the LED lightbulb. Originally at a slightly higher price and offering lower levels of brightness than the incumbent incandescent or compact fluorescent bulbs, it has succeeded due to a longer operational life and lower power consumption. The IoT, sensors, and big data give new insight into our purchasing behaviour and how we can make intelligent purchase decisions in response. Take smart metering technology for both gas and electricity consumption as an example. They are a replacement for standard meters, which required tenants to periodically submit meter readings to their supplier to ensure accurate bills. They serve a dual purpose of automatically reporting energy usage to the supplier, and through an in-home display they give users information on consumption and the cost of their energy use, making them aware of excess consumption so that necessary action can be taken to reduce future bills. Smart meter benefits include more accurate bills, better understanding of usage, helping suppliers to create a smart grid to provide low-carbon, efficient, and reliable energy, and to offer better supply deals tailored to the needs of individual households.

- **Space for life** involves the rethinking of how we live, work, and socialise. The trend for smaller living spaces is driven by a complex mix of factors. Economic factors include the ever-increasing cost of purchase or rental, with which income growth seldom keeps pace. Social factors such as increased urbanisation and the increase in single-person households also play a part. From a work perspective there are many online collaboration tools which allow teams to function remotely. Examples include: DropBox, which hosts high-volume data sharing; Google Docs and Google Sheets, which enable real-time collaboration; and Microsoft Teams events, which combine document sharing and video conferencing. Lastly, how we socialise has changed significantly in recent years. Face-to-face socialisation has changed, as evidenced by the decline in the number of pubs and clubs and the rise in the numbers of coffee shops. Much of our socialisation now takes place via email, text, and social media platforms on an ongoing basis, such as when travelling, when relaxing at home, or as a brief and welcome distraction from our work or studies!

- **The gig economy** is the move away from permanent exclusive employment to a working life characterised by a portfolio of short-term contracts, freelance work, and entrepreneurship. Gig working is commonplace in industries such as entertainment, construction, and hospitality, where there is a combination of short-term employment contracts (i.e., those that provide insurance cover, a vacation entitlement, and pay the necessary employment taxes) and freelance work (i.e., where the worker is considered to be self-employed for legal, insurance, and tax purposes, and therefore liable for their own employment costs). Take, for example, the live entertainment industry. The performer in a show may be contracted to a production company for as long as the run lasts. This may be for months or years for popular shows or those that go on tour for an extended period. However, the light, sound, and stage management technicians who work for the individual venues are most likely to be treated as permanent employees. For smaller productions, where performers or technical teams work together for days or weeks, these teams are more likely to work across a range of different projects, for different organisations, that are constantly changing over time. Gig workers have high levels of flexibility, autonomy, task variety, and complexity, but these benefits come at a price as the definition in law of what constitutes employment, and therefore employee rights, has become blurred, with many gig employees losing contractual and social security protections as a result.

9.3.1 Opportunities

The creation of flexible markets using digital technologies has significantly reduced the barriers to entry for new suppliers and offered unfathomable choice for customers. No longer does it take years to diligently build global brand reputation and logistics infrastructure. Indeed, the fundamental role of retail is being reimagined, building stronger relationships without the expense of renting large spaces and carrying a sizeable and varied inventory. There is clearly significant opportunity for our society to be more efficient by significantly reducing waste in the supply chain, and redeploying goods after they have served their primary purpose. We can also be more effective in whom we serve and how we serve them, tailoring product and service provision based on dynamic data insights.

9.3.2 Threats

Those organisations and individuals who cannot invest in the latest equipment or for whom the pace of change is simply too quick and too intimidating to keep up with risk being disenfranchised by the global economic system. Gig workers see the opportunity to grow their income and decide their own working patterns in the good times. However, in the bad times they are left vulnerable by a lack of employment protection. Although the capitalist economy is based upon concentrated ownership of the means of production, we are seeing the fragmentation of buyers and sellers in global markets, with dominant companies in rapid decline unless they learn to become agile organisations. What is clear is that our attitude to property is changing. Why own a single property when you can rent properties around the world with Airbnb, living your life as a citizen of the world and working remotely? Why buy expensive computer hardware and software when you can rent them as a service (i.e., on a pay-per-use basis) using cloud computing? Why buy a car that requires a significant sum, needs insurance and maintenance, and spends most of its time unused, stored in a garage or a parking lot, when you can call an Uber or Didi driver? While there are significant cost and choice benefits for consumers, the future of employment (see Chapter 10) is in the throes of more radical and worrying upheaval.

9.3.3 Conclusion

Depending upon your natural perspective you could see the 'asset-light' future as liberating us from debt and risk of loss of our hard-earned possessions, or you could see it as worrying that the places in which we live and the goods on which we rely on a daily basis are no longer owned and controlled by us, but instead by another individual or organisation who will have us at their mercy to provide substandard goods at exploitative prices. When it comes to property, however, the most valuable commodity in the digital world is data. This data about you and me, what we buy, how and when we interact, and our future aspirations is the lifeblood of digital marketing activity. Who owns this data and what can be done with it? We will explore this further in Section 9.4.

RESEARCH INSIGHT 9.3 How Big Is the Gig?

Eichhorst, W., Hinte, H., Rinne, U., and Tobsch, V. (2017) How big is the gig? Assessing the preliminary evidence on the effects of digitalization on the labor market. *Management Revue*, 28(3): 298–318.

This paper considers the impact of digitalisation upon the labour market. The analysis undertaken by the authors indicates an economic and social transformation from long-term exclusive employment to short-term portfolio employment. Such changes are driven by technologically enabled organisations, which better use the information available to them and can become more agile in the process, and versatile employees and consumers who through greater market transparency can select the options which best suit them. However, not all actors will necessarily see the opportunity and benefit from the platform economy or the opportunity for self-employment. The paper identifies the challenges for social protection and develops proposals to adapt social insurance systems to these new challenges.

9.4   Trust

With such an ongoing upheaval in how we communicate and transact business there are bound to be teething problems relating to the reliability and security of the system that will need to be worked through over time. During this time, several existing and emerging stakeholders will play their roles in developing systems and protocols that ensure that we can rely on robust and trustworthy digital processes.

Consumers provide essential feedback to marketers about their satisfaction or dissatisfaction with a product or service. As you will know from your studies, it can be a challenge to ensure that feedback is received with the same sentiment it is intended due to the risk of distortion and misinterpretation. Imagine, then, the havoc that can be caused by a disgruntled consumer providing malicious feedback that may be lazy, exaggerated, or untrue. Given the distance and anonymity offered by the Internet, it is easy for those giving feedback to feel immune from accountability for the harm that their words cause. If **feedback** is shared directly and confidentially with the supplier then it is possible to make a reasonable judgement about what feedback is genuine and can be acted upon, and which feedback is perhaps less reliable and could be discounted. If feedback is shared more publicly using social media platforms it can very quickly gain momentum and have a more damaging effect upon the reputation of the company and its products and services. It is important here for organisations, no matter how difficult they find the feedback, to engage in a positive way. In other words, by responding rather than reacting. Reaction such as publicly challenging, or plainly denying, the sentiment can make an organisation appear to be defensive or arrogant, neither of which are a good image to build customer engagement and loyalty. Positive responses which seek engagement for further understanding can diffuse malicious commentators or they can help those who perhaps did not communicate their concerns effectively, to enter into a positive discussion.

From the early days of the Internet, consumers have been concerned about their **privacy**, which incorporates financial information such as bank account numbers, passwords, and credit and debit cards. Thankfully, financial security and fraud detection have improved significantly, but so have the skills of systems hackers and the fraudulent operators seeking to pose as another user to either access their resources (e.g., bank transfers or fraudulent transactions) or pretend to be them to engage in criminal activity while protecting their own identity (i.e., identity theft). Risks extend beyond financial security into the protection of children and other users vulnerable to grooming activities, for whom the potential to be tracked, found, and monitored remotely as an individual is a highly distressing and potentially risky prospect. With this in mind there is a growing movement for the **right to be forgotten,** which goes beyond the requirement for a message recipient to have the choice to opt out from company communications. This is the right of the individual to have their private information removed from internet searches and other directories so that they can determine the development of their life in an autonomous way, without being perpetually or periodically stigmatised as a consequence of a specific action performed in the past. However, the debate as to the ethical robustness of such a practice continues. Those against the proposition are concerned about its impact on the right to freedom of expression, its interaction with the right to privacy, and whether creating a right to be forgotten would decrease the quality of the Internet through censorship and a rewriting of history. Those in favour of the right to be forgotten cite its necessity due to issues such as revenge-porn sites appearing in search engine listings for a person's name, as well as instances of these results referencing petty crimes that individuals may have committed in the past.

Commercial organisations who create and provide products and services have extensive legal responsibilities under the General Data Protection Regulation (GDPR), which were explored in Chapter 2 and cover the collection, storage, use, and transfer of personal data. In Chapter 6 we discussed the risks of cybercrime particularly in relation to system vulnerabilities (e.g., denial of service attacks, loss of confidential information, ransomware) that can be caused by system weaknesses or employee error. However, with increasingly fragmented markets and organisations – incorporating a mix of employees, contractors, and gig workers – it is becoming increasingly difficult to provide **oversight and guidance** of worker activity. Software applications exist to track employee activity with the organisation's hardware and programs, but it is acknowledged that they can only capture a small proportion of a worker's activity. For example, the time spent building relationships with suppliers, colleagues, and customers does not always fall within the scope of a neat reporting system. Some elements of customer relationships can be captured with customer relationship management (CRM) systems such as those discussed in Chapter 5. However, it is the activities of problem solving and opportunity identification – essentially non-linear creative activities – which are harder to monitor and quantify. Take, for example, an Uber driver who is motivated by productivity as measured by how quickly they get their passengers to their desired destination and how many passengers they can transport within a given period. To boost productivity, the driver might minimise activities such as conversation, helpful suggestions for places to visit, or assistance with luggage. This makes the driver efficient but it does not make them effective since they have diligently fulfilled the transaction (i.e., transportation for money) but have failed to build a relationship that will lead to glowing feedback or requests for repeat journeys from the passengers and their friends, leading to higher long-term income.

This reliance upon **workplace surveillance** by employers might make sound economic and financial sense, allowing for job redesign and outsourcing, but it risks showing an unrepresentative picture of employees' diverse and creative activities which will build long-term success for the firm. It could also jeopardise employees' mental health through excessive monitoring and the expectation to be always available, leading to feelings of harassment, stress, and burnout.

Finally, the organisation has an ethical responsibility to refrain from **misleading advertising and customer mis-targeting** through its marketing activities. While the viral nature of platforms such as social media actively encourage users to spread advertising messages within their peer groups so as to maximise audience exposure, there is always a risk that the product or service may not be suitable or appropriate for every user – for example, messages that promote the sale of alcohol, cigarettes, or medication being accessed by children. This is a very challenging issue for organisations and needs to be considered when designing promotional messages and when processing customer purchases and enquiries to ensure that no inappropriate sales are made which may put the buyer or community at risk.

Governments and regulators will face increasing calls to provide oversight due to the ease with which data can be created, shared, and harvested via the Internet. The openness of the system gives a voice to many, but not all of the Internet's users operate in good faith with the welfare of others as their primary concern. There are malicious and dangerous actors at play, as in any community, and their actions are disrupting organisations (e.g., through implantation of virus malware and ransomware, or through the theft of confidential intellectual property data) and jeopardising the economic and psychological wellbeing of users (e.g., through identity theft, data corruption, malware, and trolling). While one way to address these issues is through communications and education, they are not always the most effective means to address misbehaviour in society. To some degree social media communities moderate their own members by allowing members to post comments on content posted by others. Genuine mistakes and misjudgements might be dealt with through discussion of alternative viewpoints which can lead to a positive experience for all through the tolerance and understanding of the viewpoints of others. However, those with more toxic views can quickly find themselves ostracised from friends and groups at the click of a mouse to unfollow, block, or remove from a group.

Some issues are beyond the power of individuals and small groups to self-monitor. For example, stories of political manipulation through the developing of messages with a clear influencing aim (i.e., to vote for one candidate over another by providing misleading or inflammatory 'information'), the publication of offensive materials such as sexual abuse or messages encouraging intolerance and violence towards others, or the facilitation of deviant lifestyles via the **dark web**.

At its most extreme the connectivity and language of the World Wide Web has created the potential for computer code to become **weaponised**. It is no longer the fiction of TV crime dramas and Hollywood superspies to manipulate connected devices via the IoT, which includes life-support machines in hospitals, medical devices such as pacemakers, energy generation and transmission, transport infrastructure such as rail signalling and air traffic control, and possibly even military weaponry such as drones and missile systems. Governments and regulators will need to consistently develop and review packages of measures which are both 'soft' and 'hard' in nature. Soft measures are based on information and education and aim to clarify and communicate the desired norms in social behaviour of tolerance, compassion, and community. 'Hard' measures such as criminalising offences (e.g., drug dealing and human trafficking) and taking action to stop and prosecute offenders require firm and dedicated action in many different areas over time, using increasingly sophisticated methods to deter and apprehend the most resilient offenders. These measures will have impacts upon civil liberties and how we work. Surveillance and data harvesting for security purposes can track and deter offenders, but is also considered to be too intrusive into the privacy of the individual in liberal democracies. The policing of cyberspace could restrict our freedom of access to all areas of the Internet, which has been the key to its growth and massive adoption from the beginning. Regulation *may* make the Internet a safer place to be – criminals are adaptable to finding new ways to conduct their business – but it will certainly restrict the freedoms which lead to creativity, innovation, and economic growth. In other words, regulation delivers benefits but also carries significant long-term costs.

Globalisation and the Internet have enabled a more diverse and connected world. As with any integrated system, the Internet will change to meet the needs of its users, dispensing with some processes and creating new ones in response. At a minor level, companies have been more able to reconfigure their operations and supply chains quickly and at relatively low cost to take advantage of changes in demand (e.g., moving from declining markets towards growing markets) or capitalising upon changes in the factors of production (e.g., relocating jobs to low-wage and high-skill locations). Global digital companies can be a challenge to national governments who need employment and tax income to meet the needs of their populations. Since companies are usually charged corporate taxes based on where they are domiciled, these companies are choosing to report their activities from tax-favourable jurisdictions. So, even though companies may sell many products and employ many people within a given country, their corporation tax liability will often be payable at a lower rate elsewhere.

This is a frustration for national treasuries but is not nearly as disruptive as the potential of **blockchain** technology. Blockchain is an open, distributed ledger that can record transactions between two parties efficiently and in a verifiable and permanent way. Each 'block' is a record of a transaction which includes a timestamp to verify the action. Having a record of transactions is nothing new. What is novel about blockchain is the distributed nature of the system. This means that whereas secure records, such as financial transactions, would normally be kept by banking institutions whose security processes ensure that these records have a minimal chance of being lost, copied, or manipulated, the blockchain creates a fresh record on every machine that it encounters. Blockchain has given rise to cryptocurrencies (e.g., Bitcoin, Ethereum) which challenge the dominance of national central banks who underwrite currencies, and private retail/merchant banks who charge a fee to securely store and transfer money. However, despite early market speculation in cryptocurrencies, they are yet to offer an agreed standard or incite widespread confidence and use from customers. Further speculative applications of blockchain include: smart contracts which can be partially or fully executed or enforced without human interaction, but whose legal status is at this point unclear; video games (e.g., CryptoKitties) which catalogue digital game assets; and supply chain management (e.g., Everledger).

Intermediary platforms offer new ways for internet users to moderate their access to content on the World Wide Web. Social networks such as Weibo, TikTok, and YouTube help to guide us to interesting or relevant content, based on our behaviour and the behaviour of those to whom we are closely connected online. Independent commercial intermediaries help us to set a criterion to filter the vast choice of financial services such as credit cards, personal loans, mortgages, insurance, pensions, and investments. Review sites help us to choose which movies we watch, what fashions we want to wear, where to spend our vacations, and where we want to live. But to what degree can we trust these intermediaries with our data, and to give information that is in our best interests? Since intermediaries, sometimes also known as infomediaries, make little income from simply sharing information or making it easier for us to find what we need, they often generate income from advertising, commission (i.e., recommending certain products), or the sale of our data to interested third parties for their own research and marketing objectives. Therefore, how trustworthy are they? It may be convenient and efficient to accept the opinions of others, but what if these 'others' are not like-minded consumers eager to improve the common good but instead are commercial organisations seeking to maximise their financial income? Is it really in our best interests to blindly follow this advice? Intermediaries may help to make choices in a complex world, but their commercial objective and the limitations of their use of big data to anticipate new needs should qualify our reliance upon them.

9.4.1 Opportunities

Data is increasingly becoming the most valuable asset on the Internet. Without it, organisations and systems lose their usefulness. Should consumers be paid for their data? Is there a role for greater government and regulatory control?

9.4.2 Threats

There are undoubtedly risks to using the Internet. Bad actors exist, as they do in the physical world. Everyone has different objectives and different moral standards, therefore making it impossible to guarantee one universal view of what represents 'good' and 'bad' behaviour. Added to this we must accept that no system – whether company, financial, or government – is immune to security threats. These organisations deal in risk management instead of risk elimination.

9.4.3 Conclusion

For data to be a currency it needs to be robust and reliable. As financial currencies are underwritten by the national central banks, so the data that we use must be truthful to establish its value. But who should monitor and maintain 'trust' and are we not at risk of the suppression of ideas which challenge an established truth? Wars have been fought over such ideas. Or should we just take our chances with the Internet and the opinions expressed therein, hoping that the vulnerable members of society will not be unfairly manipulated into decisions and actions which unwittingly act again their self-interest?

DIGITAL INSIGHT 9.3 How Much Do You Trust the Internet?

Before we can measure trust, we need a clear definition of exactly what it is. Since trust exists on the side of the reader, it is fair to assume that it is not a behaviour of the sender of the message, but an expectation of the receiver of the message. An added complication is that, based on experience and the current situation, receivers will frequently change their expectations. This moving target makes it difficult to measure trust, yet there are factors that influence the degree to which we trust the messages that we receive. The sender's reputation may infer a trustworthy source – for example, someone who is personally known to us, a government body, or an independent news outlet. However, in all cases we can identify situations where we feel we have been misled – intentionally or unintentionally – by a friend, a campaigning political party, or by an esteemed institution. Since it is the responsibility of the individual user to differentiate 'truth' from 'untruth' given that we consume media both for entertainment and for information, where do you draw the line? Consider what aspects of the subject, media, and sender convince you to fully trust what you see and hear on the Internet.

CHAPTER SUMMARY

Using the broad themes of data, humans, ownership, and trust we have explored some of the key technologies that are influencing the practice of digital marketing. You are not experiencing these technologies for the first time in this book. We have discussed them previously as being relevant to different aspects of the digital marketing mix. By distilling them into four themes we can begin to see their fundamental impact upon the buyer–seller relationship and their potential future directions of development. For example, big data is used to great effect in the online marketplace, principally via close integration of vendor sites with social media platforms. When combined with robotics processes and the IoT we have complex autonomous systems (e.g., self-driving cars) that are capable of deep learning (i.e., artificial intelligence). Self-driving cars themselves will change how data regarding our journeys is captured and used. For example, are more efficient routes available based on data that is livestreamed from sensors embedded in transport infrastructure, or will we stick with our old, familiar route? Next, will a significant proportion of humans choose not to drive? This is common in many big cities where owning and operating a car is an expensive and frustrating experience. This may not be the case in more suburban and rural areas, where transport independence is more important. Consider also that many people enjoy driving and may not be ready to give up that joy to a robot just yet. Our attitudes to ownership are also changing by our use of cloud servers to back-up our digital data, ride-hailing services to move us around town, or accommodation-sharing apps when considering how we will live and vacation, as many explore the variety of experiences as they move on from the traditional expectation of residential property ownership. Finally, our fluctuating levels of trust in the media (e.g., 'fake news'), financial transactions (e.g., independent financial transfer services such as PayPal or alternative currencies such as Bitcoin), and commercial organisations (e.g., the loss or unauthorised use of personal data) will limit the rate of adoption and reliance upon these technologies, and as a result their marketing effectiveness.

Review Questions

- Based on your own experience as a consumer, to what degree do you agree, disagree, or challenge the suggestions made in this chapter about the marketing relationship?
- What role does data play in our day-to-day lives? Do humans use data to serve them? Does data control humans? Or do they peacefully coexist in a mutually supportive way?
- Are you excited by the potential to leave more tasks to machines, or does it worry you?
- What emerging trends have you identified that have not been discussed here? What are their opportunities and threats?
- What are the risks of systems endorsement (e.g., Trustpilot)?

END-OF-CHAPTER CASE: WHAT IF ...?

Science fiction stories have intrigued us for decades. The works of Jules Verne (*Twenty Thousand Leagues Under the Sea*, *Journey to the Centre of the Earth*), and H. G. Wells (*War of the Worlds*, *The Time Machine*) are personal favourites, as was the thrill of watching *Star Trek* when I was growing up ('Beam me up, Scotty!'). Visions of worlds which are utopian or dystopian (*The Terminator*, *The Matrix*, *Demolition Man*, *Blade Runner*) have the potential to terrify. But how real are these potential futures, and what can we do to adapt to them? What follows is by no means a definitive list, but simply highlights some examples of where technology could take us in the next few decades.

1. Bionic eyes – surgical advances have enabled artificial corneal implants, an artificial iris fitted to smart contact lenses, and glasses fitted with a camera connected via wireless brain implants that bypass the eyes altogether.
2. A flexible workforce – as data analytics, artificial intelligence, and robotics combine to replace the operational role of humans in performing tasks of increasing sophistication, the remaining work will become more fluid as some employees will be virtual, some will be full-time, some will be bots, and many of us will work non-fixed hours.
3. Robot personal carers – as you become more vulnerable in your old age, how would you feel about being cared for by a robot? Elderly citizens have responded well to the company of a robot who helps them to find items around the house, contact loved ones, summon emergency care, and help with activities such as cooking and washing. They also provide conversation to prevent the lonely from feeling more isolated.
4. Nanobots – it will soon be possible to plug our brains straight into the cloud, which will give us full-immersion virtual reality from within the nervous system. Memories and knowledge will not fade over time but will instead be held on our all-inclusive personal drive. We could couple this database with the DNA sequencing of a deceased friend or relative and be able to create a convincing virtual version of somebody who's passed on.
5. Tactile virtual reality – epidermal VR uses a flexible material fitted with tiny vibrating components that can be attached to skin. This can be used in advanced gaming applications, creating more authentic and immersive experiences. A more valuable application helps amputees renew their sense of touch.

DISCUSSION QUESTIONS

1. What risks do you foresee in these developments?
2. What opportunities do you foresee in these developments?
3. Will humanity retain control of these developments, or will it be taken out of our hands by artificial intelligence?
4. Is this a good thing or a bad thing for the future of our species and the planet?

Develop Your Skills
. . . .

What Is the Skill?
Technology business impact analysis is the process of determining the
vulnerability of business activities and identifying what needs to be done by
the organisation to ensure its ability to continue operations during and after
a disruption. It quantifies the impacts of disruptions on service delivery,
prioritises them for action, and helps to develop solutions and plans to
minimise the potential disruption and maximise the potential benefit that the
organisation could gain from a timely move to the new approach. It differs
from the broader organisation risk analysis in three important respects:

- It focuses on technology-related issues.
- It focuses on service interruptions in the buyer–seller relationship.
- Its approach is to minimise risk and identify opportunities for growth.

Why Is It Important?
All businesses can be disrupted by rapid and radical changes in their
operating environment. This includes what goes on inside an organisation
(e.g., hacking, systems viruses and ransomware) as well as outside the
organisation (e.g., hostile social media of a highly competitive new market
offering from a dominant new entrant). Since it is not ideal to produce a
response during a crisis, planning a more appropriate response in advance is
likely to lead to better outcomes. Take, for example, the need for emergency
funding to invest in new equipment or fund cashflow for employee costs.
Banks will give better terms for contingency funding than for emergency
funding since their level of confidence in the organisation's ability to
anticipate and overcome the temporary crisis will be higher based on their
level of professionalism in foresight and planning.

How to Develop It
Such a process depends on an intricate knowledge of business processes, the
technology that supports them, and their criticality to the customer relationship
in respect of the potential impact of a disruptive event. Impacts to consider
include delayed sales or income, increased staff expenses, regulatory fines (e.g.,
for GDPR infringements), contractual penalties due to a failure to supply, and
customer dissatisfaction, which can play out through social media. The key
organisational data which helps to assess the risk and opportunity includes:

- a detailed description of the process;
- all inputs and outputs from the process;

- defined maximum allowable outage time before impact occurs;
- descriptions of the financial and operational impact experienced during an outage;
- human and technology resources needed to support the process;
- a description of the customer impact;
- what legal or regulatory impacts may be created in an outage;
- description of past outages and the impacts associated with each; and
- description of workaround procedures or work-shifting options to other departments or remote workers as applicable.

How to Apply It

There are many approaches to technology business risk assessment available on the Internet. Type the term into your search engine and explore the results in images and videos. You will see assessments that range from basic descriptions to complex analyses with lots of discussion and detailed financial calculations. A good practice would be to identify three different approaches and critique them based on how useful you might find them as a marketer who is seeking to secure and extend highly satisfying customer relationships.

References

Eichhorst, W., Hinte, H., Rinne, U., and Tobsch, V. (2017) How big is the gig? Assessing the preliminary evidence on the effects of digitalization on the labor market. *Management Revue*, 28(3): 298–318.

Euromonitor (2016). 'What is the New Consumerism?' YouTube, uploaded by Euromonitor International, 12 May 2016. www.youtube.com/watch?v=0hVssoPcPg.

Hoffman, R., and Yeh, C. (2018). *Blitzscaling: The Lightning-Fast Path to Building Massively Valuable Companies*. New York: Harper Collins.

Kurzweil, R. (2005). *The Singularity Is Near*. London: Duckworth.

Lecinski, J. (2011). Winning the zero moment of truth. [online]. Available from: www.thinkwithgoogle.com/marketing-resources/micro-moments/2011-winning-zmot-ebook [Accessed 9 May 2020].

Ministry of Defence (2018). *Global Strategic Trends: The Future Starts Today*, 6th ed. London: Ministry of Defence UK.

Ng, I., and Wakenshaw, S. (2017). The Internet-of-Things: review and research directions. *International Journal of Research in Marketing*, 34(1): 3–21.

O'Reilly, C. A., and Tushman, M. L. (2004). The ambidextrous organization. *Harvard Business Review*, 82: 74–82.

10 Working in Digital Marketing

Introduction

This chapter considers how, as learners and marketing professionals, we can continue to adapt our skills to be competitive in a dynamic marketplace. We will not focus the discussion on specific technologies since they tend to be short-lived in their original form, either becoming obsolete or evolving to meet changing needs. Neither will we seek to identify trends in individual industry sectors or currently recognised professions (e.g., teachers, lawyers, engineers, or artists). Instead, we will discuss workplace competencies which fit a wide range of contexts from those working as freelancers on a gigging basis, entrepreneurs developing highly flexible ventures, and those working for large organisations which may be seeking to become more diverse or more integrated in their business operations. The employment market is in constant flux, customer attitudes are frequently changing, and our competition is global. How can we secure our future employment in the face of competitors that we cannot see, customers we do not fully understand, and markets in turmoil for myriad reasons? I will not even try to offer any certainty or insight into what the future holds, but I can be certain that over the last 20 years or so of my career, digital technologies have given me many opportunities which include the ability to work independently or in teams as I prefer, work when and how I choose, and maintain a healthy work–life balance which maximises the benefit I get from time with my friends and family. Digital technologies, and the responses to them by employers, are not perfect, but change never is. Change creates uncertainty and it is down to your individual mindset, and the active choices that you make, as to whether you will see them as threats or opportunities.

Learning Objectives

- Compare the diversity of potential routes into the digital marketing profession.
- Differentiate between the skills and competencies required for specific job roles.
- Consider the impact of different working contexts upon a digital marketer's learning needs.
- Plan for your continuing professional development.

CASE INSIGHT: BEFORE THEY WERE BIG ...

Digital marketing is not just the realm of computer scientists. There are many cases of successful marketers who achieved significant success from a wide range of backgrounds, education, and prior work experience. Here are a few success stories.

- Jeff Bezos graduated in electrical engineering and computer science and went on to work in the financial services industry before founding Amazon in 1994 as an online bookstore.
- Brian Chesky and Joe Gebbia (both designers), and Nathan Blecharczyk (an engineer) founded Airbnb in 2008 after renting out an air mattress in their living room, effectively turning their apartment into a bed and breakfast, to offset the high cost of rent in San Francisco.
- Gagan Biyani graduated in economics before moving into journalism. He wrote several investigative journalism pieces, including one about a PR firm that was writing fake reviews on the App Store. In 2009 Biyani founded Udemy, an online educational platform.
- Julia Hartz graduated in communication and broadcast journalism and began working as a development executive at MTV. In 2006 she founded Eventbrite, a global self-service ticketing platform for live events.
- Reed Hastings graduated in mathematics then joined the Peace Corps. He went on to teach high school maths in Swaziland from 1983 to 1985. After other entrepreneurial adventures, he launched Netflix in 1997.
- Melanie Perkins dropped out of her university programme in communications, psychology, and commerce to develop an idea that led to the formation of Canva in 2012, a graphic design platform that allows users to create social media graphics, presentations, posters, and other visual content.

- Natalie Massenet worked as a retail sales assistant, receptionist, fashion model, and stylist before founding Net-a-Porter in 2000 as a website in magazine format for selling designer fashion.
- Lynda Weinman worked for Dreamquest and as an independent contractor doing animation and special effects. She worked on several films, including *RoboCop 2, Bill & Ted's Excellent Adventure*, and *Star Trek V: The Final Frontier*. She taught digital media and motion graphics before launching Lynda.com in 1995, an online training library that teaches computer skills in video format to members through monthly and annual subscription-based plans.

Questions

Now it is your turn to research the people behind the digital products and companies that you use or admire.

- What did they study at college or university?
- What other professional experience do they have?
- What is said by others about their style of work?
- What do they say about their own values and beliefs?

10.1   Skills and Competencies

These terms are often used interchangeably, but it is worth making clear what they mean and how they differ.

Skills are knowledge-based, which means that they tend to relate to the performance of a specific task. It is the ability acquired through deliberate, systematic, and sustained effort to carry out complex activities or job functions involving ideas (cognitive skills), things (technical skills), and/or people (interpersonal skills) with maximum certainty that you can bring about the result you want. This could be simply described as the 'what' of a job function. Examples of digital marketing skills include:

- content design and production (e.g., audio, video, animation);
- search engine optimisation;
- user experience designing, programming, and testing;
- cloud and distributed computing;
- statistical analysis and data mining;
- web architecture and development framework; and

- middleware and integration software.

Competencies are behavioural in nature, which means that they tend to explain the way skills are used. They are a cluster of related abilities and commitments that involve the ability to meet complex demands, by drawing on and mobilising psychosocial resources (including skills and attitudes) in a context. This could be simply described as the 'how' of a job function. Examples of digital marketing competencies include:

- behavioural competencies include problem solving, self-management, and communication;
- technical competencies include application systems development, systems networking, and database analysis; and
- professional competencies include industry and professional standards, negotiation, and people management.

10.2   Working Contexts

This chapter will identify, describe, and explain the importance of digital marketing skills and competencies that have a common requirement in the workplace. The breakdown will be structured according to standard working contexts:

- **The freelancer** will work on a wide range of highly specialist projects, typically working remotely for multiple organisations. You will work in short bursts (perhaps measured in hours or days) over a period of years, at low frequencies (say annually or semi-annually). You will benefit from social media platforms, crowdsourcing, and outsourcing websites that will help you to find work. Your professional development challenges will involve maintaining and extending your reputation, and keeping your skills updated to include new tools and techniques.
- **The employee (part I – start-up and small organisations)** will work across multiple business functions to initiate and grow new organisational capabilities. You will master some specific technical skills (e.g., coding or analysis) but you will also act to co-ordinate the efforts of a few other workers within the organisation. Your work will be demanding and pressurised as you seek to gain market acceptance for your initiatives before the competition has time to act. You will benefit from real-time collaborative workplace tools, such as cloud drives, to co-ordinate everyone's effort. Your professional development challenges will involve identifying, evaluating, and exploiting market trends.

- **The Employee (part II – larger organisations)** will work within a specialist business function where the focus will be upon operational effectiveness and efficiency. Processes will be highly structured and data-driven. You will work alongside other specialists using dedicated systems which are highly integrated across the organisation. You will benefit from cloud-based systems and crowdsourced workers to augment your team as and when required. Your professional development challenges will involve ensuring that your skills both fit the legacy operations of the business and identify emerging good practices across the sector.
- **The portfolio worker** will mix employment with freelancing as their workload permits. They will combine highly specialist skills for freelance work, entrepreneurial skills for start-ups and small businesses, and broader team player/leadership skills to fit within complex bureaucratic organisations. You will be versatile and able to manage multiple dynamic demands. You will benefit from the ability to rapidly master the operational systems practices of different organisations as well as operating a standalone offering to private clients. Your professional development challenges will involve being flexible to meet client needs as they may vary from requiring traditional skills to more specialist up-to-date skills.

Please remember than none of these definitions are absolute and your actual working pattern may be an evolution of different forms, representing different challenges to your professional development over an extended and uncertain period.

10.3 Digital Creation

Here we deal with the act of making something new. The root of this creation may be in the methodological investigation of a specific phenomenon – for example, a rigorously researched and tested idea for a new product. Alternatively, it may come in a moment of inspiration from the happy accident of a collision of different ideas – for example, a theme for a new promotional campaign. The ability to articulate these ideas in a form that can be visualised, shared, and agreed upon plays perfectly to the strengths of the digital tools and techniques that we have explored in this book.

Data literacy concerns the efficient and effective use of source material that is available to us. You will already be aware that the capacity and nature of the World Wide Web means that it might feel like there is an infinite amount of data 'out there' on which we could base our decisions. But how do we know which data is useful for our purpose, and which is not? How do we know if we can trust these sources? Is sufficient data available for us to analyse behaviour over time to identify potential future trends? Data literacy is a competence that pulls together a range of techniques that we have discussed in earlier chapters. Specifically, it concerns the following:

- Collecting data through activities such as browser search criteria, database filters, and customer surveys. Look back to Chapter 2 where we covered data, analytics, and intelligence. For more on customer insight, look again at Chapter 4.
- Managing data through the appropriate classification, storage, and security systems ensures that your source material is robust, reliable, and available in a usable form when you need it. Chapter 2 will be useful to revisit this topic, specifically around the subject of the General Data Protection Regulation (GDPR).
- Interpreting data to create insights that support decision-making. Chapter 5 discussed some analytics approaches, but there are many packages on the market, both free and paid for, that will help you make sense of the data inputs. For example, Google Analytics is a great free resource to understand data from user interactions with your website. Facebook campaigns can also give some helpful high-level data about which audiences are seeing and engaging with your posts. However, for more sophisticated insights you should design your own approaches that prioritise what you want to know, and why you want to know it. Good processes will also help you to model and visualise your data. Specialist software packages such as advanced Excel, Stata, Tableau, and SPSS are helpful here.

Coding is a useful skill as the workplace becomes increasingly automated. Traditionally the skillset of the computer scientist, coding is becoming more mainstream as schools, colleges, and universities seek to include this employability skill within the general curriculum. Popular programming languages include SQL, HTML, VBA, Matlab, Python, and R. It is possible to thrive as a digital marketer without formal programming skills. Many web design, graphic design, payment systems, and social media platforms offer accessible interfaces for the non-expert to build a professional and significant market presence.

Creating digital artefacts such as images, documents, and recordings to be accessed and shared online is the lifeblood of the Internet as we know it. User-generated content is created through blogging (e.g., Twitter, WordPress), website design (e.g., GoDaddy), Adobe Creative (which includes Photoshop, Illustrator, Lightroom, and InDesign), Microsoft Office (which includes Word, Excel, PowerPoint), Prezi, video recording and editing (e.g., for YouTube), and audio recording and editing (e.g., for podcasts). There are many training resources available within these websites and packages, but YouTube can also be a valuable source of 'how to' videos.

Industry specialist tools for your industry are also a valuable professional development investment. When searching for roles in industries that you prefer, you should search within the job description or person specification to understand if they expect applicants to be fluent with specific software packages – for example, the computer aided design (CAD) packages AutoCAD and ArchiCAD.

10.4   Digital Communication

Chapter 7 explored the online communication process in some depth. It is important to remember that although it is possible to target messages more precisely at specific audiences, there is a great deal of environmental 'noise' to deal with. The noise comes from consumers themselves as cognitive dissonance occurs due to their changing needs, offerings from competing suppliers, and the existing accumulation of content and messages from within the organisation. These numerous and complex messages need careful management to ensure that the organisation is to be an influential communicator.

Content curation supports the management of the digital artefacts described in Section 10.3 so that the organisation's digital space is not overburdened with superfluous material that may confuse or distract the visitor from the key marketing messages that you are trying to convey as part of your wider campaign. Platforms will include Twitter, Instagram, Facebook, Reddit, LinkedIn, WhatsApp, and Hootsuite. This competence ensures that the right materials are in the right place at the right time. Also, we can use analytics or consumer research that maps the customer journey (see Chapter 5) to identify where there are gaps in the organisation's digital offering that require the revision or development of new materials. Another complex balancing act is in the detailed consideration of the needs of individual users (e.g., a complex report or presentation) or a wide audience (e.g., testimonies, case studies, user support videos). Not only will you need an appreciation of consumer behaviour (Chapter 4) and integrated marketing communications (Chapter 7), but also an understanding of how to ensure accessible design for a wide range of audiences with different languages, cultures, age profiles, and other factors such as disabilities.

Presentation and interaction in live online events (e.g., Skype, Zoom, Webex, Collaborate, Microsoft Teams) is a social skill that can be learned from established formats but will largely be self-developed to reflect your own style and your rapport with the audience. These events can be very challenging as it is difficult to grasp the level of audience understanding or agreement/disagreement unless the audience speaks up using the mic or chat function – which many are reluctant to do in online forums – as it is impossible to feel the atmosphere of the group since the audience's body language cannot be observed. A helpful approach here is to have shorter presentations, say 15–20 minutes, then a facilitated session where the audience can ask questions. It is also helpful to have someone to support the main speaker so that they can concentrate on delivering an engaging presentation that will stimulate the audience to action. The supporting facilitator will manage access to the online room and curate the chat contributions. As a presenter you should always try to get feedback from a wide range of people on your presentation. Perhaps you can invite a highly skilled colleague to act as your confidential critical friend to highlight and explore areas where your approach can be developed.

Media literacy affects how we receive and respond to messages in a range of digital media, to include email, chat, direct messaging, and social media commentary. The instantaneous and unhindered sending of messages can be a blessing and a curse. Positive feedback is always encouraging to receive, but those who are loyal to our organisation or its brand identify strongly with it and are unlikely to offer constructive criticism. The physical distance between senders and receivers on the Internet, along with the potential anonymity of senders, can lead to unpleasant or unhelpful contributions. The development of media literacy helps us to ascertain which messages can be ignored and which need to be acted upon. If there is a real problem with the organisation which has been identified, then we must work to put this right. Where problems occur, particularly in social media, it is because of the nefarious activities of trolls.

10.5   Digital Collaboration

The Internet and the World Wide Web enable us to work together as never before, unconstrained by the limitations of organisations, languages, or distance. Outsourcing and offshoring are commonplace, and we think nothing of ordering goods from across the world.

Cloud-based platforms, among other uses, enable us to share and co-create in real time documents such as reports, databases, and presentations. Tools that support this include Google Drive, DropBox, SharePoint, and

OneNote. Working in this manner requires a different approach to working on one's own on a project which is only released to the next stage when it is complete. The ability for live collaboration involves a wide range of stakeholders, many of whom may be non-experts, to develop a truly democratic offering. When jointly developing artefacts, it is helpful to have working guidelines that specify who has access to the artefact and what permissions they must have to download, copy, edit, or delete all or part of it.

Project management to co-ordinate the efforts of virtual teams across great distances and multiple time zones, or even in separate divisions or organisations within the same supply chain, can ease this complex and time-constrained activity. Tools including Slack, Asana, Basecamp, Podio, Projectwise, Microsoft Teams, and Trello give both visibility and accountability on the allocation and completion of tasks. They can also allow for the implications of project changes – say, the change of focus of the project or a change in those contributing to it – to be instantly cascaded to all of those involved.

Participation in the building, facilitation, and leadership of digital groups or networks is explored in Chapter 4. Whatever role you or your organisation chooses to play can offer great reputational benefits. Networks can offer collaboration opportunities, fresh marketing perspectives, or can just invoke a sense of loyalty from stakeholders who appreciate the effort put in and feel that their participation is valued.

DIGITAL INSIGHT 10.1 **Industry 4.0**

Geissbauer, R., Vedso, J., and Schrauf, S. (2016). Industry 4.0: building the digital enterprise [online]. PwC. Available from: www.pwc.com/gx/en/indus tries/industries-4.0/landing-page/industry-4.0-building-your-digital-enter prise-april-2016.pdf [Accessed 24 June 2020].

PwC's 2016 Global Industry 4.0 Survey is the biggest worldwide survey of its kind, with over 2,000 participants from nine major industrial sectors, including aerospace, defence, and security, industrial manufacturing, engineering and construction, chemicals, electronics, transportation and logistics, automotive, metals, and forest-based paper and packaging. The study's scope also included 26 countries. The study explores the benefits of digitising organisational value chains, and in so doing provides a valuable insight into the need for human competencies to support changing a digital product and service portfolio.

DIGITAL INSIGHT 10.2 Building Digital Capabilities

Joint Information Systems Committee (2015). Building digital capabilities: the six elements defined [online]. JISC. Available from: http://repository.jisc .ac.uk/6611/1/JFL0066F_DIGIGAP_MOD_IND_FRAME.PDF [Accessed 22 July 2020].

JISC's Digital Capability Framework (Figure 10.1) describes the digital skills needed by employees to succeed in a rapidly changing workplace. Although principally designed to guide curriculum development and teaching practice, this framework also enables learners to audit their own skills to inform a continuing professional development plan which sets skills goals and helps to identify development opportunities.

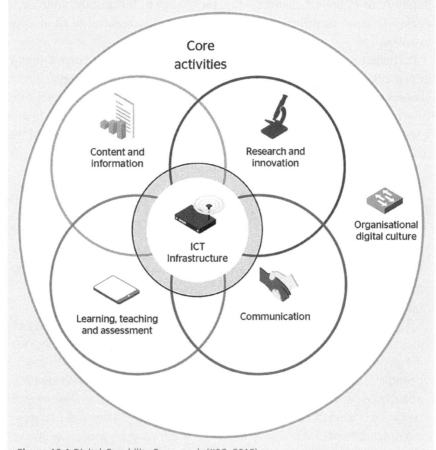

Figure 10.1 Digital Capability Framework (JISC, 2015).

> ### DIGITAL INSIGHT 10.3 Digital Marketing Skills Benchmark
>
> Target Internet (2020). Digital marketing skills benchmark [online]. Available from: www.targetinternet.com/resources/Digital_Marketing_Skills_Benchmark .pdf [Accessed 28 July 2020].
>
> This follow-up to the 2018 edition highlights a significant shift in skills needs. The environment of constant change has led to challenges for individuals and organisations. Remaining relevant relies on a constant evaluation and updating of skills. The report provides a breakdown of digital disciplines, the strengths and weaknesses of which are assessed across a range of industry sectors, including automotive, consumer goods, fashion, and pharmaceuticals. There is also a clear overall delineation of the skills need by organisational seniority, including assistant, executive, and management.

CHAPTER SUMMARY

In this chapter we have explored the practical challenges to establishing and developing our careers in digital marketing. With such a radically changing and fast-moving environment it would be naïve to declare that a specific skillset will be adequate or enduring. Instead, we have explored the role of skills (i.e., what we can do) and competencies (i.e., how we perform them) in a range of working contexts to include short- and long-term engagements in organisations both big and small. The remaining sections explore how we can develop our digital skills and competencies to create, communicate, and collaborate more effectively.

Review Questions

1. What digital marketing roles appeal to you and how does your current skillset need to develop?
2. How would your approach to work change, depending on whether a job was online-only, a hybrid of working between an office and from home, or if you were 100 per cent office-based?
3. What have been your experiences using digital tools to collaborate with others? What went well and what went not so well? What would you have done differently?

END-OF-CHAPTER CASE: HOW MARKETING JOBS HAVE CHANGED WITH TECHNOLOGY (1950–2020)

1950s: As the global economy began its post-war rebound, consumers were ready to buy homes, cars, and clothes as they emerged from the threats and restrictions of the global conflict (e.g., rationing) to a supply chain moving away from war duties and back to serving the needs of consumers. The 1950s also saw the widespread adoption of TV as a new technology that was a more powerful tool than print advertisements. Television had sound and movement. Print ads, by contrast, were unengaging. Marketers now had to develop their storytelling skills for the medium and develop an awareness of film production, scriptwriting, and media management skills.

1960s: Social changes (more women in the workforce, more children in school) influenced advertising methods. Families ate much later, which meant that working men would be home in time to eat with the rest of the family. Also, with growing family incomes there was a much wider range of potential product purchases. Marketers also noticed the influence of children in purchasing decisions. Increasingly, fun, and exciting advertisements targeted children, creating the phenomenon of pester power. With increased competition the concept of branding was born. Marketers now required solid grounding in psychology concepts as everyone in the household had an influence over purchasing decisions, not just the traditional patriarch.

1970s: This decade saw a shift from labour and services to technology-based jobs. Microprocessors, VCRs, home computers, and video gaming systems all meant that jobs in previously unknown sectors were opening up for workers. Improved technology required increased basic skills for employees. A school education was no longer enough, workers needed further education more than ever before.

1980s: This decade saw a fundamental change in the marketing relationship between fast-moving consumer goods (FMCG) brand owners and grocery retailers. Traditionally, FMCG marketers held the balance of power. They would announce that a brand was going to go on TV, provide stock to retailers, and watch it be given prime position in store to be consumed eagerly by excited customers. Grocery retailers began to feel that they had primacy in the relationship since it was they who maintained the valuable first-hand relationship with the customer. Retailers began to capitalise on this realisation by creating own-label products, led by Sainsbury's, which began to spread and were often as good as the brand leader. To support this drive for higher margins and greater independence, retailers needed marketing and advertising expertise and began to build their own departments.

1990s: This was a time of mega-brands growing ever more dominant, when Unilever, Procter & Gamble, Reckitt Benckiser, and Diageo were attempting to impose an elite portfolio on a universal consumer. These ambitious communications and loyalty objectives were supported by a plethora of mass media channels. The one marketing services sector on top of the trend was media planning and buying.

2000s: Before the Internet became what it is today, for marketers it was new – and there were a lot of unanswered questions about how effective it was as a marketing tool. Where radio, direct mail, and newspapers were the go-to media for marketing, the online space was still a bit of an unanswered question. Until the mid-2000s traditional promotion was a simple 'push' of information from company headquarters, through subsidiaries and their media channels. As web-centric promotion gained traction, marketers realized the opportunities to move from mass broadcast to mass dialogue with customers.

2010s: Digital influencers represent the largest majority group that brands have worked with for endorsement and commercial opportunities. Although new types of information and influencers may give marketers more ways to reach consumers than ever before, attention-grabbing, shareable content can work better than accurate or unbiased information, and as a result consumer trust is declining.

DISCUSSION QUESTIONS

1. How has technological change driven the development of the marketing profession?
2. What has been the role of social changes?
3. In what ways do you think the scale and rate of change will continue to increase?
4. Do you think we need to slow down to avoid burnout?

Develop Your Skills

. . . .

What Is the Skill?

Continuing professional development (CPD) is the process of improving and developing your knowledge, understanding, and skills. Many of us do this because of our inquisitive and adventurous nature. Done systematically, it helps to identify your development needs and then plan how you are going to meet them.

Why Is It Important?

Undertaking CPD is a clear indicator of professionalism, which can improve your chances of getting hired or promoted. It aims to develop both efficiency and effectiveness in professional learning by identifying your career goals then identifying your knowledge gaps and the most appropriate ways to address them.

How to Develop It

Here are a few examples of different CPD activities:

- *self-directed learning* such as general reading, research, informal networking (e.g., social media contributions, blogging);
- *practice-based learning*, including on-the-job training, work shadowing, projects outside the scope of the current role;
- *professional activity*, such as professional journals, events, and exhibitions; and
- *formal learning*, including include qualifications, training, online learning using digital learning environments such as Udemy, Emeritus, Moodle, Coursera, Canvas, and Blackboard.

How to Apply It

A CPD plan will begin by identifying a skill or competence that you want to master. Be as specific as possible when describing this, and if possible, describe it in a professional context to gain a better understanding of its practical application. These learning needs might be identified from the person specification of a job role that you are interested in. They might also come through the observation of professionals whom you admire. It is always worth getting the opinion of a trusted colleague or mentor who has relevant professional experience. They can help you to understand your development needs, describe the skill or competence in more detail, and may offer advice as to how you could achieve the learning goal (i.e., signposting to appropriate reading, identifying the best professional groups to be part of, or recommending suitable courses to attend). Remember, though, that knowledge only becomes a skill or a competence when it is practised to the extent that it becomes a habit. So, you will rarely master these when you see the first principles in a book or on a training course. As with any knowledge, its true value can only be realised when it is used in the right way, at the right time, in the right context. Practice, and reflection on how well you did, and how you might further improve your use of the skill, are key to learning and growth.

Try to plan your professional development at least annually. This gives enough time to build your skills in addition to your other commitments. It will also give you time to practise and reflect. Professional development planning in the long term in a profession as dynamic as digital marketing risks investing in skills that, by the time you master them, will have become obsolete due to the relentless and radical nature of technological change.

To be clear about what you are aiming to achieve you should write your aims as SMART objectives:

- Specific – use terms which are clear to the non-expert.
- Measurable – enables you to monitor progress and to know when the objective has been achieved.
- Achievable – objectives can be designed to be challenging, but it is important that failure is not built in.
- Realistic – do you expect that this can be done within your time and resource limitations?
- Timescaled – put a date on it.

References

Geissbauer, R., Vedso, J., and Schrauf, S. (2016). Industry 4.0: building the digital enterprise [online]. PwC. Available from: www.pwc.com/gx/en/industries/industries-4.0/landing-page/industry-4.0-building-your-digital-enterprise-april-2016.pdf [Accessed 24 June 2020].

Joint Information Systems Committee (JISC) (2015). Building digital capabilities: the six elements defined [online]. JISC. Available from: http://repository.jisc.ac.uk/6611/1/JFL0066F_DIGIGAP_MOD_IND_FRAME.PDF [Accessed 22 July 2020].

Target Internet (2020). Digital marketing skills benchmark [online]. Available from: www.targetinternet.com/resources/Digital_Marketing_Skills_Benchmark.pdf [Accessed 28 July 2020].

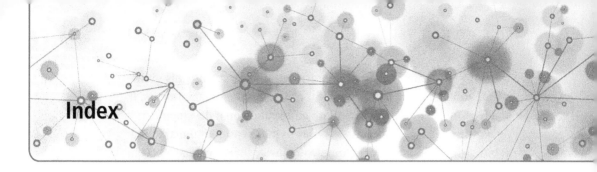

Index